ANDALUCIA

ANDALUCIA

A Portrait of Southern Spain

NICHOLAS LUARD

CENTURY PUBLISHING
LONDON

First published in Great Britain in 1984
by Century Publishing Co. Ltd,
Portland House, 12–13 Greek Street,
London WIV 5LE

British Library Cataloguing in Publication Data

Luard, Nicholas
Andalucia.
1. Andalucia (Spain) – Description and
travel – Guide-books
I. Title
914.6'8'0483   DP302.A45

ISBN 0-7126-0330-1

Photoset by Rowland Phototypesetting Ltd
Bury St Edmunds, Suffolk
Printed in Great Britain in 1984 by
Purnell & Sons (Book Production) Ltd
Paulton, Bristol

For Elisabeth

❧ FOREWORD ❧

WHEN I FIRST visited Andalucía I confess to my shame I barely even knew the region's name. To me it was simply a part of southern Spain famous chiefly as a tourist resort with winter sun. Then almost by accident I found myself living there. As I began to explore it I learned Andalucía is infinitely more than a tourist resort or even a region of Spain. It is a country all of its own, one of the many proud and singular Spains and as different from the others as Wales or Scotland are from England. It has a long, fascinating and momentous past, a robust and extraordinarily rich culture, some of the finest monuments in Europe, a landscape of haunting beauty, a dazzling flora and wildlife, a people who are bold, witty, generous and vital. More than anything it has a way of treating life as a brimming cornucopia and celebrating it to the full unparalleled in my experience anywhere else in the world.

In this book I have tried to record some of the delights of Andalucía in what for me remains a continuing process of discovery. *Andalucía* is an account of one family's experiences of Andalucian life, initially among a peasant community in the Guadalmesi valley and later on journeys across Andalucía. Scholars of Spain will notice there are whole areas of Spanish life and thought, for instance the issue of the *leyenda negra* or the influence of anarchist-syndicalist ideas on the Andalucian *pueblos*, which I do not touch on. The reason is either that I felt they fell outside the scope of what is essentially a book of anecdote and reminiscence, or that they didn't intrude on

Andalucian life as I experienced it. Others far more knowledgeable than I, for Andalucía has many immensely knowledgeable devotees, may find errors of what they see as detail or interpretation. Where they do I offer my apologies in advance. Andalucía's canvas in both time and space is broad, and I have of necessity taken a broad brush to it.

I owe thanks to many – to the authors of the books on Andalucía I have read over the years and to the people who have introduced, illuminated or shared the pleasures of its life with me. Interestingly, as the Andaluz are the first to acknowledge, some of the best and most perceptive writing about Andalucía has been by foreigners and particularly by the British. In the second category I would single out Gerald Brenan's *South from Granada*, J. A. Pitt-Rivers' *The People of the Sierras*, Alastair Boyd's *The Road to Ronda*, and Ronald Frazer's *The Pueblo*, although I could equally well mention twice as many again.

The other group, the people who have helped me in so many ways, is so large I would need a directory to list them all. I mention a few of them in the chapters that follow. All I feel I can do here is acknowledge a tiny handful whose company in Andalucía has always given me special insights or happiness. First, our long-time friend and neighbour in the Guadalmesi, the beautiful and sparkling Milet Delme-Radcliffe. With her, Maria Cristina Parkes-Lieb, Clara and Lorenzo Larios, their parents the Duke and Duchess of Lerma and the many members of the Lerma, Medinacelli and Larios clans, Joaquin and Victoria Cervera and their multitudes of relations, Juan Carlos Barbadillo and his family, the bullfighter Miguel Mateo 'Miguelin', the novelist Luis Berenguer, the master-carpenter Ramon Sosa, my old comrade David Towill, the two sisters, Anglo-Andaluz as they became, Amanda and Catherine Howard, Bill and Annie Davis, whose palace 'La Consula' Ernest Hemingway made his headquarters on his return to Spain and where the immortal Antonio Ordoñez, among many others, was a frequent visitor, little dark-haired Ana Lobato, and her cousin Juani, who looked after us for so long and so lovingly and the communities of the Guadalmesi in the valley and La Ahumada on the ridge above.

Lastly, I incurred an immeasurable debt of gratitude to my four Andaluz children, as during their years there they inevitably became. They went to Andalucian schools, they learnt to speak Castilian with the broad Andaluz accent, they made Andalucian friends, they grew up knowing Andalucian games and customs, songs and dances, history, folklore and traditions. Watching them dance Sevillanas, listening to them talk in the countryside patois, discussing with them Franco and bullfights, the old and the new Spain, flowers and birds and the price of *pipas* and nougat in the Christmas market, towed along always in their exuberant wake, I was exposed to more of Andalucian life than I would have been if I had lived there on my own for a hundred years.

I thank them and all the Andaluz from the bottom of my heart. Most of all I thank my wife, Elisabeth, who took me to Andalucía in the first place. Without her I would never have known what the Moors, those supreme connoisseurs of earthly pleasures, decided could only be the ground floor of paradise.

I

As so OFTEN, chance shaped the game.

In the winter of 1956 the Austro-Hungarian plain was chill and desolate. Black ice patined the flat and muddy plough-land of the landscape. At dawn and dusk skeins of wild duck descended on the freezing marshes, and the nights echoed with the clamour of distant gunfire. Across the border half a mile from the little Austrian village of Heiligenkreuz, the tanks and infantry of the Warsaw pact forces were in the final stages of crushing the Hungarian uprising against the Soviet empire.

Built on a low hill above the plain, Heiligenkreuz was dominated by an old Franciscan monastery. With the grudging consent of the monks, the monastery's lower floors had been taken over as a transit camp for Hungarian refugees fleeing from the struggle. The camp was staffed, supplied and run by a motley group of mainly British volunteers drawn for one reason or another to the candle lit by the Hungarian cause. As a young army officer I had been sent out to Vienna after training with a NATO special forces unit with instructions to collect two trucks laden with clothes, bedding and antibiotics, and head south to join the camp.

The camp at Heiligenkreuz was in a state of turmoil and exhaustion. The refugees from the fighting would start to arrive each evening with the onset of darkness. As the night hours passed, the early trickle would become a flood. By dawn half a dozen volunteers would be attempting to deal with as many as a thousand people. There were weapons to be re-moved, wounds to be dressed, meals to be cooked, identities to be checked, weeping children to be comforted, fights and disputes to be settled. When morning came, buses would arrive from Vienna to transport the night's intake back to the big clearing camps round the Austrian capital. Then, after a few hours snatched sleep, the cycle would start again.

Early one morning I returned from a border reconnaissance. For eight hours I'd been out on foot checking the guide lamps that marked the corridors which the refugees were instructed to follow through the Soviet-laid minefields. I was soaked, chilled to the marrow, and my eyes were aching from searching the darkness for Russian patrols. I decided to warm myself with a mug of coffee before joining the camp staff. I went into the monastery kitchen. There I found a stranger. He was an immensely tall and thin young Englishman of about twenty-five with dark curling hair and a ready smile. He wore a pair of high Spanish riding boots and had a flamboyant black leather jacket slung round his shoulders. For fifteen minutes we talked together. Then we exchanged names. According to the conventions of the border that winter no one asked what anyone else was doing there and we parted without further questions. I went out into the cloisters, where as always at that hour an anxious throng was milling round the makeshift beds on the frost-coated flagstones, and forgot about him.

Seven years later, in the spring of 1963, I flew out to southern Spain with Elisabeth, my wife. We'd been married the year before and we took with us our son of a few months, Caspar. After the dirt and damp of a long drawn-out London winter we wanted to spend some weeks in the sun. We rented a small house and settled into a peaceful existence of eating, swimming, sleeping and reading. Ten days later the holiday was disrupted by a cable announcing the arrival of an old friend of ours named Dominic Elwes. A brilliant mimic and raconteur with gentian-blue eyes, irresistible charm and the values of a seventeenth-century buccaneer, Elwes' life was a series of escapades invariably conducted in a blaze of international publicity. From his cable's anguished wording it was obvious that once again he needed sanctuary.

I collected him from Málaga airport. When we got back to the house Elwes discovered his forced departure had been so abrupt he hadn't brought any money with him. I checked our own finances. I discovered we, too, were almost out of funds. All we could muster between the three of us was a paltry £5. It didn't matter. The car's petrol tank was full. The British outpost of Gibraltar was only three hours' drive down the coast. Each of us had accounts with banks on the Rock. In the morning all we had to do was drive to Gibraltar, cash our cheques, and return well-funded for the rest of our stay.

Next day we rose early and left the house at 6.00 a.m. The road was empty of traffic and we reached Gibraltar by 9.00. With an hour in hand before the banks opened, we decided to spend the last of our resources on breakfast at the Rock Hotel. Sixty minutes later, filled with bacon, mushrooms and scrambled eggs and having given our final few shillings as a grateful tip to the waiter, we walked confidently into the main street. A moment afterwards we paused. Streams of bunting were flying from Gibraltar's roofs and the crowds in the streets were festive and laughing, but puzzlingly the shops were shut. It was only a few minutes before we learnt why. The day was the Queen's official birthday. As a loyal outpost of the British empire Gibraltar was celebrating the occasion with a public holiday. All the banks on the Rock were closed until the following morning.

As we stared at each other in dismay – we hadn't even enough petrol for the journey back to Málaga – I suddenly remembered something. A few days earlier a note had been left at the house while we were out. It had been written by the tall young man in the Spanish riding boots I'd met on the Austro-Hungarian border. His name was Hugh Millais and he'd given an address less than twenty miles from Gibraltar on the other side of Algeciras bay. The letter had invited us to visit him there.

We climbed back into the car and set off along the isthmus towards the mainland. Forty minutes later we were eating a second breakfast in Millais' house above the straits. After our

13

encounter on the border, I discovered, Millais had emigrated to Canada. Following a variety of adventures he'd returned to Europe, moved to Spain, and had just finished building the house in which we were sitting. Now he was planning to develop property in the area. Buoyant, witty and ebullient – among his many talents Millais was a professional entertainer who accompanied his own songs on a guitar – he and Elwes were well matched. They discovered friends in common. Their tales struck sparks from each other. Within a couple of hours they'd become firm friends.

To celebrate the occasion Millais opened a bottle of champagne. Then he offered to show us the surrounding countryside. We bumped down the track from his house and headed west along the winding coastal road. Fifteen minutes later we came to a halt. I got out of the car and gazed round, astonished. The Málaga plain we'd left that morning was flat, drab and densely cultivated. Even in the early 1960s the ribbon development that was to blight the coast was already seeping out from the little fishing villages along the shore to the south. The ugly clutter of highrise apartments and hotels had come to an end 40 miles behind us. Afterwards the highway had wound across low, bare hills beneath a hazy, monotonous sky.

Here the landscape, the vegetation, even the air had changed suddenly and dramatically. We were looking down on the Straits of Gibraltar, the narrow channel linking the Atlantic and the Mediterranean. Eight miles across the water rose the mountains of north Africa, their umber-coloured flanks serrated with violet shadows. At the point where we'd stopped, 2,000 feet up from the rocky shoreline, the road crossed a valley. From our feet the valley sloped down in a funnel to the sea two miles away. Above us it climbed into a jagged range of hills with streamers of cloud sweeping over their crests.

I turned and walked upwards. The valley was mantled with a forest of cork oak trees. Beneath the bright saffron-green leaves the trunks had been stripped of the cork up to the point where the branches forked out. The naked wood ranged in colour from dark bull's blood to blazing vermilion. Dense, rosin-scented maquis, threaded by goat and mule tracks, covered the ground. From time to time the tracks opened into little glades. Under the trees the air was cool but in the glades the sunlight was hot and clear and butterflies clouded the turf.

I climbed higher. A quarter of a mile above the road a fold in the hillside had formed a hidden shelf two or three acres in area. At the back of the shelf a stream ran from a waterfall through a clearing thick with reeds and marsh orchids. The cork oaks here were taller and older than the ones below, and the waterfall was surrounded by great lichen-marbled rocks. High overhead caravans of migrating eagles were using the morning thermals to reach the sierras, their shadows flecking the grass as they passed. A pair of hoopoes were feeding on the turf and, as I watched, a golden oriole rose from beneath my feet and swirled away.

I lifted my binoculars and looked down at the straits. A tiny square-rigged sardine boat was bending in towards the shore with dolphins leaping in front of its bows. Then I heard a clatter of stones behind me. I turned. An old woman on a mule had appeared on a path that led down from the hills. She was dressed in black with a scarf half-hooding her face. As she passed she raised her hand from the rope bridle.

'*Vaya con Dios,*' she said, using the old countryside greeting. 'Go with God.'

Hoopoes

15

The straits from the valley

The woman and the mule left the path and vanished sound-lessly into the trees. I reached out with my foot and probed the soil. Further down, the ground had been rocky and hard. Here it was covered in a layer of thick dark loam produced by centuries of decomposing leaves. Only an inch below the surface the earth was still moist.

'There used to be a smallholding here,' Millais said, striding up the hill to join me. 'It was abandoned during the Civil War. Now the place is known as "El Huerto Perdido", the lost orchard.'

We stood together looking south. The wind was fresh and scented. Eagles continued to soar overhead, dolphins were still jumping far below in the sea, the air dazzled in bars of sun and shadow.

'I like your friend,' Millais went on, referring to Elwes. 'Most of the valley's up for sale. We've been discussing the possibility of buying it and building houses. Why don't you join us? You could build a house for yourself right here on the Huerto Perdido.'

❦ 2 ❦

THE FIRST VIEW most visitors have of Andalucía today consists of an oil-smeared stretch of chipped concrete at Málaga airport. It was mine, and as I discovered that morning standing with Hugh Millais above the straits, it is not only a dismal but also a totally misleading introduction. Behind the artificial and hermetic tourist belt on the Mediterranean coast is another world. Ancient, complete, austere and yet incomparably rich, it might belong to a different planet from the Costa del Sol. The best approach to it, I learned later, remains the one taken by the armies of the Catholic Kings 500 years ago as they moved implacably south across Spain's central plateau.

For mile after mile the flat Castilian landscape is bare and arid, the sky grey with heat, the air stifling. Then abruptly the road angles down, twisting and plunging through the pass of Despeñaperros. As the road falls, the shimmering haze dissolves, wells of shadow start to darken the ravines on either side, birds lift from the rocks, and drifts of wild flowers glow in pockets in the soil. When the road levels out at the foot of the pass the heat is even fiercer than on the high plateau above, but something fundamental in the countryside has changed. The earth is rich and shot through with colour. The rocks are threaded by streams. The reflected sunlight is no longer opaque but clear and golden. Water pulses beneath the land, trees crowd the horizon, at evening the air is fragrant with oranges, herbs, lemons, jasmine and magnolia, in the distance there is the icy presence of snow-flanked mountains and chill trout-filled streams.

17

For the true traveller Despeñaperros is, and always has been, the proper gateway to Andalucía.

No one knows for sure the derivation of the name. In the most popular view it is a corruption of Vandalicia, the land of the Vandals who overran the area in the sixth century AD. Another theory interprets it as a legacy of Spain's Moorish occupation when all the territory under Islamic control was known by the Muslim name 'Al Andalus'. There are several other considerably more arcane explanations. I have the same opinion about this as I have about a number of other Andalucian puzzles. The Moors occupied Andalucía for almost 800 years. The print they left on the land, people and language was deep and lasting. Whenever various suggestions are advanced to explain some Andalucian term or practice and there is no overwhelming evidence on any one side, I tend to favour the Arabic answer. Andalucía for me is 'Al Andalus' – Islamic Europe.

Although for reasons of administrative convenience Andalucía now has precisely defined borders, it is not as is sometimes believed a province of Spain but something much vaguer – a region, an area, a general description of the southernmost part of the European landmass. Its present boundaries date from the second half of the eighteenth century when Spain

Antequera

adopted a provincial structure. Andalucía was divided into eight provinces, each named after its most important city: Almería, Granada, Jaén, Cádiz, Córdoba, Málaga, Sevilla, and Huelva. The provinces' own borders were fixed in 1834 and with minor adjustments they have remained the same ever since. They encompass and delineate modern Andalucía but they have not won universal acceptance. Several scholarly Andaluz insist the region's name should be applied only to the Guadalquivir valley. The rest of so-called Andalucía, they maintain, is in reality the kingdom of Granada with its own distinct history and culture. Rightly or wrongly I accept the more traditional view, a view held by the large majority of the people who live there. Any inhabitant of the eight provinces is an Andaluz. By definition, therefore, the provinces are Andalucía.

Between them they embrace an area of 98,280 square kilometres – 17 per cent of the land surface of Spain and roughly the size of the entire United Kingdom or a US state like Kansas. The infrequency and imprecision of Spanish censuses, coupled with the continual migration of people from the countryside to the cities, make it difficult to reach an accurate estimate of Andalucía's population. In 1983 the total was probably rather over 6 million. The average density of their occupation of the land, a favourite statistic of Spanish demographers, is about 70 per square kilometre, the lowest in Europe. By contrast the figure for Britain is 600.

Physically this sparsely occupied territory consists in essence of two great wandering chains of hills and mountains separated by an immense valley. To the north, bordering the plateau from where the staircase of Despeñaperros winds down lies the Sierra Morena, a forest-covered rampart of dark umber rock which gives the hills their name. At the base of the cliffs of the Sierra Morena the land opens out into the sunken basin of the Guadalquivir river – the 'great river' in its Arabic name. Rising in the Sierra de Cazorla to the east, the Guadalquivir runs westwards for over 200 miles, the valley it carves broadening with every mile, until it drains into the sea through the plains and marshes south of Sevilla. South again of the Guadalquivir basin the Andalucian terrain rises into the Penibetic chain, a range of mountains, hills and uplands which fringes the Mediterranean and climbs only 35 miles inland from the coast to Mulhacén in the Sierra Nevada, at 11,408 feet the highest peak in the Iberian peninsula.

From the air Andalucía appears a huge and mountainous inverted triangle, slashed through by the valley of the Guadalquivir, its base walled securely by hills, its tapering arms bordered by the Atlantic and the Mediterranean, and its apex resting delicately on the narrow sea-lane of the Straits of Gibraltar. Within the sea and mountain-bounded triangle the range of climate, landscape and vegetation is extraordinarily broad. The torrid sapping heat of the Guadalquivir basin in summer gives way after only a few hours' drive to the icy air of the Sierra Nevada, where deep snow lies on the mountain peaks all year round. Spaces of coastal and upland plain so fertile they yield three successive crops in a single season alternate with barren flinty hills. There are places where rain has not fallen within living memory and plumes of bone-dry soil blow away like sieved flour in the lightest air. There are others close by where each autumn massed clouds darken the sun, the deluges are so heavy that lamps burn in the farms at midday, and the earth in the storms' wake has the colour and consistency of a sodden, emerald-green sponge. An apparently dead water-course turns a corner and becomes an oasis with deep pools, thickets of trees, and pastures of rippling waist-high grass. The cool and shadowy aisles of a towering forest are suddenly sliced away by stunted scrub. A mud flat changes into a fat-eared cornfield and then within yards back into salty, sun-baked mud cakes again. A ribbon of flowers fades into stone only to explode once more on the neighbouring meadow in a Roman candle of colour.

Elsewhere in Spain the land, the seasons and the life they nourish are largely predictable. The Castilians, for example, know their climate all too well. 'Three months of winter,' they say in a resignation bred of years of experience, 'followed by nine months of hell.' South of the plateau there is no such fixed pattern. Without warning, vast areas of Andalucía, traditionally well watered, can experience a decade of drought. Sierra villages, for centuries considered safe, comfortable enclaves, can be swept away overnight in some freak torrential downpour. Andalucian life is precarious. Only one thing is sure: the constant underlying richness, the fecundity of the earth. Drought may cause it to lie fallow for years. Then, when conditions are right, it erupts, hurling up flowers, cereals, fruits, nuts, and meadow grasses with the exuberance of an overspilling cornucopia. The entire region is nothing less than one vast granary. It is this that has drawn man to Andalucía from the beginning.

In the hills 17 miles north-west of Ronda is a group of caves known as the Pileta caves. Radio carbon-dating of the pigment in the simple but graceful red and black drawings on their walls, older than those at Altimira, has shown the caves were inhabited at least 25,000 years ago. (Further evidence in the form of skeletons and weapons indicates that they remained inhabited as late as the Bronze Age or until about 1,500 BC.) There is almost nothing to suggest how those early Andalucian dwellers lived or what their antecedents were, but if *Homo sapiens* emerged on the central African plains it seems likely they were direct descendants of the first hunter-gatherers who crossed from Africa into Europe. Certainly, 25 centuries be-

fore the birth of Christ, humans had penetrated the sierras a hundred miles inland from the Mediterranean shore.

With rare exceptions like the painted leavings in the Pileta caves the records of Andalucía's early human history are blurred and fragmentary. In about the eleventh century BC the first Phoenician expeditions setting out from Asia Minor reached the Spanish coast. There they found settlements of a small and stocky dark-skinned people, the Iberians. Several hundred years later still the Iberians were overrun by an invading wave of Celts from the north. The intermingling of the two races produced the Celtiberians who, as far as the term has any meaning for a quintessentially mobile and parasitic species like man, form the Andaluz rootstock.

Over a period that lasted perhaps as long as six centuries after the Phoenicians' first landfall, the Phoenicians themselves and then the Greeks founded random trading posts along the Andalucian shore. It was a fragile and tentative attempt at colonization which has vanished virtually without trace apart from the Greek legacy of the vine and the olive. Then, in 540 BC, the Carthaginians displaced them and firmly took control of the Iberian peninsula. Their domination lasted until Hannibal's defeat and the destruction of Carthage in the wake of the second Punic war, when the Carthaginians gave way to Rome. Under the Romans, who called Spain 'Iberia' or 'Hispania', Andalucía became known as Baetica after Baetis, the old name for the mighty Guadalquivir river. In 151 BC the Romans founded Córdoba to provide an administrative centre for the huge colony, and Baetica was made a province of the empire. Among the Roman citizens born and bred there were the philosopher Seneca and the future emperors Trajan and Hadrian.

At some stage, possibly between Carthage and Rome, possibly earlier still, western Andalucía appears to have been the home of the kingdom of Tarsus or Tartessos. Known only from allusions in the Old Testament and from references by a few historians like Herodotus, Tartessos seems to have owed its existence to the wealth of the Sierra Morena mines at the

source of the Rio Tinto. Whatever happened to Tartessos, whose uncharted site has become a magnet for archeologists and treasure-seekers like an inland Atlantis, when Rome's empire began to crumble and retreat, the Vandals flooded in. The Vandals were supplanted in turn in the fifth century by the Visigoths. The Visigoths, basing themselves on Toledo, created a monarchy which lasted until the early eighth century. Then, in 711, the most significant event in Andalucía's modern history took place: Spain was invaded by the Moors and the Visigoths were swept away.

Within a few years of their arrival the Moors had conquered the entire country and were pouring north into France. Although they were forced to retreat behind the Pyrenees soon afterwards, it was a further seven centuries before they were finally dislodged from the south. In 1492 their final stronghold and the capital of their last kingdom, Granada, fell to the advancing *Reyes Catolicos*, Ferdinand and Isabel. After a short and unhappy exile in the hills of the Alpujarras the Moors departed for Africa, and Spain was united under what was in effect a single crown. Since then Andalucía's chronicled history has been in large part the history of the country as a whole: the golden age of the sixteenth century, the remorseless economic decline over the next 200 years, the turbulence and divisions of the 1800s, the twentieth-century crisis over the monarchy which led to the Republic, the carnage of the Civil War, the harsh dictatorship of the Franco years, and ultimately the restoration of the monarchy and the introduction of today's democratic government.

❧ 3 ❧

THE UPPER SECTION of the valley was named El Cuarton. Six months after I first saw it, a Spanish property company had been formed and the 4,000-acre El Cuarton estate had been bought.

The chief entrepreneurs behind the company were Millais and Elwes. Starting with an almost virgin tract of forest their plan was to develop the land slowly and carefully. Totally opposed to the ugly, cramped schemes already scarring the coast, both were the sons of considerable painters and both were exceptionally gifted as artists themselves, they envisaged a time when El Cuarton would have a small number of widely spaced houses, an Andalucian-style village of studio-apartments linked by cobbled streets, a Franciscan monastery, and a little harbour at the valley's foot – all without violating the intrinsic beauty of the landscape and trees.

It was a bold and almost quixotic vision, conceived with a flair and style typical of the two, but it never quite worked out. Fifteen years later the first arm of the Andalucian studio-village, a scattering of houses and a few roads had been built, but most of the valley was untouched. The monastery, the harbour, and many other features of the original plan remained dreams.

The valley was too remote and the world's economic climate too harsh for the venture to have succeeded. Those who could have afforded a second home in El Cuarton's forests preferred the security of their Paris, New York, Madrid and Geneva apartments. By then the scintillating Dominic Elwes had died,

24

Hugh Millais had moved on to employ his formidable talents in other fields, and the company they'd created was a shadow of its brave beginnings.

Although I bowed out of the scheme early on, both Elisabeth and I remained enchanted by the valley. Elisabeth had spent much of her childhood in Madrid and Latin America. Spain was her second home and Spanish her second language. For her the idea of living in Andalucía was as natural as breathing. I had no such links; I was simply captivated by the towering cork oaks, the shadows of the passing eagles, and the clean fresh wind on my face as I'd stood gazing at Africa. When we were offered land and building credits in return for my modest share in the company, we accepted without hesitation.

Choosing someone to design a house on a distant and untouched piece of land, let alone in a foreign country, is inevitably a matter of chance. The orthodox approach is to engage a native architect familiar with the idiosyncrasies of the climate and the local conventions of style and construction. We abandoned orthodoxy. We went instead to a young Australian-born designer named Jon Bannenberg, who had already built up an international practice. His work was strong, simple and uncluttered, combining great sensitivity in the handling of materials with an exuberant disregard for convention. Lacking any of the inhibitions about size and scale which seemed to fetter his European contemporaries, he was happiest working on a scale that was almost monumental. Southern Spain was unknown territory to him but Bannenburg needed only two short visits to the valley before he'd decided what he wanted to build. One evening after dinner he retired to his studio. He worked throughout the night and by morning he'd finished.

'I want the house to be like a great white bird,' he explained as he went over the drawings. 'At rest beneath the trees but with its wings poised for flight.'

The site where the white bird was to be built was the fold in the hillside I'd explored on my first visit to the valley, the lost orchard or Huerto Perdido. It consisted of two distinct areas.

At the back, cupped by the hill which rose steeply above, was the waterfall and marshy glade through which a stream ran. Then, in front, the ground rose to form a small, oval plateau. It was on this plateau, looking down over the valley and across the straits to the African coast, that Bannenberg set the house.

The building he'd designed was large and rambling with white walls and a honey-coloured tiled floor. At the centre was an immense living-room almost 100 feet long. This opened into an internal courtyard with a glass-walled cloister passage running round three sides. Leading off the courtyard were a huge kitchen and six bedrooms, with another bedroom at the other end of the house. All the bedrooms were large, airy and high-ceilinged. Finally there were two further rooms, both cantilevered above the ground and approached from the outside by sloping ramps like ship's gangplanks. One was a service area for the kitchen. The other, hanging like a crow's nest high above the stream, was my study.

On the little plateau were some of the finest cork oaks in the forest. From the moment he first saw them Bannenberg was determined none of the trees should be lost. Instead of the oaks being felled to accommodate the design, the house was planned so that it folded round the trunks. Barely a branch had to be removed. There was even a great shady oak in the courtyard at the centre. When the building was finally complete it rested on the ground just as Bannenberg had envisaged from the start, a white bird poised for flight beneath the trees.

Instead of ordinary windows every room had one or more pairs of tall and wide glass doors with wooden shutters outside. In winter the doors would be closed and the shutters pulled tight against the rain, but sometimes in high summer we would throw all the doors in the house open. On those occasions the Huerto Perdido seemed to become part of the forest. By day, warm air and butterflies and the scents of the turf swirled through the rooms. By night they were full of owl calls and the sound of the stream in the glade and reflections of stars on the panes of glass.

El Huerto Perdido

Work on the house, which once it began continued in fits and starts, lasted for over two years. In the course of many visits during those two years I came to know considerably more about the valley. In 1820 a British infantry officer, Captain Rochford Scott, set out from the garrison at Gibraltar to travel by horse round the coast to Cádiz. On the second day of his journey he wrote: 'The road is now very bad, being conducted across the numerous rough ramifications of the mountains on the right and midway between their summits and the sea. At about seven miles from Algeciras it reached the secluded valley of the Gualmesi or Guadalmesi, celebrated for the crystalline clearness of its springs and the high flavour of its oranges, and crossing the stream whence the romantic dell takes its name, directs itself towards the sea-shore, continuing along it the rest of the way to Tarifa.' (*Excursions in Ronda and Granada*)

The coastal road no longer turns down through the valley to follow the shore. Instead it winds through the hills parallel to the straits. Apart from that, the 'romantic dell' must have changed very little since Rochford Scott rode through it 150 years before. Three miles in length and falling 4,000 feet until it reached the straits the valley had the shape of a broad and regular V. At its widest, just below the ridge, it stretched for almost a mile. By the time it tapered down into the sea the distance between the two arms had narrowed to a couple of hundred yards. Between those arms was a small, self-contained world.

One of the valley's most immediately noticeable features was its climate, part of a micro-climate formed by the convergence of two oceans and two continents. Several years later I was given a NASA photograph of the southern Mediterranean taken on one of the Apollo space probes. Portugal, Spain and north Africa lay tranquilly under a clear summer sky, but over the Straits of Gibraltar ribbons of cloud were being sucked down like suds into a whirlpool. It was a vivid illustration from the skies of what by then I'd come to know well on the ground. Whatever the weather along the coast on either side, in the valley there would almost always be turmoil.

Cloud and wind were the Guadalmesi's main irritants. Often the clouds would hang sullenly for days on end above the ridge, casting a grey shadow over the forest. Sometimes they would descend into the valley itself. Then, depending on the wind, they would either pour racing through the trees or coil slowly in dense banks of mist. I'd occasionally be sitting in my study and glance up to see a huge bird, a griffon vulture or a migrating eagle, hovering a few feet from my face through the window. Disorientated by the haze the bird would have blundered down from the ridge until it was brought up in confusion by the glass.

The winds that swept the valley were known locally as the *levante* and the *poniente*. Blowing from the east the *levante* was the equivalent of the mistral and the other hot winds that scourge the Mediterranean. Harsh and dry, it could gust monotonously for weeks without a break, rattling windows, shaking leaves from trees, raising dust spirals along the tracks.

'This place would be paradise if it wasn't for the *levante*' a shop-keeper grumbled to me once as the wind clattered his shutters beneath a cloudless sky. 'All it allows us to do is murder our wives. Providing the *levante*'s blowing when you take an axe to her, no court will ever find you guilty.' It was a widely held and often expressed belief along the straits, although I never knew it to be put to the test.

The *poniente* from the west, named after the place where the sun 'puts itself to bed', was milder and less frequent although it too could be tormenting. Once or twice a year in the intervals between the two winds a curious meteorological event took place: under certain atmospheric conditions the straits would suddenly be filled by a thick white belt of fog. The fog, known as the *taro*, rose to a height of only a few hundred feet and stopped abruptly on either shore. Looking down in bright sunlight from the house it was as if a layer of cotton wool had been draped over the sea. While the *taro* lasted, the shipping passing through the straits, one of the busiest sea-lanes in the world, would inch cautiously forward and the normally silent valley would echo to the booming roar of sirens and hailers.

The final striking consequence of the Guadalmesi's micro-climate was its rainfall. Although as unpredictable as every-thing else in the valley, the rains usually fell at two separate periods – first in the early autumn and then in the winter months following Christmas. The autumn rains tended to be light, a swift, welcome freshening of the baked soil at the summer's end, but those of winter could be awesome in their violence. The clouds would close in and the water would start to fall in monsoon-like cataracts. The stream behind the house, a narrow trickle for most of the year, would rise and flood the glade before cascading away in a yellow-brown torrent down the hill. The air would darken, the forest would be obliterated, and it would be necessary to shout from room to room to make oneself heard above the uproar of the drumming on the roof. Then abruptly the skies would clear, the sun would reappear, and the trunks of the cork oaks would seem to float like blood-red lances in a sea of mist as steam lifted from the sodden turf.

It was the rains, of course, that fed the valley's springs whose clearness struck Rochford Scott. There were several of these like the one that emerged in the rocks behind the Huerto Perdido. They burst from the hillside and poured downwards. By the time they passed under the coastal road most of them had been funnelled into a single channel which formed the course of the Guadalmesi, the river that gave the valley its name. Running beneath the valley's eastern arm, for most of its course the Guadalmesi resembled an Alpine riverway. Tumbling in a succession of waterfalls through miniature rocky gorges, in winter it was a foam-flecked torrent, in summer a chain of dark rippling pools over which kingfishers darted and from whose banks terrapins splashed down into the water. Then, half a mile before it reached the sea, it suddenly levelled out to run through a tiny fertile delta with rivulets branching this way and that, until it drained over a pebble-strewn shore into the straits.

Cloud, wind, *taro*, and rain. They all played an important role in the life of the Guadalmesi. Each could be enervating, depressing, even dangerous. Yet they also singled the valley out and gave it its character. Along the coast the quality of the light seldom changed, the air was leaden throughout the summer, and the seaward horizon was always the same bare line. In the valley the light varied minute by minute. Whatever the heat, there were always gullies and clefts swept by breezes from the hills above. Instead of a blank horizon, the mountains of north Africa reared up across the straits and the sea channel between was thronged night and day with ships.

At the same time as I was learning about the Guadalmesi I started to become familiar with the surrounding countryside. The area known as the Campo de Gibraltar, the plain of Gibraltar, was one of Spain's three military zones, the other two being the Balearic and the Canary Islands. The Campo had been designated a military zone because of the general strategic importance of the straits and also to emphasise Spain's claim to Gibraltar. Apart from a large although not intrusive military presence, the main effect of its status had been to keep the region insulated from urban development. Most of the post-war building which was blighting Spain's Mediterranean coast was directed at foreigners and often financed by foreign companies. Under the military regulations for the zone no foreigner or foreign company was allowed to own land there.

The restrictions, coupled with the relative absence of sandy beaches, meant that the countryside of the Campo had changed little for several hundred years.

What little development had taken place was largely restricted to the two sentinal towns at either end of the 20-mile length of the straits: Algeciras to the east and Tarifa to the west. Tarifa, the most southerly point of Europe, was a fishing port with steep, cobbled streets and densely-packed houses inside a ring of crumbling, medieval walls. Battered and faded by the Atlantic waves and winds, it announces itself proudly to the visitor as the 'most loyal and noble millennium city of Tarifa'. In fact, it has undoubtedly stood there for much longer, guarding the western approaches to the straits. The Phoenicians may well have colonised it over a thousand years BC, and by one (although much disputed) account, it gave the word 'tariff' to the English language as the tax the Phoenicians levied on the Greek trading vessels which used the port's facilities.

Tarifa's main claim to fame comes from the actions of its Spanish commander in 1292 during the Moorish occupation. Early that year the little town was captured by the Christians. Alonso Perez de Guzman, later known as Guzman el Bueno, Guzman the Good, was placed in command of the garrison. When the Moors returned to besiege Tarifa, Guzman barricaded the town and put up a valiant defence. During a sortie by the Christians in search of supplies the Moors managed to capture Guzman's teenage son. They brought the young hostage, bound and manacled, in front of Tarifa's walls and threatened to execute him unless the town surrendered. Guzman leaned over the battlements, tossed down his dagger, and shouted: 'If you're short of a weapon to murder my lad, use this.'

The Moors, quite unmoved by sentiment or heroics, promptly picked up the dagger and cut the boy's throat. Guzman nonetheless held out. The siege was eventually raised by the Spaniards and he retired to the Andalucian uplands covered with glory. Guzman's gallant gesture, although his son may not have seen it in quite the same light, was the high point of Tarifa's recorded history. Afterwards the town slipped back into the role of a small provincial harbour. Tuna and sardine boats set out from its quays, and Guzman's stronghold, the shoreside castle, was only saved from crumbling away by being requisitioned as a barracks by the nationalist army during the Civil War. Now, an agreeable army major escorts visitors round the castle battlements and towers, after asking them to leave their cameras at the gates in order not to prejudice the security of the nation.

Tarifa is white, windy and a little forlorn. Its position and its past should have conferred on it a status more in keeping with the grandiloquent greeting at the entrance. Somehow the world, like the coastal road which unequivocally skirts the ancient walls before heading west, has passed it by.

Its inhabitants have always seemed to me to include a far higher proportion than usual in small Andalucian towns of cripples, grotesques and the mentally deranged, as if the

Tarifa

32

population has been subjected to intensive in-breeding. Yet Tarifa has its virtues. A tiny and attractive municipal garden where blue plumbago glows in the shadow of the sturdy church. A winding high street mercifully free of traffic where chess can be played and the local newspaper, the *Diario de Cádiz*, read at pavement cafés away from the stench of diesel exhaust and the roar of container trucks. A little market where fishwives from a Brueghel canvas cleave steaks from swordfish, caught the night before and sold by Dutch auction where the price, instead of rising, drops until a buyer comes in.

Over the years Tarifa endeared itself to us. More than once on our frequent visits its merchants, by then long-time acquaintances, denigrated the town to us, 'bad-tongued' it in the Spanish phrase of *mala lengua*. Tarifa, they assured us gloomily, was a mean, sorry place, peopled by *inalfabeticos* (the illiterate, a grave Andaluz insult), and rightly ostracised by persons of education. The merchants had far less to apologise for than they believed. Apart from anything else Tarifa, as we later discovered, had two crowning delights in its annual fair and its little wood-framed bullring.

Algeciras was the same distance from the valley as Tarifa, but at the other end of the straits. Much larger than Tarifa, not a village or a town but a real city although it didn't proclaim itself as such, Algeciras was a noisy and bustling deep-water port. Its vigour derives, and always has done, from its position on the encircling bay. Algeciras bay is simply one of the finest and most sheltered anchorages in the Mediterranean, perhaps in the world. If Tarifa was colonized by the Phoenicians centuries, even millennia BC, Algeciras was surely familiar to them even earlier. Tarifa is at the edge, an outpost and point of departure. Algeciras is a place to come back to, a haven and sanctuary.

A mile across the bay is Gibraltar. To the ancients, the Rock, Mons Calpe, was one of the two pillars of Hercules. The other 'pillar', Monte Hacho or Jebl Musa, rises a further nine miles away on the African coast on the far side of the straits. From the Heurto Perdido, Gibraltar was hidden by the valley's eastern arm, but except in the fiercest winter storms or when cloud had rolled down from the sierras, Jebl Musa was always visible. Sometimes at night I would walk out on to the house's front patio and gaze down on the channel at the brilliantly-lit ships passing through in the darkness, wondering how the old people of the Mediterranean had viewed the sea-lane. Did they really think, as I had been taught at school, that if one sailed westwards between the two mountains one would fall off the rim of the world? Until I came to the valley I never doubted it. Afterwards I was less sure. I went out with the sardine boats. Their skippers were quite prepared to follow the shoals far out to sea. The small boats of the Mediterranean and the habits of their sailors have changed, I would guess, very little in thousands of years. Stories of the world's end at the pillars of Hercules may have been believed in the cities of Asia Minor, but I doubt the old mariners at the other end of the sea would have had any truck with such stuff and nonsense. They would simply have sailed into the Atlantic, cast their nets, and got on with their job.

The original site of Algeciras was on an island in the bay, the Isla Verde, or green island, long since joined to the mainland. It must have been still recognisably an island in 711 at the start of the Moorish invasion for the Moors on landing named it 'Al Djezirah', the Arabic for island. Like many ports it seems to have been almost continuously redeveloped ever since to accommodate the changing patterns of sea transport, and little remains of its past. Few writers on Spain, native or foreign, have a good word to say about the town, but as I came to know it over the years I felt Algeciras had been much maligned. It certainly does not have anything very obvious to offer. At the foot of the hill which dominates the town is the market, housed beneath a splendid and elegant pre-cast concrete canopy, one of the earliest and finest examples of the technique in the country. On the hill's crest is the *plaza alta*, the little upper square with a fountain, orange trees, crowds of scampering children wheeling and clamouring like gulls, and delightful gaily tiled benches. But apart from the market, the square, and

34

a few eighteenth-century houses which have somehow escaped demolition, Algeciras today is a sprawl of office blocks, high-rise apartments, shoebox-like residential developments, and the jangling paraphernalia of the quays and harbour. It is also for much of the year hot, dirty and high-smelling – whenever I come across an open drain anywhere in the world some association in the memory makes me think instantly of Algeciras on a Monday morning.

In spite of that, the town has a certain gritty individuality. It is utterly without pretension. Every other town in Spain boasts of some monument or other, however tawdry and neglected, to which the visitor will be directed from any bar. Algeciras has none and doesn't pretend to. Its people are there to live, work and provide services for the huge cosmopolitan throng that passes through – upwards of 4 million passengers a year use its ferries to north Africa – and they do so plainly and honestly. There are cafés for Christians and tea-houses for Muslims, fairly priced shops for everyone, ship's chandlers on the front, and, because Algeciras was and remains above all a sailors' town, a street called Calle Alejandro Fleming in honour of the discoverer of penicillin and appropriately a few blocks away some renowned whore-houses.

Over the past fifteen years the town has grown and changed more swiftly than at any time in its history. Its mounting problems, or opportunities as both local and international entrepreneurs see them, stem largely from its relationship with Gibraltar across the bay. Gibraltar too owes its name to the Moors. The commander of the force which took the green island of Algeciras was Tariq-ibn-Zeyad. At the same time as he seized the port he took possession of the Rock, named it Jebl-el-Tariq, Tariq's mountain, after himself, and built a castle at the top. The Rock and the castle remained in Moorish hands for over seven centuries until on 20 August 1462, only 30 years before the fall of Granada, it was captured by Spain. The day it capitulated was the feast-day of St Bernard, who was made the town's patron. Some 250 years later, in 1704, it was taken by the British led by Admiral Rooke during the war of the Spanish succession. Britain's occupation of the Rock, although not its sovereignty over the citadel, was formally recognized under the treaty of Utrecht in 1713 – and the hornet's nest of disputes which has hummed malignly ever since began.

One summer morning not long after the Huerto Perdido was finished I was driving down the coastal road towards Algeciras. On the way I glanced out of the car and saw to my astonishment the improbable but unmistakeable figure of an old-fashioned British nanny. Dressed in a severe grey coat and skirt and wearing the traditional grey felt hat on her head, she was striding purposefully down the hill in the blazing heat past laden donkeys and old peasant farmers trudging to market. Then I remembered Dominic Elwes had arrived to spend a holiday at a nearby house and had brought a nanny to look after his three children. I pulled into the side and offered her a lift.

'Where are you going?' I asked as she got into the car.

'Gibraltar,' she answered crisply. 'To buy a reliable kipper.'

Her reply summed up everything generations of British have come to feel about the Rock. Enduring and changeless, it has lodged in the national consciousness as the shining symbol of all that was best, of all that was safe and secure, about the empire. In Gibraltar the policemen wear the British bobby's uniform and helmet, and are totally incorruptible. Warm draught beer is sold in pubs where horse brasses gleam under Tudor beams, darts are played, and cricket teams selected. Scones with cream and raspberry jam are available for tea. The streets have names like Drumhead Court, Martial Lane and London Pride Way. A colour photograph of the Queen looks out from every window. At dusk, trim young soldiers in khaki shorts and shirts stand stiffly to attention as bugles call and the Union Jack is lowered. On the Rock the gates have not yet closed on the gardens of the raj.

Or so with incontestable skill and on a very modest advertising budget the present-day inhabitants have managed to project Gibraltar. They have been remarkably successful in winning the support of both the major wings of British political opinion. The conservatives uphold the Rock's present status as a jewel of individual freedom, free enterprise and traditional British values. On the other side socialists defend to the death the rights of Gibraltar's trade unions. The essential rightness in both views was overwhelmingly confirmed by the 1967 referendum, held in accordance with a United Nations resolution, when the colony voted by an extraordinary margin of 12,138 to 44 not to sever its links with Britain and axiomatically therefore not to move towards integration with Spain.

For the moment, attitudes to Gibraltar are not only deeply ingrained but apparently inflexible, and the wishes of the people, expressed in a free and open vote, undisputed. Yet even as a patriotic Briton I found the reality of Gibraltar rather different from its image. Unlike Algeciras, I discovered, to know the Rock is not necessarily to love it. The living space is cramped and claustrophobic. The air, under the canopy of levanter cloud which hovers interminably above the Rock's peak, is smoke-grained and humid. Traffic clogs the streets. The rare breezes reek of gasolene and, puzzlingly, of sulphur. The stridently-proclaimed nationalism of the locals is, in spite of all its fervour, somehow graceless and unreal. Even the photographs of the Queen don't always produce the intended response. Not long ago I asked a teenage Gibraltarian girl what she felt about her monarch, a reproduction of whose portrait by Annigoni was hanging in the parlour window of her home. 'Queen Sofia is very pretty,' she answered in Spanish. Spain's Greek-born present queen is certainly very pretty. What she is not is Elizabeth ii of Britain and Gibraltar's sovereign.

The girl's confusion, and the language in which she instinctively replied, was understandable. In a sense the Gibraltarians suffer from an identity crisis. Under one of the provisions of the treaty of Utrecht, the British undertook that the Rock would never harbour Jews or Arabs. For years now, as the Spanish quietly take pleasure in pointing out, Gibraltar's prime minister has been Sir Joshua Hassan. There are no racial undertones to the observation. Jews and Arabs have played a long and honourable role in Spanish history, and most educated Spaniards are proud to claim the blood of both in their ancestry. Yet Hassan's very name highlights the absurdities of Britain's present position as the protector of a group of largely Spanish-speaking Indian and Levantine merchants, who are forced to be something they are patently not.

On the other hand, in the light of the Gibraltarians' express wishes, Spain's demands for the return of the Rock are equally fanciful. With Spain's impending entry into the European common market some compromise solution will have to be found, but for years the issue appeared to be intractible. It was certainly regarded so by Franco who, partly from stubborn personal conviction and partly for political reasons, would admit of no compromise at all. In June 1969 after a period of increasing harassment he suddenly closed Spain's borders with the Rock. Until then access had been virtually unrestricted. Now as so often in the past Gibraltar found itself a citadel under siege. For the large British community which had settled in southern Andalucía the effect was mainly psychological. Reliable kippers were no longer available. On the Rock itself the consequences at first appeared disastrous. The immensely lucrative trade with Spain had been cut off, Spanish labour had been withdrawn, and Gibraltar's expanding role as a tourist gateway to the Costa del Sol had ended. In fact, within a year the damage to the economy proved small. Quick-witted and adept, the Rock's merchants turned their eyes to north Africa. With imported Moroccan labour, support from Britain, and a successful campaign to develop a tourist trade of their own, life on the Rock continued much as before.

The only real hardship caused was among the 10,000 Spaniards from Algeciras, the border town of La Línea, and the villages round the bay, whose entire livelihood depended on their employment in Gibraltar as day workers, mainly in the naval dockyards. Overnight they and their families were left penniless. In an effort to help them and eliminate the area's dependence on the Rock, the Franco government launched a crash programme to attract investment to Algeciras bay.

The results were to affect the whole region and not least the valley itself, but in the mid-1960s as the Huerto Perdido approached completion and we prepared to move in, Gibraltar's closure was several years away. The winding coastal road was still little more than a rutted track. The valley was largely undisturbed. Apart from our own house only two other new buildings had been erected on an area covering 10,000 acres. Nightingales sang in the trees, clouds raced through the forest, the sun shone, the wind blew, gorse flared yellow on the hillsides, and we began to meet the people of the Guadalmesi.

ও২ 4 ৩৯

WHEN THE BUILDING was finally completed and the last truck pulled away, the grounds of the Huerto Perdido were scarred and corrugated with dry mud. As a formal garden would have looked incongruous in the forest, we decided to surround the house with close-cut turf that would stretch away and blend into the trees. If the earth wasn't to be invaded by bracken and scrub it clearly had to be planted and tended. For all its wilderness setting, the Huerto Perdido needed a gardener. The builders' foreman, an authority on local affairs, returned, consultations took place, and José appeared from the valley.

José was in his early thirties. Of medium height, stocky and muscular, he wore faded blue overalls, a rain-flattened straw hat and a pair of thick glasses behind which his eyes blinked with shyness. For a while he stood awkwardly outside the house in the drive. Then, in response to the foreman's beckoning finger, he removed his hat and entered the living-room. He stood quite still with his head lowered as the foreman interrogated him. Was he aware of the responsibilities he was taking on? Would he dutifully look after the house and garden? Would he do all in his power to protect the *señor*, his wife, and his family? As the questions came to an end José lifted his eyes and stared through the glass towards the straits.

'I come from the Guadalmesi,' he answered. 'I will work hard and be loyal. I can say no more.'

'He is an *hombre bueno*,' the foreman said as José went out.

José started work next morning. In Andalucía the term *hombre bueno*, signifying honesty and reliability, is one of

40

high praise. As we found out, José more than merited it. Patient, courteous, and unfailingly good-humoured, he exemplified all that was best in the Guadalmesi community.

There were in fact two groups of people living in the valley. One, those of the Guadalmesi proper, lived on or round the fertile little delta at the valley's foot where the river levelled out before draining into the sea. The other group, who called themselves the people of La Ahumada, lived in the uplands behind the Cabrito ridge, the ridge of the 'little goat' which encircled the valley to the north. Neither group inhabited what could be called a village or even a hamlet. The Guadalmesi was a scatter of little houses and smallholdings, La Ahumada a straggle of much more widely dispersed cottages among the hilly woods and pastures.

Even without the usual focal points of a church or village square both groups, separated only by a few miles, had developed quite distinct personalities. In each almost everyone was related to each other. Both in the Guadalmesi, which numbered some 80 inhabitants, and in La Ahumada, with perhaps twice as many, it was difficult to find a family which hadn't some kinship through marriage or more often through blood with its neighbours. Yet in spite of the short distance between the two communities, and the fact that both knew all about the affairs of the other – from children's nicknames to the most trivial local gossip – each kept to its own. When new blood entered either, it was invariably from the comparatively remote towns of Algeciras or more often Tarifa. Somehow the different ways of life dictated to them by the land had also determined that their genes should not mix. The people of the Guadalmesi on the plain were agriculturalists, those of La Ahumada in the high rocky meadows above pastoralists. *Trigo* and *bichos*, grain and livestock, do not interbreed. That was the only explanation offered to me by the valley's dwellers. They looked puzzled I had even asked the question.

Across the length and breadth of the valley between the hills and the sea was a small number of other dwellings, each owing allegiance to one or other of the two settlements. Once there were clearly many more. On either side of the Guadalmesi river in its lower reaches were at least thirty deserted cottages and small-holdings, flagged in spring with the blossom of long-neglected pomegranate and almond trees. Most were abandoned in the course of the Civil War, some earlier still. Apart from the effects of the war's turmoil the reasons in every case were the same: the drying-up of the Guadalmesi's waters meant that the tiny pockets of land, deprived of irrigation, were no longer able to support the families which lived on them.

José came from one of the few smallholdings outside the delta or the hills which were still inhabited. It was at the very centre of the lower part of the valley, a whitewashed cottage perched on top of a rocky outcrop and surrounded by a few acres of soil which were irrigated by hand from a well above an underground spring. The cottage had only two rooms; in one of these José had been born and had grown up with his six brothers and sisters. His childhood spanned the years immediately following the Civil War when deaths from starvation, particularly in the rural areas of Spain, were common. The family were lucky in having the well and the little farm, but with twelve mouths to be fed – apart from the parents and the children three aunts shared the cottage – the yield of the few acres had to be supplemented from any source available.

Then as now the Guadalmesi valley was home to several pairs of eagle owls. The largest owls in the world, capable of taking young deer as prey, the birds are magnificent cream and tawny-breasted creatures with immense orange eyes and talons that can span a man's face. One pair nested in the rocks above the river close to José's cottage. Each spring when the owls were feeding their young, José, from the age of five on, was sent out by his father to watch the nest. Whenever one of the owls returned with a hare, a rabbit or even a bird, José would call across to the cottage, his father would run to the ravine, climb up to the nest, and seize whatever the owl had brought back. The owl's prey would then become the family's evening meal.

'When the owls provided for us my father always said a blessing,' José told me. 'He said it would be the sweetest meat we would ever taste. It came from the skies and therefore from God and He had not even asked from us sweat to enjoy it. My father told us to pray and offer thanks before we went to bed.'

José chuckled. 'If it was a hare we gave thanks. But often the owls came back with starlings or crows. Then with my brothers and sisters I used to pray they'd have better luck hunting next day.'

When he grew up José served for the statutory period in Spain's conscript army. Then he was signed up by a labour agent to work in a factory abroad. It was a pattern followed by hundreds of thousands of young Andalucians. José wasn't even sure for several weeks after he arrived which country he was in. It turned out to be Germany although it might just as well have been anywhere in Europe. For three years he seldom left the former barracks opposite the factory gates where he and the rest of the work force lived, except to cross the street to join the production line. When his contract ended he returned to the Guadalmesi, unable to stand the prison-like monotony of the life any more.

By then his parents had parted, a common feature of Andalucian peasant life. When the children have grown and moved away, the father and mother will often follow and move in with one of them, leaving their partner behind. Afterwards husband and wife will only see each other on feast-days and at family gatherings, if they live reasonably close, or at intervals of years if they are far apart. The reasons are, of course, economic. People wed and rear children to provide themselves with a source of support in their old age. After perhaps three decades of toil in the fields under the Andalucian sun, the onset of old age and its penalties can happen remarkably early by northern European standards. By his mid-fifties the countryside Andaluz could well be spent as a worker, even if work is available to him. It is then that he and his wife need the shelter and support which only their children, bound to them by family ties, can be expected to provide. Few children are able to roof and nourish both. So father and mother, without resentment and without in any way breaking the marriage contract, go wherever their offspring can produce a stew on the stove and a pallet for a bed.

In José's case, his father had left to live with an older married sister of José's who had settled in Tarifa, while his mother had remained with two of his aunts at the cottage in the valley. While he was abroad José's task had been to support the truncated part of his family which had stayed on in the Guadalmesi. In addition to his mother and aunts it included a younger sister and brother. As a result, although his German factory earnings had been remarkably handsome by the standards of an Andaluz field-worker's wages, José's own savings were pitifully small. José had put them by as the financial underpinning of his own marriage: he was engaged to a beautiful girl who worked as a sempstress in a village between the valley and Algeciras. Not long after José's return from Germany his mother died and his younger brother and sister moved away from the Guadalmesi. This still left him with the burden of providing for himself and his two aunts. He did so by working the smallholding and taking whatever casual labouring jobs became available. The offer of permanent employment as gardener to the Huerto Perdido came as a godsend.

Soon after we moved into the house Elisabeth decided to acquire a donkey. After various Byzantine negotiations, the local horse-dealer, Manolo the gypsy, led Bernardo up the drive. Bernardo was plump and shaggy. His ears were long, his dark eyes speculative, his coat a greying mixture which blended the colours of the valley's forest acorns and its tumbled rocks. He inspected the property, spotted the lush grass in the glade, and ambled confidently forward to take up residence. Bernardo turned out to be everything a well-bred donkey should be. His duties were hardly demanding – to give an occasional ride to the children and for the rest of the time to wander as a sun-dappled living sculpture through the trees –

but whatever he was called on to do, Bernardo remained tolerant and agreeable.

José, who'd worked with donkeys all his life, at first greeted Bernardo's arrival with delight. Then in the days that followed he fell unaccountably silent. His habitual smile turned to a frown, and he would stand for minutes on end gazing at the sea and shaking his head. Although he was far too polite to say so, something about the donkey was clearly troubling him.

Finally Elisabeth decided to have it out with him.

'Is there something wrong with Bernardo?' she asked.

'Not exactly, *Señora*,' José answered. 'Bernardo's a fine beast. The problem's with his dress.'

Elisabeth looked puzzled.

'He's got nothing to wear,' José explained. 'It's very important for a donkey to be properly dressed. If you arrive with one that's shabbily turned out, people aren't sure who you are and they treat you accordingly. But with a well-dressed donkey you're welcome everywhere.'

Elisabeth and José got into the car and headed for Algeciras where there was a saddlery shop. An hour afterwards they returned. José climbed out beaming. He was carrying a full harness consisting of a brightly woven bridle, a saddle, girths, pannier bags, and an embroidered tail-band. He dressed Bernardo and led him proudly to the door.

'You will of course notice the difference immediately, Don Nicholas,' he said. 'Bernardo is no longer just a donkey. He is a donkey of *categoría*.'

During his first winter's work José planted the churned-up areas of mud round the house with couch grass, laboriously inserting each shoot into the ground by hand. When spring came the shoots sprouted and grew, and soon the earth was covered by thick springy turf. Then the garden was invaded by moles and overnight the grass was disfigured by dozens of molehills. José was enraged. The lawn had been his creation, and so was the responsibility of preserving it. He immediately launched his counter-attack.

José's technique for dealing with the moles required a spade,

45

Bernardo

a club, and infinite patience. He'd dig a hole in the mole-run and retire, club in hand, to the shade of a tree to wait for the mole to surface and repair it. When the unfortunate creature emerged he leapt forward, clubbed it over the head and triumphantly bore the carcass to the house. Sometimes an entire day would pass without a mole emerging. José was unmoved. All other work at the Huerto Perdido ground to a halt as he sat grimly for hour after hour in the shadow, his eyes fixed on the trap he'd set. Fortunately one morning the moles vanished of their own accord as quickly as they'd appeared. José reluctantly put away the club and the spade and returned to his normal duties. Long afterwards he still spoke wistfully of the great mole campaign and its victorious conclusion which he was certain was due entirely to him.

As a small network of roads began to spread through the forest and a few more houses were built, El Cuarton's management company instituted a rubbish collection service. Rubbish was the responsibility of Manolo the dustman, so named to distinguish him from the many other Manolos in the valley. As in Wales, although in Andalucía the practice applies to first names, a man is distinguished from others named the same by adding his occupation or the place he comes from. Manolo the dustman was the second of the valley's inhabitants we came to know well. Manolo, who lived at La Ahumada, was a short, broad man with immensely powerful shoulders, an imposing belly, and bright blue eyes under grizzled hair. Illiterate, deceptively slow-moving and easy-going, Manolo was in fact immensely shrewd and a prodigious worker. His dustman's job at El Cuarton was simply a well-paid interlude in a working day that started long before dawn and ended as often as not after midnight.

Manolo's main occupation was breeding pigs at his cottage behind the ridge. Working with him on the tiny farm were his three muscular daughters and his wife. His wife, beside whom Manolo looked like an emaciated child, was a local legend. Once, I was told, a bull maddened by hornet stings broke out of a corral in La Ahumada and went rampaging between the houses. The men fled in terror and barricaded themselves indoors. Manolo's wife strode out, gripped the bull by its plunging horns, wrestled the animal to the ground, and sat on its neck until its legs had been roped. I heard the story several times before I met her. Until then I'd been a little sceptical. After shaking her hand and seeing the massive bicep muscles rippling on her arms, I no longer doubted it for an instant. My sympathies were transferred to the maddened bull.

Everything Manolo did, and his wife and daughters too, was turned to account. He rode to work and back again to La Ahumada in the evening on a mule. Always he'd be carrying a pannier of vegetables some neighbouring farmer was sending to market, or taking back a sack of cement dropped off at the roadside by a truck from Algeciras. Inexorably, through his thrift, energy and sharpness, Manolo's wealth accumulated, earning him the nickname of the valley's millionaire. It wasn't far short of the mark. Five years after we arrived the management company sold its original Land Rover, which among other jobs was used to carry the rubbish away, and replaced it with a new one. The former vehicle, still in excellent condition and worth a considerable sum, was bought by the company's book-keeper – a professional man from Algeciras.

Seeing him sitting proudly at the wheel a few days later, I asked him jokingly how he'd managed to find the money to buy it. Somewhat embarrassed he told me he'd first approached the bank for a loan. When the bank turned him down he'd gone to Manolo. Manolo had produced the full purchase price in cash without hesitation.

'The old scoundrel's making me pay through the nose,' the book-keeper added. 'But where else could I have found the money?'

As he drove away I saw Manolo, bulky thighs spread wide on the mule's back, riding into the hills. Behind him on the animal's withers were sacks of fertilizer someone had ordered from the local farmers' cooperative. Manolo reached a bend in the track, dismounted, and began to walk. He and the sacks together were too heavy a load for the mule to carry. It left Manolo with a steep climb on foot. I knew Manolo wouldn't mind. Another few coins would soon be jangling in his pocket.

El Cuarton, the upper part of the valley, was divided in two by the coastal road. One of the first actions of the development company was to run a narrow track from there down towards the sea. The track continued for barely half a mile and came to an end well short of the rocky outcrop crowned by the cottage that was José's home. At the end of the track a delightful and effervescent Irish woman, who'd fallen head over heels in love with Andalucía, built a house for herself and her French

Hacienda near Ronda

husband. The house, in impeccable taste, was large, elegant and expensive, a skilful and lovingly recreated version of an ancient Andalucian *cortijo*, or manor. The pair, who enjoyed entertaining, were an excellent host and hostess with many friends. When the house was finished they engaged a couple from the valley as cook-housekeeper and manservant. The couple were named Juana and Domingo. Juana, a grim, tight-faced woman who became a competent plain cook, was efficient if cheerless. The reason for the cold eye Juana cast on life wasn't hard to find. She was married to Domingo.

The imagination of Kafka would have been taxed to create someone less suited to the role assigned to him than Domingo. If José was one of nature's gentlemen and Manolo the archetypal letterless peasant entrepreneur, Domingo in the name given him by the people of the Guadalmesi was simply *El Loco*, the madman. Lean, gangling, and stubble-jawed with staring eyes, a maniacal laugh, and hands that plucked compulsively at anyone he was speaking to, Domingo's spirit surged and ebbed with the moon. Each month, as it approached the full, Domingo would leave the house and take to the hills behind the Cabrito ridge. There he'd lie up in the grass, strangling foxes with his bare hands whenever he could catch them, or firing cartridges at the stars from a rusting wire-bound shotgun. Then as the moon began to wane and the frenzy passed Domingo returned to the valley.

Travelling as he invariably did at night, he would sometimes get back to the house in the middle of one of the dinner parties at which he was meant to be serving. During his lunar absence his daughter would have been delegated to take over his job, but on his return Domingo would always insist as a matter of honour he assumed it again immediately. Whenever that happened a guest at the table would glance up to find to his astonishment that the demure and neatly dressed young girl who'd handed him a plate a few minutes earlier had been replaced by a grinning, mud-spattered scarecrow with bloodshot eyes and hair matted with thorns.

What Domingo did have – and for this reason I came to

know him well – was a remarkable fund of information about the valley's wildlife. All the inhabitants of the Guadalmesi hunted when the season was right and the chance arose. Domingo hunted all year round, obsessively-driven by some dark predatory impulse in the blood. Any bird, any animal, any fish or reptile was considered game. He placed traps, he limed twigs, he set lines in the river, he sat out in the moonlight with his ramshackle gun slanted down over the rabbit-runs between the Guadalmesi's coverts and thickets. Sometimes Domingo kept his captures alive. Once he trapped a fox. As a new moon was shining, Domingo's daemon didn't instruct him to strangle it. Instead he built a cage and penned the fox inside. The fox, perhaps diseased, perhaps wounded in the trap, soon sickened and died. I went to visit Domingo the morning afterwards. Scowling and bewildered, he was kicking the fox's body across the dusty floor of the yard.

'Look how it's betrayed me, Don Nicholas,' he said. 'I made him a house, I gave him food, and then to spite me he dies. I should have cracked his skull as soon as I saw him.' He gave the dead fox another malevolent kick and invited me into the kitchen for a morning drink.

Domingo's attitude to the Guadalmesi's birds and animals, although haunted and extreme in his case, was not unusual. The valley's wildlife was a crop and was there to be harvested. Whenever I suggested the nature of any crop, whether wheat or partridges, meant that seed had to be saved, stored and put back to yield for the following season, eyes would glaze over and foreheads crease in puzzlement. I clearly didn't understand, I was courteously but silently being told, that there was an immeasurable difference between the wheat and the wild *bichos*. Man had to sow the wheat himself. The countryside birds and animals were bounty. They came from afar. They had nothing to do with the valley. They were God's lavish gift and inexhaustible.

In spite of stubbornly persisting with my arguments, for years they had no effect whatsoever. Then, with the arrival of television and the screening of wildlife programmes, attitudes

began to change. Not of course Domingo's. Asking him to modify his views would have been like inviting a leopard to become a vegetarian. What I did gain from him were insights into the valley's ecology. If I wanted to know how genets hunted the hills, whether there were otters left in the river, why I regularly found mongoose droppings in the centre of the tracks, if peregrine falcons bred in the Cabrito's crags, all I had to do was walk down to the 'Molino Viejo', the old mill, as the house where he was employed was named, and ask him. Some of the answers I was given, as his fingers tugged at my shirt and his wine-reeking breath billowed over my face, were as extravagant and improbable as tales in a medieval bestiary. Yet sifting Domingo's words for the truths tangled up in the lies and the fantasies, I learned a great deal. He was moon-struck, but with a true hunter's hunger he knew and understood much about the Guadalmesi.

For the first few years after the house was finished we went to the valley at Christmas, Easter and for a couple of months in the summer. Then we took stock of the situation. We had a pleasant but small apartment in London, a large and beautiful house in Andalucía, and four young children. Elisabeth was determined that the children, as she had done, should grow up to speak a second language – not from a few hours classroom learning a week, but as spontaneously and fluently as if it were their own. The only way to achieve that was to immerse them in another country. The answer was obvious. We would reverse the year's pattern. We would live in Andalucía and make the occasional trip back to London. So, in 1972, we settled permanently into the Huerto Perdido.

Until then Elisabeth had employed a number of temporary

maids to help clean and run the house. Now we needed someone to work there on a more regular basis. One of the other new houses in the valley was looked after by a couple from Algeciras named Fernando and Maria. They were already friends of ours but an incident in the spring of that year cemented our relationship with them for ever. Fernando and Maria had a small and sickly mongoloid son of six, Francisco, whom they adored. One day, while their attention was distracted, Francisco wandered away and disappeared. When the alarm was raised the entire valley joined in the search for him. As the hours passed and there was no sign of the little boy his parents became more and more distraught. Dusk was approaching. Heavy rain was forecast for the night. The spring had been grey and chill, and frosts were still being recorded on the Cabrito ridge. Everyone knew that if Francisco wasn't found before dark, the chances of the frail child surviving the night were slim.

On impulse as the light began to fade I left the main body of searchers, which by then included the local military and the police, and made my way up through the rocky defiles that led to the ridge. Even for a fit adult the terrain was hard and the lowering ridge had been ignored in the certainty the boy could only be lost somewhere in the forest below. All day the search had been hampered by a howling *levante* wind which made any call impossible to hear from more than a few yards away. I reached the gulley just below the crest, the wind suddenly dropped, and for an instant there was a freak silence. In the silence I heard a child sobbing somewhere in front of me. The wind gusted up again as I ran forward but I'd fixed the source of the sound in my mind. A few moments later I found Francisco lying huddled and shivering beneath a rock. I picked him up, wrapped him in my jacket, and carried him down the hill in the gathering darkness.

From that day on there was nothing I could do wrong in Fernando and Maria's eyes. When Elisabeth visited Maria to ask her advice about finding a full-time maid, Maria immediately volunteered her younger sister. A week afterwards

Ana took up residence in the house. Later Ana was joined by her cousin Juani. For the rest of our years in Andalucía the Huerto Perdido was never without one or other of them. Utterly different in appearance, temperament, and character, both were striking illustrations of some of the forces uneasily attempting to find a compromise between the old and the new Spains.

Eighteen when she arrived, Ana was small, compact and olive-skinned, with long, shining black hair that reached to her waist. Her eyes, darker even than her hair, sparkled, and her smile was ready and enchanting. Utterly fearless, she had no hesitation in standing up to anyone. When Elisabeth was in the house Ana accepted her unquestioningly as the *señora* and sought her advice on a whole range of matters. But when Elisabeth was away Ana came into her own, ruling the Huerto Perdido with a rod of iron. I quickly learned to give way meekly rather than risk her wrath by disagreeing with anything she proposed. The children loved her. At night she'd gather them on her bed and tell them stories of the terrible wolf-men in the woods outside, terrifying both them and herself until they all clung together squealing in fear.

Juani by contrast, whom the children also adored, had wide brown eyes, frizzy mouse-coloured hair, and a nervous, fretful manner. Several years older than her cousin and lacking any of Ana's grace, Juani in a different way could be just as stubborn. Where Ana achieved her ends through four-square boldness, Juani got to the same point by relentless persistence. Talking, explaining, justifying, worriedly rubbing her hands and creasing her forehead, she bore down on an issue like water dripping on a stone. In the end Juani usually got her own way too.

Both Ana and Juani had an identical background. Both came from the same little quarter of the same town. Both had had the same few and interrupted years of schooling. Neither could read or write except with difficulty. Yet a gulf separated them, a gulf created by Andalucía's brutal code of sexual morality. Ana was a good girl and Juani was a bad one. The difference had nothing whatsoever to do with any real or imagined activities either might have got up to. By any normal standards the pretty, flirtatious and self-assured Ana was a far more likely candidate for a tumble in the hay than her prim and hesitant cousin. Juani's disgrace stemmed from the conventions of the *noviesca*, the Spanish system of courtship and engagement.

Throughout Spain, once a young man has been formally received at a girl's house the two are considered engaged. The engagement can last anything from a few months to fifteen or twenty years. José had been engaged to his fiancée for seven years when he came to work for us and it was a further four before they married, a fairly normal period for the countryside. During the engagement neither can go out with anyone else and both, to a greater or lesser extent depending on the circumstances, are chaperoned by the girl's family. To that extent the system is little different from engagement practices in several other European countries. The problem for girls is the way the Spanish *noviesca* is entered into and what happens if it ends without marriage.

At the start, the decision to open the door to a young man is not the girl's but her family's. It means that suitors of unwed girls, particularly in Spain's poorest regions like Andalucía, very seldom have the key turned against them. With only minimal support needed from the family a man can effectively force himself on any girl he chooses, regardless of her own feelings or wishes. That in itself has been the cause of more than enough misery across the centuries. Far worse are the consequences of terminating the engagement. While theoretically either can do this, in practice it invariably happens at the whim of the man. For while the man is entirely free to walk away and find a new *novia*, or fiancée, without any repercussions, the girl is not. Her virtue is considered forfeit. Smeared and contaminated by the past, her chances of acquiring another *novio* are almost non-existent. Indeed, the man's rights over the girl are so absolute that in the rare instances of a discarded *novia* finding another suitor, it's not uncommon for the original *novio* to challenge the newcomer and warn him off. He might have moved on to pastures new, but the girl is still his property and no one else can touch her.

Such was poor Juani's fate. For no particular reason her *novio* had walked out on her. Without, I would guess, even the memory of a chaste kiss to console her, it had turned Juani into a fallen woman and consigned her to a life of spinsterhood. At that stage Juani was quite stoical about her lot, although she was to change later, but from the beginning Ana was a bitter critic of the system that in a sense had imprisoned her too. Her own *novio* was a dour and sullen-faced young iron-worker named Juan, who arrived at the house each evening and sat silently at the kitchen door watching her at work. What the vivacious Ana really felt about Juan I never had any idea. All I knew was that she'd accepted her lot. She was going to bear his children, tend his hearth, and keep her peace. Whatever life brought her in the years ahead, it could certainly be no worse than the destiny thrust on Juani.

'They say the *noviesca* is God's will,' Ana said to me. 'Well, I don't believe in God or in the church. They were just invented by the old people to frighten us and keep us under control. But if He does exist and one day I meet Him, then, believe me, Don Nicholas, I'm going to tell Him straight what I think about His tricks and lies. Not even a dog should be made to live the way we Andalucian girls do.'

One of Ana's bitterest complaints against the church was at the way it forced her and countless other pretty young Andalucian girls to dress almost constantly in black. Mourning periods even for quite distant relatives were long and strictly enforced, and every family always seemed to have at least one member who had just died. For Ana a great bonus in living at the Huerto Perdido was in being away from the social and clerical pressures of her *pueblo*. Each time she came back from a visit home she rushed into her room, took off her severe black dress, and emerged happily in a brightly-coloured skirt and blouse or sometimes, even more daringly, in jeans.

Theoretically young women turned to the local priest for

advice and guidance on matters they couldn't discuss with their parents. In practice they and everyone else invariably went to a witch. There are two sorts of Andalucian witch, black and white. Their powers overlap to some extent but the black is strange and fearsome, a creature of the night who flies the skies on broomsticks and communes with evil spirits, while the white is a pharmacist, a dispenser of ancient wisdom, and a dealer in potions and spells. Most communities have at least one of each type. The Guadalmesi was so small it only had a white witch. She was called Curra and she lived in a tiny foul-smelling cottage near the Mesón de Sancho, a roadhouse on the coastal road at its western entrance to the valley.

Curra was boisterous and cheerful, a stumpy old peasant woman with a cackling laugh and lank and filthy grey hair that reeked, like her clothes, of her cottage. The people of the Guadalmesi consulted her about everything from the calving of difficult cows to their marital problems. For a few pesetas or more often a payment in kind – in the sierra villages it was still quite normal to pay the local prostitute for her services in eggs or olive oil – Curra would provide the solution. Apart from herbs, potions and spells, which she kept tightly guarded secrets, Curra's world was dominated by the moon. The moon's power was common knowledge along the straits and she was quite prepared to talk about it.

'It controls everything,' she used to explain to me as I fell in beside her on her walks up the valley to her cottage. 'Children, for instance. They slide best and easiest from the womb when the moon is filling. Their blood is stronger and healthier. They have more heart and spirit in them. It's the same with animals at a *matanza*, a killing. If you slaughter a pig at a thin moon, its blood will be weak and thin too and the black pudding will be tasteless. You have to wait until the moon's rounded and growing. Then you'll get twice as many sausages from the beast.'

Some of Curra's most regular customers came from the little peasant farming community at the mouth of the Guadalmesi. The settlement had a tiny bar and *venta*, a shop, owned by a couple named Fernando and Maria. Fernando was the Guadalmesi's equivalent of Manolo the dustman, a burly, energetic man who worked upwards of 18 hours a day tirelessly looking after his few acres, running the bar and shop, or driving an old Land Rover which he used to bring goods into or out of the settlement. Maria was a jovial, lumpy woman of forty who looked twenty years older. To her great regret she had only managed to produce one child. Finally, realizing time was running out, she went to Curra. A few days afterwards Fernando came home in the early morning and enjoyed his marital rights. Nine months later Maria gave birth to a daughter.

'What have you named her?' I asked Maria the first time I saw the baby.

'El Milagro del Rocío,' she said smiling delightedly. 'The miracle of the dew. Well, what else could I have called her, Don Nicholas?'

~~ 5 ~~

IT WAS EARLY autumn and the start of the academic year when we settled permanently in the Guadalmesi. One of our first requirements was a school for the four children. At nine the eldest, Caspar, was an alert and adventurous boy. He was followed by the three girls. The dark and solemn Francesca, Poppy, fair-haired, forthright and uncompromising, and Honey the youngest, an anarchic and irrepressible four-year-old. The four had arrived in Andalucía with barely a word of Spanish between them, so to begin with the school couldn't be too demanding.

The coastal road crossed the ridge that formed the valley's eastern arm through a 3,500-foot pass known as El Bujeyo, an archaic word that meant 'the pass of the moving earth'. A mile or so on the far side, as the road wound down towards Algeciras it passed through the village of Pelayo. Somewhat bigger than the settlements of La Ahumada and the Guadalmesi, Pelayo possessed its own village school. It was there we enrolled the children.

Like hundreds of others throughout the Andalucian countryside the schoolhouse was a small weathered building with a single classroom and a yard at the back. Funded by the state its purpose was to combat rural illiteracy. Once the pupils could read and write they were considered educated, and left. As the children were needed to help on their family's farms and smallholdings, classes were only held in the mornings. Some thirty boys and girls attended, ranging in age from five to sixteen, and all were taught together. Apart from reading,

58

writing, and a little simple arithmetic, the emphasis was on practical lessons in countryside skills, which took place in the yard. One week the children would be shown how to catch, skin, and quarter wild rabbits, the next how to shape wooden stakes for fencing, the week after how to repair a *trillo*, the mule-drawn wooden sled used for threshing corn on a baked earth floor.

The end of the school year was celebrated by an excursion to the sea. Every child who'd attended the past nine months' classes with reasonable regularity was allowed to join in. Gathering at the school early in the morning, each carrying the elements of a picnic lunch, they were led by the school-mistress down through the forest to the little bay at the mouth of the Guadalmesi river. There they'd light a driftwood fire, roast chickens donated by the richer parents over the flames, and spend the day singing – being Andalucian, invariably one or more of the children played the guitar – and playing games. Finally, exhausted, they'd wind back up the hill in the dusk.

Next morning the annual parents' meeting was held. The meeting was always packed and attentive. Several of the grey-haired peasants clustered on the wooden benches were themselves pupils at the school, attending evening classes in literacy. That day their proud and sometimes anxious concern was to learn the progress of their children, receiving an education quite unavailable to them at the same age. The school-mistress would speak to them one by one and end with a rousing speech, urging them to make sure attendance improved the following year. Then after a vigorous round of applause school broke up for the summer.

In its curriculum, time-table, and values, Pelayo's village school belonged to another century. The school had no frills. It taught the three Rs, it encouraged self-reliance, it gave lessons in the basic rural skills. Its one teacher, the school-mistress (she was helped in the practical classes by volunteers from the surrounding farms), was dedicated to what she considered a vocation. After learning, she believed in God, laughter, and discipline. The day began with prayers. The lessons were given with enthusiasm and pleasure. Discipline was largely a matter for the conscience of each child. They should attend whenever they could, she believed, and while they were there they should give their studies their total attention. The Pelayo school, and others like it in Andalucía, served its local population conscientiously and well.

After nine months there the children all spoke fluent Spanish. More accurately they spoke the Andalucian version of Castilian. When the Catholic Monarchs, Ferdinand and Isabel, finally united the country after their conquest of Granada in 1492, they took great care to call themselves not the king and queen of Spain but *Los Reyes de las Españas*, the king and queen of the several and distinct Spains, a group of countries loosely linked by common borders and a more or less common language. The language was Castilian, the tongue adopted by the people who had sheltered for several hundred years behind the constantly expanding line of *castillos*, the castles which marked the shifting frontier of the Christian reconquest. Pure Castilian belongs to Madrid and the central plateau. Andaluz is a regional dialect. Its relationship with the parent tongue is not unlike the relationship between West Country English, spoken with a thick Devon accent, and the English used by the BBC news announcers.

One particularly hot August day I was talking to a Spanish visitor from the north when Maria, the mother of little Francisco, appeared at the door of the house to see her sister.

'*Que calor, Maria!*' I said to her as I let her in. 'My goodness, how hot is is.'

'*Más que nada,*' she answered.

As she headed for the kitchen the visitor, bewildered, asked me what she'd said. Maria's reply – meaning the heat was the worst ever – had been spoken in typical Andaluz fashion without sounding the 's' or 'd'. To the visitor's ear, accustomed to orthodox Castilian, it had been incomprehensible.

While all the Spanish regions have developed their own variations of Castilian, Andalucía's is particularly rich in vocabulary, and strong, sometimes impenetrable, in accent. Its vocabulary's wealth comes partly from the Moorish legacy, which has left the region with so many of its place names, but more from Andalucía's dependence on the *pueblo*. The concept of the *pueblo*, a many-layered word but meaning at its simplest a village or town, is so fundamental to an understanding of Andalucian life it seems more sensible to examine it later in greater detail. But in the context of Andalucía's vocabulary the *pueblo*, whether a hamlet, village, town or metropolis, means a self-sufficient world with its own system of naming.

The naming embraces everything from common household objects through birds and animals to social activities. A group of words in use in one village will be replaced by an entirely different collection a mile away in another. Accents too vary from village to village. A commercial traveller who covered some fifty little Andalucian towns and villages told me that after working his territory for twenty years, he only needed to listen to someone talk for a few minutes to know which of the fifty they came from. In addition, in informal conversation the Andaluz has a passion for diminutives. Virtually no word is immune, ranging from proper names like Ana and José, which became Anita and Joselito, to nouns like *café* or *coche*, a car, which in turn emerge as *cafelito* and *cochecito*. Hearing two Andaluz speak to each other often seems like listening to an exchange conducted wholly in baby-talk. The reason, I think, is that the diminution somehow makes the words more intimate and turns the language into a private shared code.

One irritating characteristic of the rural Andaluz' attitude to his language, as many people have noticed, is his conviction that outsiders do not speak it. There is no problem if he is unaware one is an outsider, but unless a lengthy dialogue has been established first, as soon as he discovers the shutters come down. Quite often I would have stopped in some sierra village and be talking to one of the local inhabitants, when he or she suddenly noticed my car had a foreign number-plate. Instantly the face would go blank and the eyes glaze over. Any attempt to continue the conversation afterwards would be met with silence and a state of mystified incomprehension.

In time I developed a technique to bridge the credibility gap. I would pause for a few moments. Then I would ask politely, 'Do you speak Castilian, *señor*?' The response would be a wary nod. 'So do I,' I would go on. 'Let's please start again, this time in Castilian.'

And the conversation would continue exactly as before. Somehow the mention of Castilian acted as a password, convincing the Andaluz we were now using a common language. Years afterwards I discovered that the writer Gerald Brenan had hit on the same solution half a century earlier when he was living in the Alpujarras mountains.

The same forms of address are used in Andalucía as everywhere else in Spain. A man is *senõr*, a married woman *señora*, although all women married or not acquire the status of *señora* at a certain undefined age, and a girl *señorita* – a title also often used by the Andaluz as a compliment when addressing young married women. *Señorita* has a masculine equivalent, *señorito*. This is usually translated and explained as 'master', the form of address, now largely out of fashion, for the sons of the British squirearchy until they reach manhood. Once it did indeed have much the same meaning in Spanish. Now, although sometimes still used as a playful formality to a child, it is almost always a term of scorn. The '*señoritos*' are the idle, the *nouveau riche*, the absentee landlords, the jumped-up speculators and money-lenders – everyone, in short, the rural Andaluz most dislikes and resents.

In addition there are the titles *Don* and *Doña* used in front of a christian name. *Doña* is reserved for older women of a certain standing in their family or community, a grandmother or the widow of the head of a large household. *Don* is much more common. It does not imply nobility or grandeur, as the Spanish *Don* of popular mythology outside Spain has led many people to believe. It is used simply as a gesture of respect, courtesy and often affection – old peasants are often fondly referred to and addressed as Dòn Andres or Don Antonio. I was called Don Nicholas because it was the normal country way of addressing an employer – it would have been the same if I'd owned a large farm or store.

One requirement of being addressed as *Don*, which involves the use of a christian name, is of course familiarity. Before I began to know the people in the valley, and they in turn came to know my name, I was referred to for convenience as 'El Inglés', the Englishman. This led to some confusion. Matching the Andaluz' passion for diminutives is their obsession with nicknames. Everyone must have one, however bizarre or inappropriate. A goatherd may be stopped on a road by a pair of French tourists asking for directions. If someone spots their car as they question him and the goatherd hasn't already been given a suitable nickname, he's likely to be known for the rest of his life as the 'Frenchman'.

That, often for reasons no one could remember, was exactly what had happened in the Guadalmesi. The valley's population included *El Americano*, *El Francés*, and inevitably *El Inglés*. The 'Englishman' was a 60-year-old former share-cropper named Fernando with rheumy eyes, a leg crippled by a Civil War bullet, and a curious whistling way of speaking that made him sound like one of the valley's migrant warblers. Employed at El Cuarton as a watchman against fires, Fernando lived with a pair of lurchers in a lonely cabin in the forest. He was looked after from a distance by a niece who lived in the Guadalmesi. Until I arrived there was no problem. Afterwards the valley had not one but two 'Englishmen'. For several years I would be called to the door of the house to be handed a tiny reed basket containing some cheese rinds and a hunk of bread, while if I made my way down to the cabin in the trees I'd find a famished and baffled Fernando poring over a package of galley proofs sent express from New York for delivery to *El Inglés*.

After their year at Pelayo's village school the children had not just learned to speak Spanish. They had also learned, as Caspar pointed out, enough about trapping wild rabbits, sharpening fencing stakes and repairing a Bronze-Age threshing sled, to last them for the foreseeable future. In his view, and his sisters agreed, it was time to move on.

Following the closure of the Gibraltar border two years earlier, the bay of Algeciras had been declared by Spanish governmental decree a zone of major industrial importance. The decree, designed to be particularly attractive to foreign companies, granted the bay a whole range of subsidies and tax concessions. As Franco intended, it triggered an investment boom. To service the boom, built on a refinery, a steel plant, a paper mill, and a number of other rapidly erected factories, an army of lawyers, accountants, engineers, architects, doctors, and planning consultants poured into the town.

Almost overnight Algeciras acquired a substantial middle-class population with professional skills.

To house the new middle class, who wanted something better to live in than the small apartments of the crowded city centre, residential developments sprang up like October mushrooms on the town's outskirts. As soon as the neatly planned houses were sold and occupied, their owners demanded schools – schools that could reflect and cater to their own values. The transformation of Algeciras happened with bewildering speed. When we came to the valley the town slumbered above its serviceable but little-used harbour, a modest and well run port like some rarely visited fuelling station in the South China Seas. Apart from a few lawyers and shop-keepers a middle class barely existed, and secondary education was in the grimly clenched hands of the church. Five years later the entire bay was teeming, Algeciras' population had doubled, the waterfront was choked with cranes, tugs, ferries, merchant ships, cargo boats and liners, and the city was spreading out on every side.

One of the new schools was set in the *barrio*, as the quarters of Spanish towns are called, named Los Pinos. The 'College' of Los Pinos was outward-looking, almost aggressively modern, and largely secular, although the staff included the statutory religious advisor. Its buildings, like the trim villas which

64

surrounded it, were smart and functional. English as a second language was a required study. The curriculum included chemistry, physics and biology; there were laboratories, playing-fields for organized games, judo and drama clubs, and three times a year expeditions were made to cultural centres like Granada and Córdoba. The teachers were young and enthusiastic, and the school hummed with ideas, debates, and projects.

It was a world away from Pelayo, yet the two schools continued to operate within a few miles of each other, serving in their different but complementary ways both the old and the new Andalucía. Even among the microscopes and electronic calculators of Los Pinos the Andalucian countryside was never very remote. One of Caspar's best friends at the school was named Toni. Toni was the son of the school's night watchman and was given his education free. As soon as school ended for the day the two boys would head out into the hills behind Algeciras. There Toni would teach Caspar the skills he'd learned from the country people from whom he'd been plucked only a few years before when his father moved to the city.

Toni was extraordinarily skilful with his hands. His favourite pastime was to make and fly a baited kite with which he caught darting swifts, among the fastest of all birds, on the wing. The bait was a fragment of dry grass which hung glittering like an insect from a thread below the kite. Attached to the piece of grass was the noose of a draw-string. When the kite was flown, the swifts would swoop to take the bait, the draw-string would pull tight, and Toni would haul the birds down from the clouds like a fisherman reeling in trout. When he'd caught enough, a fire would be built, the birds would be plucked, and the boys would roast and eat them.

How ancient the technique was I have no idea – I suspect very old. In the harsh Andalucian landscape some inventive peasant must have devised it as a means of augmenting his lean diet, just as José's father had learned to increase his by robbing the eagle owls' nest. When Toni finished at Los Pinos he left

65

Algeciras to study economics at Madrid University with the ultimate intention of becoming a banker. It always gave me pleasure to think that 30 years on, in the twenty-first-century world of international finance, there would still be someone who knew the old Andaluz art of fishing the skies.

Toni's progress from peasant boy to teenage aspirant banker heading off to university in the capital illustrates the remarkable mobility available in the apparently rigid structure of Andalucian society to someone offered a genuine chance to advance himself. Like most of Spain, Andalucía has traditionally been populated by three classes: the peasants, the landowning nobility and the bosses. The bosses, who ranked between the two tiers, did not in the commonly accepted sense constitute a middle class with a culture and values of its own. They were foremen, agents, managers, opportunists, a bully-boy group who rose from below to serve the landowners by filling positions of authority over their own people, often abusing them as they did so, and generally sinking back at the end of their usefulness to the level from which they'd come. There were naturally exceptions, but lacking education in the main, the *caciques*, as the bosses were known when they become political brokers, were doomed. The emergence as happened in Algeciras in the 1970s of a true middle class, professional, durable, conscious of its own identity, demanding education almost as a natural right, changed the equation. From then on anyone with determination and given the chance of learning, as Toni was, could throw a grappling-iron over society, haul himself up to a chosen level, and anchor himself there permanently. A new dimension had been added to the old tri-partite structure of Andalucian life. It no longer had three levels but four.

The peasants such as those of the Guadalmesi were largely unaffected. The bosses divided into two streams, sandwiching the new middle class from above and below. Below, they continued to perform their role of petty entrepreneur, foreman, and neighbourhood agent. Some became immensely successful brokers. Shrewd, tough and avaricious, they knew the countryside and realized its potential in the booming local economy. To exploit it they needed to buy services – legal, accountancy, architectural, engineering, and medical. They made themselves fortunes and because of their purchasing power they acquired the status of a new elite. Meanwhile the nobility, like the peasants, continued much as before. Andalucian life often reminded me vividly of the American South chronicled in William Faulkner's novels. There was the same sense of contact with the land, the same deep passions and ancient feuds, the same dynastic awareness, the same dark sagas that spanned generations. It operated at every level but most strongly among the aristocracy, whose fortunes touched on the lives of everyone.

Not far from Algeciras was the immense estate of Benalmin. Embracing forests, hills, rivers, valleys and villages, together with a castle or two, it belonged until shortly before we came to the Guadalmesi to a ducal family named Montalbi. In mid-life the previous Duke of Montalbi, riding one day past the house of one of his many farm managers, saw the silhouette of the manager's young wife in the doorway. He was instantly obsessed by her and in due course the woman became his mistress and remained so for many years. Finally the Duke's wife and mother of his two daughters, the Duchess of Montalbi, died and on his deathbed soon afterwards the Duke married his long-time consort, by then a widow herself, legitimising their relationship and conferring on the former farm girl the title of Duchess too. The new Duchess had an only child, a son by then an adult. Whether the son was fathered by the Duke or the farm manager was never established. In any event it was unimportant. As soon as the Duke died mother and son jointly challenged his will, which left the estate to his daughters, and laid claim to Benalmin themselves. Their contention was that the paternity of the son, Miguel, was irrelevant. There were no male children of the Duke's first marriage, the second had legitimised Miguel in the eyes of the church and the state, and he was therefore Benalmin's rightful heir.

The 'legitimate' family, as they understandably considered themselves, were appalled. They had treated the Duke's second marriage as the dying whim of a foolish old man, vulgar but trivial. Now it seemed possible it might lead to the loss of their patrimony. The prize was vast but more than money was at stake. Benalmin was the family's past, their birthright, their mark on history. The two sides joined battle in the courts. The hearings dragged on for years and in the end the second Duchess and her son won. Miguel was refused the family title, but the courts awarded him and his mother all the Benalmin lands. Soon afterwards his mother died and Miguel became the sole owner. A coarse and dissolute man who quickly grew bored with the estate and spent his nights drinking with a group of sycophantic cronies in the Algeciras waterfront bars, he eventually ran off with a plump little Swedish secretary who was already married. When she divorced her husband to wed Miguel they both had to leave Spain to avoid prosecution, their marriage being illegal under the country's existing laws. For a while they drifted through a series of international hotels. Then, growing even more tired of the acres he owned but never saw, Miguel sold Benalmin on impulse to a glib Andalucian entrepreneur who had built up a ramshackle conglomerate. The conglomerate shortly went bankrupt, the government in Madrid picked up the wreckage of its operations, and the now badly neglected estate passed into the ownership of the nation.

After Franco's death and the subsequent liberalisation of the marriage laws, the two returned to Spain to continue their hotel-room existence, this time in Algeciras. I used to see them often in the Reina Cristina. Their few years of exile had not been kind to either of them. Miguel's eyes were bleared and the former secretary's figure had thickened and drooped. They sat in the hotel lobby drinking American cocktails and anxiously watching the door in case someone they knew came in. Few did. Benalmin's sale must have left Miguel an enormously wealthy man, but during his absence even the sycophants seemed to have found better things to do and most nights the couple drank alone. Watching them I sometimes wondered if it had ever occurred to either that a silhouette glimpsed in a doorway and an old man's lust had briefly turned them into royalty and given them a kingdom, for Benalmin was nothing less, and that they had traded it all for a few Martinis and the occasional scrap of conversation with an uninterested barman.

When we first came to the valley the court's verdict on Benalmin and the turmoil it created was comparatively recent. Twenty years later the issue was still being debated as pas sionately and contentiously as ever. Entire villages and their populations had come in a sense under a new ruler, and everyone, directly involved or not, had their own personal view of the matter. The dispossessed family, who became close friends of ours, bore the loss, at least on the surface, with grace, fortitude and good humour. Underneath, their bitterness was immense. To reach Sevilla from the east of Algeciras it was necessary, or rather logical, as the journey was an hour shorter, to take the inland road which passed through Benal min rather than the coastal one. Yet from the day of the court's decision neither of the old Duke's daughters ever used the inland road. The journey was one they made almost weekly, but in spite of the extra hour they chose not to set eyes on their lost lands again. I suspect their children and grandchildren will do the same. In Andalucía time and memories are measured by a different metronome.

৫৯ 6 ৩৯৯

BEFORE LONG THE valley's year took on a recognisable and clearly defined shape. The winter months of January, February, and March were dark and damp. Perhaps once or twice each year the temperature at night fell below freezing. In the morning the grass in the glade was rimed with frost and there was ice on the pools of standing water in the drive.

In the main, however, winter was the season of rain. Storms raged across the crests of the Cabrito ridge. The water swept in black sheets through the trees. The air was moist and chill. Throughout those months two huge log fires burned in the house from dawn until after midnight. One was in the living-room. After supper everyone would gather round it, the children with their books, Elisabeth with her sketches, I with my papers, the maids with their sewing, guests and visitors, sometimes the night watchman or a passing Guardia Civil patrol, all of us clustered round the blaze, like the garrison of a medieval castle under siege, until it was time for bed.

The second fire was in our bedroom. Running behind the bed and reached by a curving flight of steps was a tiled walkway that led to my study. The fireplace was set into the wall midway along the walkway and immediately above the bed itself. Facing it on the far side of the room was a large mirrored cupboard. Lying in bed at night we would go to sleep with the warmth of the blaze spreading over us and the play of the flames reflected in the glass as the wind clawed at the shutters and the rain clattered down. During the worst of the wet spell I would get up at intervals to keep the fires in through

70

the night, but nothing kept out the damp. Mushrooms grew on the tiles, stains appeared on the walls, the drains ran over and the cellar filled with water.

By early April the rains had lightened and the storms were interspersed with days of clear sun. José was always cautious about welcoming the spring prematurely.

'You can never trust the valley until after the Algeciras fair,' he'd say, shaking his head suspiciously as he looked up at a cloudless sky.

Every year he was proved right. The Algeciras fair took place in mid-June. The rains would continue intermittently right up to it, and sometimes even during the fair itself. But as soon as the fair ended, so did they.

The April sun brought out an explosion of the wild flowers which had been beginning to appear since February. In the valley they blossomed in three successive waves of colour, first white, then blue, then pink. For years I was puzzled why the predominant hue changed every few weeks (there were exceptions of course in individual species). I never found a conclusive answer, but there seem to be two probable explanations. Either the plants have evolved so that the pigmentation in their petals changes in response to the increasingly steep arc of the sun, and so the growing intensity of the light, or alternatively the colours reflect the feeding preferences of the different bands of the flowers' pollinating insects, which hatch in succession as the temperature rises over the passing weeks.

Outside the micro-climate of the straits the effect was less noticeable. Beyond the valley the flowers seemed to erupt in a single dazzling outburst. Fifteen miles across the hills to the west was a bay named Bologna where there had once been a Roman settlement built round a harbour. The sea's erosion had left the port buried underwater, and all that remained of the Roman presence were a few columns propped up on the beach and the half excavated foundations of a villa, but the Tarifeños enjoyed going to the bay for Sunday outings and a retired fisherman had opened a bar there in a little wooden

71

shack. Hills and headlands sheltered the beach from the *levante*, and when the east wind was blowing we sometimes took a picnic there ourselves.

The track to the bay, which led off the coastal road, climbed up between meadows over a low range of hills and then wound down to the shore. For most of the year the meadows were drab. A dull grey-green in winter, they were quickly burned by the summer sun to a barred and dusty brown. Columns of rock ringed by heat-haze stared down over them and occasional flints tossed back the light from the dry, chalky earth. But for a week or two each spring the meadows were transformed into a landscape that might have been created in the studios of Walt Disney. Overnight the arid pasture was flooded by an ocean of violet, turquoise, saffron, and rose. Clover, iris, buttercup and dandelion, crane's-bill and camomile, orchid and the endless species of wild sweet-pea overwhelmed and obliterated the soil. Even the dusty road vanished beneath rolling breakers of pale-blue convolvulus. It was a recurring miracle that seemed to daze even the fighting bulls grazing Bologna's meadows. Sullen, fly-haloed, and combative throughout the rest of the seasons, they stood in spring wide-eyed and amiable, as the rainbow of blossom lapped up their flanks and garlands of petals tangled with their horns.

The hills' flowering was little more than an eye's blink in the year's passage. As it happened, spring was announced in the Guadalmesi by another signal, the arrival of the migrant birds from Africa. Like the flowers they too came in waves, species by species. For me the final confirmation that winter had ended and the log fires were no longer needed was the appearance of the first bee-eaters. Flashing green, bronze and gold, they streamed across the straits from Africa and skimmed whistling over the forest, before lifting into the sierras where they dispersed to nest in colonies in the sandy walls and gullies and ravines.

By mid-June and the Algeciras fair, the last of the bird migration was over. Soon afterwards the flowers began to wilt and die back into the ground.

July and August were the valley's months of summer. The earth contracted under the heat, the Guadalmesi river shrunk, the air was heavy with dust, and the days long and listless. In the glades beneath the cork oaks, tall yellow thistles rose from the cracked soil, and brimstone butterflies and whirring day-flying moths circled the sun-bleached grass. September brought the annual season of forest fires. Most of them were started by natural causes, a bolt of lightning or the sun's rays concentrated through a discarded fragment of glass, but there was little doubt that their incidence and ferocity grew as the Franco régime declined. Arson had long been a favourite weapon in the battles between the peasantry and the land-owners, and the Andalucian woodland in early autumn was a favourite target.

'Communists and anarchists,' a local estate-owner re-marked to me bitterly one year as we watched the flames rage along a ridge, 'they're responsible for all this. They should be brought out here, every one of them, shot in the knees and dropped from a helicopter right where it's hottest. Then let's see if they can crawl their way out.'

The fires were terrifying wherever they broke out along the coast, but they were at their most dangerous on the hills bordering the straits where the swirling winds could change their direction from moment to moment. One instant, a wall of flame would be advancing towards the west; the next, it would have doubled back on itself and be racing the other way. In the valley there was no need for an organized system of alarms. Within moments of a fire starting a plume of smoke would be rising over the trees, everyone would have seen it and have turned out to fight the blaze. If the fire became serious the two little communities of the Guadalmesi and La Ahumada were reinforced by the local fire service from Pelayo, the Guardia Civil, the military, and sometimes by specially adapted planes which dived down over the forest and dropped loads of sand on to the flames. Often a fire seemed to have burnt itself out only to erupt again a few hundred yards away several days later. Feeding on tree and scrub roots the flames would have eaten their way underground before re-surfacing in a fresh patch of bush.

One obvious method of limiting the damage the fires caused would have been to cut breaks in the forest. The problem was the cork oaks. Every oak in the valley, like all the oaks in the Campo de Gibraltar, had been declared part of the *patrimonio nacional*, the national heritage of Spain. Technically, not even the smallest tree could be felled without permission from Madrid. Inevitably of course if someone wanted to clear a little area in the woods a series of 'accidents' caused by reversing trucks took place. The owner reported the trees as casualties and avoided the normal heavy fine. The clearance of a firebreak was another matter. The number of oaks that would have had to be felled was considered unacceptable because of the value of their crop, the cork. Harvested about every nine years, cropping intervals were strictly-controlled and depended on weather cycles, the cork was a significant factor in the local economy.

One mature tree could provide the equivalent of a week's wages for an average peasant family. Forest land was, not surprisingly, highly valued – a thickly wooded *parcela*, a plot, like the Huerto Perdido's was capable of supporting one hundred trees. In fact when land changed hands the buyer, unless it was specifically included in the contract, did not acquire the rights to the cork. These were retained by the seller in perpetuity. If the purchaser wanted the trees, he had to buy, in the local phrase, *suelo y cielo*, the floor and the sky, and he would pay correspondingly more.

When the bark was taken, the trunks were stripped bare from the roots to the start of the branches. Every year that followed produced a new layer of crinkly grey-brown fungus – the cork 'bark', in spite of its name, is not part of the tree but a parasite that grows on it – until the cork was one or two inches thick and the oaks were deemed ready for cropping again. In the case of the Huerto Perdido it was an extremely moot point who owned the cork. As foreigners we were barred from owning land in the Campo de Gibraltar. The El Cuarton company had hoped to get round this by obtaining a decree from Madrid giving the estate a special exempt status, but the wheels of Spanish bureaucracy moved slowly and consent was taking a long time to come through. Until it did the house technically didn't exist.

When our first approved cropping year came round I took the law into my own hands. I got hold of Manolo the wood-man, a wily and gap-toothed peasant entrepreneur from Pelayo who provided us with logs. Normally we'd have made a straightforward share-cropping deal, dividing whatever the cork-processing factory in Algeciras paid us. But in view of the considerable uncertainty, to say the least, about the cork's ownership, I reckoned the further back I stood from the venture the better. So I offered Manolo the cork outright at a very reduced price.

Manolo, who was aware of the problem, listened to the proposal and chuckled. 'What you mean, Don Nicholas,' he said, 'is if the Guardia Civil start looking for three missing truck-loads, they'll come after me first.'

'Exactly, Manolo,' I answered. 'On the other hand you've got more experience than I in not being at home when they call.'

Manolo haggled the price down a few more pesetas a kilo. Then he agreed. The bargain was too good to refuse. As the sun rose at 5.00 next morning, he returned to the house with his ancient wood truck and six helpers. By midday they were finished and the cork, cut by machete and peeled away in long strips, had gone. Manolo returned the same evening with the money after being paid by the factory where he'd delivered the load.

'If the Guardia come searching for me,' he said, 'tell them not to bother. I'm off to Granada for a week.'

The decree protecting the cork oaks was issued at a time when there was virtually no building in the forest. What little there was consisted of stone cottages. The cottages were often gutted by the autumn fires but the oaks themselves seemed little affected. The flames swept through, devouring the under-

75

growth and the leaf canopy above, but making no impression on the hardwood trunks. Next spring as the sap rose the leaves budded again. When development started to spread out from Algeciras and the hazard to life and property increased, the decree was amended and fire-breaks were finally cut. Until then the months of September and October were often a tense time in the house. If a blaze had swept down from the ridge or jumped the channel of the Guadalmesi and come rolling up the hill, the white bird in the trees would have been entirely unprotected. Sometimes we went to bed surrounding by a horse-shoe of flames on the crests of the Cabrito and with the crackle of blazing scrub echoing through the darkness. In the morning the house would smell of smoke and charred wood, and the fires would still be burning under the sun.

Apart from fire, the trees were attacked periodically in summer by a pest well-known in the USA but relatively uncommon in western Europe, the *oruga* or gypsy moth. Local lore along the straits held that the moth went through a seven-year cycle. For six of the seven years the moths were dormant. In the seventh year they erupted and covered the trees. Then they would vanish for another seven years before returning to strip the forest again. In fact gypsy moth populations are controlled by the level of predation on their eggs. The number of insects eating the eggs depends in turn on sun, rain, temperature, and a range of other variables. Yet checking the local records in Algeciras I found the rough and ready reckoning was remarkably accurate. For over half a century the forest had been attacked regularly every seven years.

The gypsy moth invaded the valley twice while we were there. Both times the effect was like a biblical plague. Rising one morning I noticed the tree trunks were swarming with tiny green caterpillars striped with bands of red. By evening they had reached the branches and were spreading out towards the leaves. At midnight they started to feed. That night the sound of millions of tiny mouths munching was no more than a background murmur. Next day the *levante* blew and drowned out every other noise in the valley. With dusk the wind dropped and the sound returned. This time it was no longer a murmur but a voracious shredding gobble that reverberated through the rooms. It continued until dawn and through the following day, growing louder every hour as the caterpillars gorged themselves and grew until they were ten or fifteen times their size when the eggs hatched.

Sleep became almost impossible. Apart from the noise, the caterpillars invaded the house, tumbling through every chink and crack, rippling over the floors and the furniture, and layering the food in the kitchen. Outside they spun webs to help them move from branch to branch. Soon the house was shrouded in a sticky grey cocoon and the trees were half hidden behind swaying gossamer curtains. Then, as swiftly as it had started, the infestation was over. The caterpillars anchored themselves in clusters to the trunks and turned into cocoons. The sound of munching disappeared and the clinging webs were blown away. Afterwards, the trees stood incongruously bare and leafless in a winter landscape under the July sun.

Until Gibraltar's closure triggered the investment boom in Algeciras, the gypsy moth eruptions were treated as little more than an irregular inconvenience. Afterwards, with houses spilling out from the town into the forest, the caterpillars changed from an inconvenience into a problem. As well as the oak leaves, they started to attack the newly planted gardens and orchards. To combat them the local authorities made available supplies of DDT-based insecticide at subsidised prices. By then the lethal toxins in DDT were already common knowledge in many countries – not, however, in Spain and certainly not in southern Andalucía. To the peasant communities of the straits, the insecticide's availability transformed the caterpillars from a natural hazard like lightning into a legitimate enemy, an enemy that had the sanction and support of authority to be attacked.

When the caterpillars now appeared, the peasants hunted them enthusiastically, pumping DDT powder indiscriminately over the trees, the undergrowth, and the grass. The effect on the gypsy moth larvae was marginal, but the consequences for

77

the rest of the wildlife were devasting. Insects, butterflies, bees, birds, and mammals died in their thousands. A few days after a spraying, the ground beneath the trees looked like an open air morgue littered with tiny corpses. Although it was less noticeable, the poison in the food chain inevitably affected the larger animals too, and the area's population of foxes, badgers, otters, mongoose, genets and wild cats must have suffered appalling losses.

'I'm sure they know what they're doing,' José said to me unhappily one summer as a Calandra lark fell dead on the earth at our feet, 'but it does seem a great waste to achieve so little. The leaves come back anyway, they always have done. All the *orugas* do is clean the forest.'

It was true. Within a month of the trees being stripped the leaves would shoot again. By late August the winter landscape would have taken on the colours of a spring flowering, bright and pale yellow-green. Afterwards there would be nothing to show the valley had suffered a gypsy moth visitation.

To my lasting regret I was as badly informed at the time about the evils of chlorinated hydrocarbons as the most self-confident official in the Algeciras office at the Ministry of Agriculture. The swarming caterpillars were an unpleasant irritant, and the ministry's magic powder appeared, from the claims made on its behalf, to be a swift and effective way of dealing with them.

Fortunately, well before we left the valley legislation had been put through to ban its use. By then the communities of the straits had largely abandoned using it of their own choice. Like José, they had seen the slaughter and come to the realisation something was profoundly wrong.

After the intermittent raids of the *orugas* and the invariable autumn fires came the first rains. As unpredictable as anything else in the valley they sometimes began in late August, before the summer was even drawing to its end, and sometimes not until November. More often they started in the early weeks of October. It was the season I liked best of all. The valley's harvest was home, the days were long and golden, the river was refreshed by the showers, the entire Guadalmesi was quiet and reflective. José leaned on his fork and contentedly studied the contours of the land below the house. Manolo the dustman had time to pause and discuss the affairs of La Ahumada before heading back on his laden mule towards the Cabrito ridge. Even the moon-plagued Domingo lost some of the frenzy in his rolling eyes, walking up to the Huerto Perdido to show me some little bird or animal he'd trapped and for once hadn't felt doomed to kill. The air was keen, the ground bright with autumn crocuses, pale violet in colour and lifting their petals straight from the still-bare earth, and across the straits the hills of Africa quivered in the sun. Soon afterwards it was Christmas, the rains thickened, and the annual cycle began again.

If the seasonal shape of the valley's year soon became well defined, so too did the pattern of the human calendar. Throughout Spain and in Andalucía above all, the year revolved round *ferias*, fairs, and *fiestas*, festivals. The principal difference between the two is that a *feria* is a general and often quite lengthy celebration, lasting as much as two weeks, while a *fiesta* celebrates a particular incident, day, or occasion. Some of the fairs and festivals have unquestionably taken over from much more ancient pagan celebrations, but the vast majority are firmly rooted in the traditional calendar of the church. First there are the great religious anniversaries like Easter, Whitsun, and Christmas. After them come the newly-instituted national holidays with names which to visitors often sound puzzling: the Day of the Race, an affirmation of national unity, the Day of the Migration, reminding the nation of its citizens who have left the countryside for the cities, and the Day of *Hispanidad*, of 'Spanishness', celebrating the links between Spain and its former possessions in the New World. Finally, and most important of all, there are the local celebrations held all over the country in honour of the patron saint of every town, every village, even every hamlet.

For the Andaluz the region's fairs and festivals are far more than holidays from the year's work. They are the very reason and justification for the year, occasions to be immersed in with passion and commitment. No one would dream of rising late when *fiesta* or *feria* come round. As in Yeats' poem of the marriage feast, the holidays are times to be packed with banneret and pennon, trumpet and kettle-drum, although unlike the poem the celebration doesn't end with darkness. It continues throughout the night until the sky lightens with morning. Then, without sleep, the Andaluz goes about his business again.

'I work harder getting ready for *feria* than at any other time of the year,' Manolo the dustman said to me one August as we were discussing the forthcoming Tarifa fair. 'I spend more money, I sleep less, it haunts my dreams for weeks before. Yet when it's ended I feel well-fed.'

He patted his belly and smiled. 'It gives me the spirit to survive for another year. However much I dread the expense and the time and the trouble, I'm always waiting for *feria* to come round again. I'm like a child. If I didn't have it to look forward to, I would have nothing.'

There were two main fairs on the straits. The first was in Algeciras in June, the second in Tarifa in September. The length and variety of any Spanish *feria* depends on the size and wealth of the local community. During the two-week San Isidro celebrations in Madrid, in addition to a host of other events, there are at least one, sometimes two, bullfights every day. The *feria* of Algeciras, an affluent medium-sized town, also went on for two weeks but only included three or four bullfights, the most the town could support. During the two weeks the streets would be decked with flags and banners, the bars and restaurants would be on holiday and the children wearing party suits and dresses. Each day's celebrations would be launched by a specific activity: the crowning of the *feria* queen, a horse-drawn carriage parade, a performance of singing and dancing in the town's little park. If a bullfight was on the day's programme, it would follow at 6.00 p.m. Afterwards the festivities would begin in earnest.

The heart of a *feria* in any Andalucian town is the fairground itself. In Algeciras this lay just outside the city centre to the east. Throughout the two weeks it was a gaudy, raucous fairyland of dazzling lights, deafening music, soaring ferris wheels, and careering dodgem cars. There were candyfloss stalls, bingo parlours, shooting galleries, lucky-dip stands, packed bars, and glittering circling carousels. One of the favourite attractions was Manolita Chen's Chinese Theatre, an itinerant vaudeville group which wandered from fair to fair performing bawdy knock-about sketches that revolved round carping mothers-in-law, cuckolded husbands and endlessly-mislaid pieces of underwear. Next to Manolita Chen, an immensely fat Spanish lady with breasts of blue-veined marble and cold, needle-sharp eyes, was the arcade of the *insolitos*, the unusual ones or freaks. There the children would stand for hours gazing in fascination at the mustachioed and bearded lady, the mermaid and the shark-woman, both in tanks of water that looked like transparent Victorian bath-tubs, and the maned lion-man who snarled at the bars of his cage and at feeding time nibbled unenthusiastically at a very small piece of raw steak.

Dominating everything at the *feria* were the *casetas*, literally meaning 'small houses' but referring to the half-tented private clubs where the members and their guests could meet, drink, talk and dance. There were ten or twelve of them, although the number grew each year. Some belonged to the industrial corporations which were colonizing Algeciras bay, some to the town's clubs and institutions, some to private groups like the fan-club of the famous local bullfighter, Miguelin. A pass to a good *caseta*, as difficult to obtain as a pass to the Royal Enclosure at Ascot, was the essential passport to all the pleasures of the *feria*. Outside the closely guarded doors the crowds jostled and sweated and squealed. Inside, families met together, dancers whirled on the floor, waiters raced between the tables with ice-cold half bottles of sherry, friends gathered in laughing gossiping circles, and business deals were struck between the town's portly merchants, inevitably wearing heavy dark glasses and their grey black suits. All the while music from a dozen bands – each *caseta* had its own – fountained up into the sky, mingling and blending with the tunes rising from the carousels and ferris wheels.

Algeciras' *feria* was by the standards of the straits large and sumptuous, a kaleidoscope of sound, colour and entertainment which acted as a magnet to people from miles around. By comparison Tarifa's fair at the other end of the straits was a very modest occasion. It lasted for only a week, its little wood-framed bullring between the fishermen's cottages and the Atlantic staged a single low-key *corrida*, and its attendance consisted entirely of the town's citizens and country folk from the immediate vicinity. Yet what it lacked in ostentation the 'most noble and loyal millennium city' more than made up for in dignity, quality, and sheer delight. Its religious relics were few compared to those of Algeciras, but they were lovingly decorated and fervently applauded as they were carried in procession through the narrow streets. Its *feria* queen, the Tarifeños proudly insisted, was without peer for beauty in Andalucía. Its tiny public gardens, even at the end of the long summer, were always scrupulously clean and ablaze with flowers. Above all there was the setting of the fair itself.

Twenty-five years ago most Spanish *ferias* took place where they had always been held, in the everyday streets and squares of the towns. Today many local authorities, reluctant to disturb local business and confronted by ever-increasing crowds at the annual celebrations, have set aside land beyond the city limits as the fair's site. Shortly after our arrival in the valley, that became the case in Algeciras, but for years after Algeciras succumbed to the pressures of commerce, Tarifa held fast to the old habits. Its *feria* took place on a shelf of sloping ochre-coloured earth that ran down beside the ancient city walls to the sea. There, up against the crumbling ramparts and beneath a few withered palm trees, Tarifa mounted its own celebration.

There were no soaring ferris wheels or clanging dodgem cars, no lavishly costumed bands or crowded private *casetas*. Instead, quietly, without fuss or ceremony, the little port offered its own side-shows and attractions in the September dusk. Many of the most popular stalls that lined the fair's single dusty lane offered contests of true skill. The equipment for one particular favourite consisted of no more than a large wooden plank, a heavy mallet, and some long steel nails. The object was to drive a nail through the plank with only three blows and without the nail bending. For the old craftsmen of the town, the carpenters, wheelwrights, and ship-builders, it was no problem. They'd gather round the stall chuckling as they demonstrated their skill. Then they'd hand the mallet to one of the younger Tariteños and roar with laughter as the nails buckled, or some unfortunate youth howled with pain as a misjudged blow hit his thumb. It was a game Odysseus must have played and no doubt it would have been considered ancient even then.

For the children Tarifa's fair, as well as all the wonders of the stalls, had two pleasures unrivalled even by Algeciras' mermaid and Manolita Chen's falling knickers. First were the little balls sold by old women from the hills outside the town. The balls were made from sun-dried chicken skin, cut, stuffed, and sewn, and then attached to a length of rubber. Custom required that every child was bought one, and the fair clicked and snapped with the games and battles the pinging, bouncing balls provoked. The fair's other delight was its ghost train. It must have been the smallest and oldest ghost train in all Spain. Pulled by a tiny petrol engine with a single carriage behind, it chugged round a little circular track, half in the open and half through an improvised tunnel. Inside the tunnel were skeletons, cobwebs, bloodstains, and fluttering bats, but the real terror was in the open. Each time the train came out into the starlight a fearsome wolf-man would leap from hiding, race along beside the carriage with blood-curdling yells, and belabour the children with a mangled hand attached to a stick. The children would shriek and cower, the train would bucket back into the tunnel, and the wolf-man would hurriedly change into the costume of an old witch. Then, armed this time with a swishing broomstick, he'd begin the chase again.

Over the years we visited or took part in *ferias* and *fiestas* the length and breadth of Andalucía. Some were rich and glittering like the spring fair in Sevilla which attracts visitors from all over the world. Others lasted only an afternoon and evening, and were attended by no more than a hundred people. All had their own traditions and idiosyncrasies. At Gáucin, on the sierra road from the Guadalmesi valley to Ronda, a solitary young bull was run through the narrow streets, echoing the famous early-morning stampedes at Pamplona during San Firmin. At one little hill village *feria* starts on Palm Sunday. The night before, every house, street, and square is covered with fresh-cut green branches. When the sun rises the next day the white houses have vanished and the village has become part of the surrounding forest. On Christmas Eve in another, *misa del gallo*, the cock's-crow mass to celebrate Christ's birth, is also a service of blessing for animals, and the church is filled with horses, mules, donkeys, pigs, sheep, and goats, braying, snorting and stamping as they jostle for space with the villagers.

Another form of *fiesta* common throughout the Andalucian countryside is the *romería*, or pilgrimage. Set at a distance from a number of villages is an isolated hermitage or chapel, almost always dedicated to the Virgin, which commemorates some long-ago event – perhaps a miraculous deliverance or, as at Andujar, the appearance of the Virgin herself to a thir-

Romería near Tarifa

84

teenth-century shepherd. Wherever these shrines exist, once a year the village's inhabitants gather together and walk in procession, or more often now drive, to the chapel. After mass has been celebrated and the Virgin has been paraded round the meadows, the occasion turns into a huge open-air picnic with the roasting of chickens and singing and dancing until darkness. Some shrines attract pilgrims from more than one village. The best-known in all Spain, the *romería* to the Virgin of Rocío in the marshes at the mouth of the Guadalquivir west of Sevilla, lasts for a week and draws its pilgrims from all over the country.

In spite of Sevilla's glitter, the attractions of the sierra village *fiestas*, and the splendours of the Rocío pilgrimage, from the start Tarifa's modest little *feria* became and remained my favourite of all Andalucía's celebrations. The town was local and familiar. Every turn brought invitations to a drink or friends to be greeted, including several who'd trekked across the hills from the valley to celebrate with Tarifa's own citizens, many of them relatives. More than that, the fair had a gentleness and contentment all of its own. It may have lacked Algeciras' exuberance and excitement, but every laugh and every guitar chord, every squeal of delight from a child and every triumphant clang of a bell from a stall, rang sharp and clear through the soft autumn air. The year was done and the harvest gathered. The scattered family of the straits had reunited for a party. It was time for reminiscence, enjoyment and companionship. In the background the crumbling walls of Guzman's castle gleamed golden-brown in the lamplight. An orange hunter's moon hung in the sky. The stars shone, the Jerez wine was cold, and the wind blew fresh from Africa.

85

✌ 7 ✌

As in most small peasant communities the valley's life had a certain formality. Everything had its proper time, its proper place, and its proper way of being attended to. One of the yearly rituals was to *encalar*, or lime-wash, the houses at the end of the spring rains.

Lime is used inside and out on almost all southern Spanish dwellings, from a gypsy hovel to a great landowner's *cortijo*, and the dazzling white villages are one of the most characteristic sights of the Andalucian countryside. Although the villages somehow give the impression of having been painted white for centuries, the universal use of lime is relatively recent. Not long ago the clay, brick or stone of most villages was left untouched. Then, in a move to limit the spread of disease and improve the country people's standard of health, a series of government decrees made lime-washing obligatory because of lime's strong disinfectant properties. In some remoter areas, like the Alpujarras mountains, the laws are still sometimes ignored and the grey villages blend with the rocky slopes, but more generally there is no longer any need to enforce them. Lime-washing has become part of rural Andalucian culture. It is pretty and clean – 'healthy' is the favourite Andaluz' expression to describe it – and after half a dozen coats it has the added virtue of helping to waterproof a building.

The cork trees that surrounded the Huerto Perdido gave off a powdery yellow-brown dust which settled in a fine layer on the house's roof. When the rains started they washed the dust off the roof and down the walls. By the end of the winter the white bird, like all the cottages in the forest, looked dirty, bedraggled, and moulting. As soon as the Algeciras fair ended I would see José wandering round the house and gazing fretfully at the stains through his glasses. I knew it was time to *encalar*. We bought our lime from a kiln up a winding track on a hillside outside Algeciras. The raw lime was quarried from the hill behind and lay in mounds of sharp-edged ochre-coloured boulders round the kiln's entrance. The kiln itself was like a cattle byre built above a trench in the ground. Many Andalucian kilns are open-sided but this one, lying on the straits, had to be walled because of the rains. Inside the trench was a blazing, ferociously hot fire fuelled by logs cut under special dispensation from the forest. Above the fire, resting on a massive iron grid, were the raw boulders. It took two days to refine them for use as lime-wash and the temperature had to remain constant throughout. If it dropped the lime was spoiled. In practice the kiln burned for months on end and the fire was tended day and night by a guard who lived in a little cabin to one side.

José chose as much as he thought we needed, sifting carefully for pieces of exactly the right texture. Then the chalky lumps were weighed, paid for, and taken back to the house. There a few of them were steeped overnight in water and by the morning they were ready to use. Once prepared the lime had to be put on at once or it would curdle and go bad. In a few places people added a coloured powder to produce a pale pastel wash, but like most Andaluz we preferred to apply ours in its pure form. The mixture had the consistency of silk and José spread it on with a long cane-handled brush. Lime-wash can be applied to virtually any surface. When first put on the wash is transparent. Then, as it dries, the sparkling snowy whiteness appears. Gradually over the years it builds up into a thick blanket, softening and rounding the edges of doorsteps, mouldings and porticoes.

'Well, Don Nicholas,' José remarked happily every year when he had finished, 'the white bird's ready to fly again. She can go looking for her summer *novio*.'

87

Liming was a mid-June ceremonial. A few months later, in September, another of the valley's rituals, equally regular although this time entirely uncontrollable, took place – the loosing of the pigs in the forest.

One of Andalucía's greatest gastronomic delicacies is *jamón serrano*, the sweet smoked ham cured in the mountains. The ham comes from two varieties of pig, the white and the red. The white is a domestic hybrid. Large, well fleshed and slow moving, it is reared on farms and smallholdings. The red is a very different creature. Swift, muscular and lean – although some of the boars can reach a spectacular size – it is closely descended from the boars of the ancient wild-wood. Both are highly valued but when it comes to smoked ham the red, particularly a red fed on forest acorns, is considered peerless.

It was the reds which were turned loose in the valley when the acorns started to fall. They appeared, untended, overnight. Unlike goats or cattle they needed no herd. They seemed to avoid the coastal road by instinct; each group settled and stayed in a small area, and they could be gathered by their anonymous owners at will. The acorns from the Huerto Perdido's tall oaks were renowned as the plumpest and most succulent in the Guadalmesi. Inevitably a group of reds always attached itself to the area round the house. As with every type of Andalucian land use, it was normal for the owner of an area of oak forest to make a share-cropping agreement with a pig breeder over the acorn crop. Most often the pigs would be weighed before and after they were set free beneath the trees. The value of the weight gain at the end would be divided between the landowner and the breeder, with the owner taking his share in cash or in pork. As owner of the Huerto Perdido's few but acorn-rich acres we were entitled to strike a bargain with the peasant who grazed his pigs there, but the sum involved would have been tiny and we never bothered. So, every autumn, we allowed the pigs to roam the garden without even knowing who they belonged to.

For several years all went well. Then the problems began. Abandoning Bannenberg's idea of leaving the land round the

88

house wild, I started to fashion a proper garden. It was very modest: some clumps of indigenous iris and oleander along the stream, a few orchids from the sierras, the geraniums and pelargoniums that frame every Andalucian cottage, cuttings of cistus and rock rose Elisabeth had brought back from our journeys. The trouble was, the pigs seemed convinced that whatever I planted was to mark and camouflage a source of food in the earth beneath. José and I would dig, plant, and water all spring and summer. As soon as autumn arrived and the acorns began to fall, the pigs would appear and launch a scorched earth strike on our efforts, ploughing through and upending everything we'd painstakingly put in. José, a son of the valley, was philosophical.

'It is their nature, Don Nicholas,' he'd say, watching with unconcealed admiration the sleek, sinewy flanks of a yearling sow as she battered some carefully-transplanted wild lily into submission, and then gobbled up the bulb. 'They have their ways, we have ours. Besides, look at the red of their hides and the red of the *chaparros* trunks. They make a fine picture together.'

I had neither José's phlegm nor his artist's eye. The pigs' assaults enraged me. Autumn, until then my favourite season in the valley, became a time of battle. The enemy was swift-footed, cunning, and extremely vocal. I took to hunting them by night, tracking a piglet through the scrub, hurling myself on top of it, and dragging it squealing through the thorny bush to a shed, where I'd imprison it in the hope the animal's owner would be forced to identify himself in order to reclaim it. Somehow by dawn the shed's lock would have been picked and the piglet would be gone, only to return next day and resume its attacks on the garden. I had almost reconciled myself to accepting defeat when one October I was provoked beyond control.

Getting up early one morning I walked into the living-room and saw through the windows at the front of the house the largest red boar I had ever seen. Mahogany-coloured with a bristling spine, trumpet-shaped ears, and huge, splayed feet, it was standing on the patio. As I watched it casually butted over a tub and began rooting in the spilled earth for the orchid rhizomes which represented a month's laborious collecting in the hills. I hurled open the glass doors and raced towards it bellowing in fury. The boar took off like a rocket. It galloped along the terrace. Then for a split-second it paused.

To its right was the forest, to the left the towering French windows opening off our bedroom. With the windows closed and the curtains drawn inside, the glass had become a mirror, reflecting the sky and the trees on the far side of the patio. To the boar both the real and reflected forest must have appeared the same, except the one in the glass was closer. It barely hesitated. The animal launched itself forward, gathered speed, and hurled itself through the window. Elisabeth was lying asleep inside. One moment she was on her own. The next, three hundred pounds of trumpeting boar haloed by shattered glass had ricochetted off the floor and was in bed with her. Elisabeth understandably screamed. The boar, even more terrified, whirled round, tossed off the clinging sheets, and smashed its way back into daylight through the other panel of glass. Then it bolted away into the scrub beneath the oaks. I watched it disappear in fury and anguish.

For the next twenty-four hours we tried to trace the boar's owner. In a community as small as the Guadalmesi it should have been easy. It wasn't. Either no one knew or if they did they weren't prepared to say. Then Manolo the dustman was called to the house. Manolo was a recognized authority on the valley's affairs. Also, as its major pig breeder, he was more likely than anyone else to know who the animal belonged to.

For a time Manolo scratched his head gloomily as Elisabeth questioned him. Then an idea struck him and he suddenly brightened up.

'I've just remembered, *señora*,' he said. 'From your description I'm sure the *bicho*, the animal, belongs to a gentleman from Málaga.'

'Málaga?' Elisabeth looked sceptical. Málaga was a hundred miles away.

'Yes, I'm certain it's him,' Manolo struggled on. 'He drives up here every morning to check on the animals. Much too early, of course, for you to see him. He has to get back in time for his business in the city. Maybe if I rode down very early from La Ahumada I could catch him before he leaves.'

Manolo's voice trailed away. The improbabilities in the story were becoming too great even for him to keep up.

'It doesn't belong to a man from Málaga,' Elisabeth said crisply. 'It belongs to someone in the valley. You know who he is and I want to know too, Manolo.'

Manolo went pink and shuffled uncomfortably.

'Even if I knew, *señora*, I couldn't possibly tell you. I'd never be forgiven.'

'Well,' Elisabeth said after a moment's reflection, 'if you won't tell me his name, I'm still going to tell everyone you did. That way you get the worst of both worlds. You'll be blamed by me and you'll be blamed by everyone else. Think about it until tomorrow, Manolo.'

Manolo stared at her appalled. The Machiavellian subtlety of the threat was unlike anything that had ever been put to him. Scowling and scratching his head again he stumped away. Next day, for the first time anyone could remember, he didn't appear for work.

A day later with still no sign of Manolo and the great red boar still harrowing the garden I invoked the ultimate sanction. I went to the Guardia Civil and denounced the unknown owner. The denunciation, a formal laying of complaint, was the equivalent in Spanish law of a civil action, although its effect was rather more complicated and the same process could be used in criminal cases too. The police investigate the charge. If they find substance in it, both parties involved are required to present themselves before a local court where the dispute is heard and settled.

I had little confidence my denunciation would ever come to hearing. If I who lived in the valley couldn't trace the owner, it seemed most unlikely the widely feared and disliked Guardia Civil would have any better chance of success. I was wrong. To my surprise I returned to the house a week later to find a message. The owner had been identified. Would I please be in court at Tarifa the following morning when the case would be heard.

Tarifa's courthouse was a small and old building above the port, looking over a tiny square whose garden was decorated by a number of bright green and rather endearing glazed pottery frogs. When I arrived at the doorway I found the usual morning throng of petitioners, defendants, lawyers, and bureaucrats, perhaps a dozen in all. Among them I was puzzled to see an old friend of mine from the valley named Gaspar. Gaspar was a stocky, cheerful peasant with greying hair and strong, splayed hands, who worked as a casual labourer in the Guadalmesi. On several occasions he'd helped José with jobs at the Huerto Perdido.

'What are you doing here?' I asked him.

Gaspar looked furtive and uneasy. 'I happened to be in town, Don Nicholas, and I came along to see what was happening.'

We talked for a few minutes. Then my case was called. I went into the bare little courtroom and sat down. A moment later to my astonishment I saw Gaspar enter and sit in the seat reserved for the defendant. He glanced at me, gave a shrug of resignation, and turned to stare impassively at the judge, who was sitting behind the desk.

When I was called to give evidence I said I'd just discovered the whole issue had arisen from a misunderstanding. The matter had now been resolved to my satisfaction and I wished to withdraw the complaint. As he had the power to do under the denunciation process, the judge refused my request. Gaspar, he said, had been investigated by the police and found to have allowed his animals to roam my land; he was therefore guilty of a misdemeanour. He was to pay for the broken windows and be fined 5,000 pesetas, worth about £25. Gaspar nodded without comment and slipped out. I caught up with him in the patio of the glazed green frogs.

'Why didn't you come to see me?' I demanded. 'You know I'd never have made the denunciation if I'd realized it was you. What happened and how did the Guardias find you?'

'It's *muy complicado*, Don Nicholas,' he answered. 'In strict confidence I will try to explain.'

I listened. *Muy complicado*, very complicated, was Andalucian shorthand for matters of almost impenetrable complexity. It certainly described Gaspar's story. He didn't in fact own the pigs. They belonged to a syndicate in which Gaspar had a minute interest in return for keeping an eye on them in the forest. The syndicate, which included a couple of small traders from Algeciras, had acquired the pigs in the first place under extremely dubious circumstances. From Gaspar's evasive account it seemed quite possible they had been rustled in one of the traders' vans from somewhere else in the sierras.

When the windows were broken Gaspar had wanted to come to me but the two Algecireños, frightened of any contact outside the syndicate which might lead back to them, forbade him. Then when the Guardia Civil was brought in another council of war was held. Much more frightened a police investigation would uncover the pigs' background, the syndicate decided Gaspar as a front man should go voluntarily to the Guardias and declare himself the pigs' sole owner.

As a peasant, it was reckoned, he would be dealt with more

93

leniently by the judge. The investigation would then be dropped and everyone could breathe again.

'So that's what happened,' Gaspar finished. 'Please don't concern yourself about me. My associates have plenty of money. They will pay for the broken windows and the fine. It will cost me nothing. I will even charge them for my bus fare to court.'

Gaspar grinned. 'To show there are no hard feelings, Don Nicholas, permit me to buy you a drink.'

We headed for the nearest bar.

That afternoon Gaspar moved the boar and its companions to a distant part of the forest. For the rest of the year the garden was left in peace, but next autumn I woke one morning to the now familiar grunts outside. By then I'd given up. The peasants and their pigs had been cropping the Huerto Perdido for centuries. They had a better right to its acorns, I decided, than I could claim for our flowers. I barriered the plants I was determined to save with stakes. Then like José I tried to enjoy the chestnut hides moving through the sun and shadow beneath the ox-blood trunks.

The para-military Guardia Civil with whom I'd filed the denunciation are one of the four separately administered police bodies which, as everywhere else in Spain, regulate Andalucian life. In addition to its complement of Guardias each town of sufficient size has its own corps of municipal police who control traffic and deal with minor local offences like parking violations. Then there are the highway police, patrolling in pairs on fast motorcycles. Because of the importance attached by Franco to Spain's relatively few roads, strategically and as sources of intelligence about the countryside, the highway police are the best trained and most efficient of the four groups. Lastly there are the secret police. Based in key towns and ports, such as Algeciras, their role is almost entirely intelligence-gathering, and they have a particular responsibility for foreigners and 'subversives'.

Among the four bodies by far the most numerous and noticeable, with their distinctive green uniforms and black

94

tricorn hats, are the armed members of the Guardia Civil. The highway and secret police, in spite of their often better educated, better paid and notionally more powerful officers, are only props to the maintenance of the law and the state. In a very real sense the Guardia Civil *is* the law of Spain. Although created to serve and answerable ostensibly to the judiciary, in many places, particularly in the remoter country areas, it metes out its own rough and ready brand of justice without any reference to the courts. A peasant may be suspected of theft. If the grounds seem good enough the Guardias are capable of arresting him, thrashing him mercilessly in the station cells, and tossing him out with a firm warning not to steal again.

As a system of law, backed up by the courts, it is very little different from the one that operated acceptably in Andalucía for hundreds of years. The difference under the Franco regime was that it was administered to 'foreigners'. Because of the country's strong regional loyalties – the endless problem of the different Spains – the Guardia Civil, like the highway and secret police, were always posted for duty to areas far away from the ones where they had been brought up. In the past, largely for practical reasons, the practice had been limited mainly to senior servants of the state such as governors, treasurers and military commanders. During the Franco years it became a fetish. Virtually no one, however lowly their position, could serve the state in their home territory.

Inevitably, the Guardia Civil's traditionally tolerated ideas of justice soured in the views of local populations all over Spain. An Andaluz might ruefully accept a beating from a uniformed symbol of authority who at least spoke his own tongue and shared his habits, customs and culture. But to be assaulted by a man like a Catalan or a Basque, whose language he barely understood and whose values and way of life were totally alien to his own, was unendurable. Throughout the country resentment and bitterness against the Guardia Civil accumulated. By the time of Franco's death they had become an even more hated symbol of the repressive regime than the military, the real base on which his power rested.

Along the straits collisions between the Guardias and the local communities were, with one exception, few. From time to time a Guardia post would have to deal with an incident like the boar and the broken windows. There was the occasional robbery, the occasional drunken assault, the occasional crash on the coastal road when a car would skid on the slime dropped by a leaking refrigerated fish truck and the highway police weren't on hand to deal with the accident. In the main, however, life in and around the Guadalmesi was peaceful. The Guardias patrolled the valley regularly on foot, they visited the house at least once a week to check all was well, and the peasants steered carefully clear of them, keeping their own counsel and dealing with their own domestic disputes in their own fashion.

The one exception was over smuggling. In a passage aptly quoted by Alastair Boyd in relation to the sierra town of Ronda but even more applicable to the straits, the nineteenth-century English traveller in Spain, Richard Ford, wrote: 'The masses in Spain go heart in mind with the smuggler as they do in England with the poacher. They shield a bold and useful man who supplies them with a good article at a fair price. Nay, some of the mountain curates whose flocks are all in that line, just deal with the offence as a *pecado venial* and readily absolve those who pay for a little detergent holy water.'

Ford, the best of all commentators on Spain, was writing 130 years ago. The smuggling tradition goes back at least two centuries further still. In the Campo de Gibraltar it still flourishes. There are several reasons. One of the Civil War's many unhappy legacies in Andalucía were small bands of guerrilla soldiers from the defeated Republican army who took refuge in the sierras bordering the straits, either too fearful of the reprisals to rejoin society or else refusing to accept the nationalist victory. With Gibraltar, the tax-free Spanish enclaves of Ceuta and Melilla on the African coast, and the then-free port of Tangiers all less than an hour away in a fast launch across the water, many of them gravitated naturally to smuggling for their livelihood. The last band had been killed in a Guardia Civil ambush half a mile from the valley only eight years before we arrived there.

Then there was the gradual growth of consumer spending power in Spain over the next two decades. It brought with it a demand for goods that were either prohibitively highly taxed or simply unavailable. The merchants of Gibraltar and the other free ports were happy to supply them. All they required was a purchaser who, at a handsome discount, was prepared to buy and run their stock under darkness for re-sale on the mainland. Finally, and in a way, most important, there was the nature and traditions of the people of the straits. Secretive, resourceful, implacably hostile to authority of any sort, smuggling had been part of their life and culture for generations. No doubt when the Phoenicians first colonized Tarifa and imposed their contentious 'tariff' on other traders using the port, little sailing barques had slipped out from tiny bays like the mouth of the Guadalmesi and returned with cargoes of untaxed wares.

Thousands of years later the valley's peasants were not only still enjoying the small illicit luxuries the boats continued to bring in; some of them were actively, if intermittently, engaged in the trade as casual deckhands, muleteers, couriers, or look-outs. In fact there was virtually no one, I came to realize, from the children to the old, who hadn't worked at one time or another with the *contrabandistas*. At the time Ford was writing about, the smugglers' main commodity was *picadura*, real coffee from beans imported into Gibraltar as opposed to the weak acorn-based brew made in the countryside. Coffee was still being smuggled in the early 1960s but by then it had been largely supplanted by Scotch whisky, Virginian cigarettes, contraceptives, nylon underwear and tights. Apart from a little mechanization the technique remained the same as it had always been. Launches would take on a load of contraband from a cargo ship lying in international waters. The launches would run into the Andalucian coast at night and land at some lonely beach or inlet. There the goods would be transferred to waiting mules or porters.

97

'Sometimes we use dogs,' Bartolomeo, an old inhabitant of the Guadalmesi and the valley's most renowned smuggler, explained to me once. 'They're only suitable for light loads like condoms, but they're the safest carriers of all. We train them to wear harnesses and make sure they're kennelled in the hills. When a boat comes in, all we have to do is load them up, give them a whack on the backside, and off they go. No Guardia has a hope of catching a dog on its own at night in the forest. By morning they're miles away in the sierras waiting to be unloaded at the farms where they live.'

For many years condoms, which couldn't be sold in Spain because of the church's teaching on birth control, were one of the smugglers' favourite lines. Then the condom was overtaken in popularity by the contraceptive pill. More portable still, the pill won an even larger market among the country's devout but prudent women. Unfortunately for the *contrabandistas* the lucrative trade in the pill was dealt a mortal blow within a few years of its appearance. With the grudging agreement of the church, Spanish medical opinion pragmatically decided the pill was not primarily a contraceptive device, but a treatment for various menstrual disorders. Accordingly it became available for sale everywhere and the demand for the smuggled consignments dried up. 'Everyone who helps,' Bartolomeo went on, 'gets paid in kind with whatever's being run in. Say it's cigarettes. A couple of cartons goes to a lookout. If we're using mules another couple of cartons to someone who lets us water them half-way up in the sierra. If they provide us with fresh animals, then that's worth maybe twenty cartons. It all depends on the service and the risk. When the mules are far enough back they meet up with a truck on a little road. The goods are transferred to the truck, and the truck sets off for town. Even the driver gets paid with what he's got in the back. No money changes hands until the stuff's sold to the public.'

Some of the smuggled merchandise appeared for sale locally and openly. In both Algeciras and Tarifa it was quite normal to buy contraband cigarettes from the kiosks in the town centres.

The only concession to their source and the presence of a Guardia Civil patrol a few yards away was the formality of wrapping the packs in brown paper. The police were well aware what was happening but it was so widespread, so much part of the fabric of Andalucian life, that once the goods had reached the streets they turned a blind eye. Their efforts were reserved for the boats and the landing parties. Both the Guardias and the smugglers were armed, and their encounters in the darkened coves along the shore were often bloody. No quarter was given or asked on either side. More than once at night I heard the sound of distant gunfire echoing across the valley.

Although the warfare between the Guardia Civil and the *contrabandistas* was unending, the authorities periodically intensified their efforts to stamp out the trade. Whenever they did they depended largely on intelligence about the smugglers' movements from informers. Just outside Algeciras to the east was a small village named Palmones. For reasons no one could ever fully explain to me the population of Palmones was known to consist entirely of police spies. No one from the Campo de Gibraltar would set foot in the village unless it was absolutely necessary. Palmones' *feria* was boycotted; when its people came into Algeciras they were shunned; the very mention of its name was accompanied by a curse and a shower of spittle on the street. Whether deserved or not, the depth of feeling against the people of Palmones was typical of the straits' loyalty to the smugglers and its antipathy to any hint of collaboration with the Guardia Civil against them.

One major problem the Guardias faced with the smugglers was the communications system of the Campo de Gibraltar. To a casual visitor armed with a map it seemed simple enough. There was the coastal highway and a few roads leading off it towards the sierras, but that was all. In fact the whole area was a labyrinth of unmarked roads, tracks, lanes and paths. Some were the ancient rights of way found all over Andalucía like the *cañadas reales*, the old drovers' roads, or the *caminos de heradura*, the bridle paths. Others had been made by the

99

passage of animals across the years – goats and cattle moving down to winter in the valleys or mule trains carrying supplies up to the hill villages. Others still had been created by the smugglers themselves. Their routes were passed down from generation to generation as part of the inherited lore of the little communities. Yet more were a legacy of the straits' long and turbulent history. There were hidden Phoenician tracks, Roman tracks, Moorish tracks. Some quite large and equally unrecorded roads were of a later date. In the eighteenth century the Spanish forces besieging Gibraltar built ten miles of road on the inland slope of a low range of hills behind Algeciras, designed to allow them to move ammunition and supplies out of sight of the garrison on the Rock. The road was still widely used, but it did not appear even on the secret Spanish military maps of the area.

To the Guardia Civil this warren of tracks was a nightmare. If they failed to stop a party of *contrabandistas* at an ambush on the shore they normally gave up. From any one landing point there might be as many as 50 routes up into the hills. To have guarded them all would have required an army. Some of the tracks led up through the valley. Occasionally very late at night there would be the clip of a muffled mule's hoof or the panting of a dog in the darkness outside the house. The children learned early from Ana to follow Kipling's advice and watch the wall as the gentlemen rode by. Sometimes out walking in the hills I'd stop to talk at a tiny farm and be invited in for a drink. More than once I was offered not wine or the local brandy but whisky bottled in Scotland. I accepted it with pleasure and without question. In the sierras one does not ask gentlemen how they fill their cellars.

One of Spain's many reasons for claiming Gibraltar is in order to bring smuggling to an end and so stop the damage which the Spanish argue it does to the economy. There may have been some substance in the charge immediately after the end of the Civil War, but in more recent years its effect has become negligible. More and more, the expanding Spanish home market is being supplied with the *contrabandistas*' traditional goods from the country's own resources. In spite of that, and in spite of increased police pressure, smuggling still survives. I believe the reason is that to the people of the straits and the sierras it represents far more than a source of luxuries or even money. Among the country people the smugglers, just as in Ford's day, are true heroes, symbolic figures who typify defiance against oppression and the occupying forces of the Guardia Civil. By hiding them, supporting them, and working with them, the Andaluz affirms his dignity and freedom. While one laden mule still climbs undetected through the darkness, he retains some measure of control over his destiny. No remote dictator or king will ever be able to levy taxes on the goods that pass by night.

๙ 8 ๙

Sometimes on still, hot summer days we took the children down the valley and picnicked by the Guadalmesi river a mile below the coastal road. The river was at its deepest there, spreading out in wide pools between rocks overhung by alders and pink-blossomed oleander bushes. It was a tranquil, private place. Sleepy-eyed terrapins basked on the stones, water-snakes zig-zagged through the shallows, firecrests flashed in the trees, and the air was drowsy with the humming of bees. Sometimes a pair of griffon vultures passed high overhead, trailing their shadows across the warm grass, and once I saw a hunting otter. While the children fished we read in the shade. Then at the end of the afternoon we'd light a fire, grill the catch over the flames and head back up the hill.

One day, restless because of the heat, I set out to explore the river downstream. For a further half mile the Guadalmesi ran through a steeply shelving ravine. Then it angled to the west and flowed down into the little delta where most of the valley's inhabitants lived. It was hard work but by swimming, wading and clambering I managed to reach the bend. From there on, the ground was much easier. The ravine fell away and the river flowed between a ridge on one side and a high bank on the other. I climbed the bank and walked on. A hundred yards later I almost plunged 30 feet straight down on to a stone-floored courtyard which suddenly appeared beneath me. I leapt back startled and looked round. A moment afterwards I worked out what had happened.

I was standing immediately above an immensely old water-mill built at the foot of the bank. Behind me at the bend in the river there was a sluice gate half-hidden by oleander. From the gate a stone channel, overgrown by grass and wild flowers, ran along the bank to my feet. Obviously neither had been used for some time which was why I had missed them, but when the gates were closed the water was directed along the channel and over the lip below me to fall on to the mill wheel paddles and turn the grinding stone.

I found an equally overgrown flight of stone steps and climbed down into the courtyard. An old man was asleep on a chair in the shadow of a vine. A dog barked and he looked up. I introduced myself and asked if I could see the mill.

'*Mi casa es su casa*,' he answered using the old-fashioned courtesy to a visitor. 'My house is your house.'

His name was Fernando. He was well over eighty and for the valley extremely tall and broad-shouldered. In spite of his age he still had a barrel chest and I could see he must once have been extraordinarily strong. I learned later that in his youth Fernando had been a legendary smuggler, outlaw and woman-iser. Ambushed by the Guardia Civil he killed two of them before escaping, and spent years as the most wanted man in Andalucía living as a bandit in the hills. The mill, which he'd owned for half a century, also had one of the richest riverside plots on the Guadalmesi, and he had other properties in Tarifa, all bought with his contraband earnings. Long since retired, he lived in town but still came back to visit the valley from time to time.

We walked round. On three sides of the courtyard were the stables and the living accommodation. On the fourth was the mill itself with the wheel beside it and a huge three-storey granary behind.

'Look at the stones,' Fernando said pointing at the massive walls of the room which housed the grinding wheel. 'Over a metre thick all of them, cut by hand, and fitted together without cement. You can't get a knife between them any-where. See for yourself.'

He handed me a slender bladed knife. The great blocks had

been so perfectly hewn and matched that the knife's tip would barely slip a millimetre into the cracks between them. We climbed the stairs at the back and went into the first floor of the granary. There was a delicate open arch at one end, and the floor was made out of narrow patterned bricks. I realized then what I should have guessed below. The mill had been built by the Moors. It must have stood there virtually unchanged for six or seven hundred years. There were a couple of rather forlorn-looking sacks in one corner and a faint smell of flour in the dusky air.

'Do you still grind?' I asked.

'Maybe once or twice a year,' Fernando said. 'It's not like it used to be. Once they'd bring me the wheat from miles around. You couldn't move on any of the three floors and there'd be more in carts outside. The river was higher then and the wheel would be going night and day for weeks and weeks. But it still works as well as it ever did. I'll show you.'

He scrambled up the steps to the top of the bank and walked to the sluice gate. A few moments later, as water came pouring down the channel and over the rim at the top, the grinding stone began to revolve. Fernando tossed a handful of wheat into a wooden hopper and a trickle of finely ground flour emerged below.

'The *Moros* left good work behind them,' he said as he watched it. 'The mill saw them out, it'll see me out, and no doubt many more too. In my view, *señor*, they were the best thing that ever happened to Andalucía.'

Fernando reached up and affectionately patted the great lintel in the doorway above our heads.

Scrambling back up the river to rejoin the others I thought of a lunch we'd had in Málaga the year before. We'd been invited by the widow of a Spanish air force officer. Her husband had been a much-decorated nationalist hero who had often piloted Franco during the Civil War. His widow lived in a comfortable apartment with her 30-year-old son, an articulate and informed young lawyer who was a member of Spain's emerging middle class. He was keen to discuss international politics, and after a while I asked him how the Spanish felt about the Soviet nuclear arsenal.

'We don't look that way,' he answered. 'We don't believe there's a nuclear threat from Russia, only from its subversives and they're not important. We can handle them. No, the real danger comes now where it's always come from in the past.'

He paused and pointed through the window towards the sea. Somewhere beyond the haze on the horizon lay the coast of Africa.

'When the Moors were here last they almost conquered all of Europe. They stayed 800 years in Andalucía and they'd like to come back. Believe me, they'll try. It's already started. You can see them now at Algeciras and that's only the tip of the iceberg. But this time we'll stop them. They were the worst thing that ever happened to this country.'

In mentioning Algeciras the young lawyer was referring to the annual migration of Moroccan workers across the straits, drawn like José to the factories of western Europe by the apparently insatiable demand for cheap labour. Twice every year hundreds of thousands of Arabs poured through the town. The timing depended on when the holy month of Ramadan fell. On the outward journey from Morocco, which started the day after Ramadan ended, they'd land and immediately head north for their destinations. Eleven months later the flow built up in the opposite direction as they returned home to celebrate the festival.

Unlike the Spaniards, the Moroccan labourers often took their entire families with them. They'd arrive at the port in ancient French-made cars, largely it seemed held together with rope and carrying eight or more passengers. Then if the ferries were delayed or they were waiting to join up with other groups, they'd set up camp on the quayside where they'd remain for a week or more. Forty-eight hours before Ramadan began the Algeciras front looked like an Arab shanty town. Between the endless rows of cars, blankets were hung to make improvised tents. Meals were cooked over charcoal braziers on the pavements, and the air in the town was thick with the smell of coriander and burnt meat. Chickens ran squawking between the wheels, children tumbled in the dust, and circles of tall dark-skinned men in jellabahs squatted playing dominoes and drinking mint tea. Sometimes when the pressure became too great the police would move some of them out, and the encampments would spread up the coastal road towards the valley. Then the ferries arrived. Somehow everyone boarded and overnight, like gypsies, they would vanish.

The best thing that ever happened to Spain or the worst? For all Spaniards the question has an endless fascination. In Andalucía it sometimes verges on an obsession difficult for the outsider to understand. One of the chief barriers, I believe, is a problem of the imagination. Franco's assertion that Europe ends at the Pyrenees has little meaning for most Europeans outside Spain. Spain, they feel, has always been an integral part of Europe and Europe is largely homogenous. Its peoples come from the same stock and their culture, values and historical background are also much the same. All its countries in fact belong to a common family with common antecedents. Across the Mediterranean lies another world. To accept that for eight hundred comparatively recent years a large part of Europe was inhabited, ruled and moulded by invaders from that alien world is as difficult as accepting it was ruled by Chinese mandarins. Yet even to the most casual visitor to Andalucía the legacy of the Moors' presence is inescapable. How did the Arab occupation happen and what apart from the towers, castles and monuments that mark the landscape did it really bequeath? The answer to the first is easier than the second.

Islam was founded in the Middle East in 622 AD when the prophet Muhammad made the *Hegira*, the flight from Mecca to Medina. Ten years later Muhammad was dead but his austere and expansionist message was still spreading like one of the valley's raging forest fires throughout the Arab world. By 711 it had reached the Berber tribes in the mountains of north Africa. On 27 April that year a force of 7,000 warriors commanded by Jebl-el-Tariq, the governor-general of Tangier who shortly before had captured Gibraltar and given the Rock his name, landed at Algeciras bay. The assault of the *Moros*, as the Spanish invariably refer to them, had begun. The invaders are often depicted as negroes in Spanish paintings and tableaux, and in English the word moor, with its resonances of blackamoor, the Moor of Venice and many other negro usages, has unequivocally become identified with black-skinned. In fact, as a number of historians have pointed out, the designation of both words is vague and imprecise. For at least the first two centuries of the conquest the majority of the invaders were almost certainly fair-skinned mountain tribesmen, with a sprinkling of true Arabs only among their leaders – and even they were dark rather than black. Nonetheless to this day there is a conviction in the Spanish national consciousness that the occupation was carried out by blacks.

Nine months after they landed, the Moors had captured Córdoba, 200 miles north of Algeciras. Barely fourteen years later they'd conquered all Spain, crossed the Pyrenees, and penetrated into France. The swiftness of their advance was breathtaking. Sometimes travelling across the countryside I left the road, climbed up to some spur in a range of hills, and gazed down trying to visualize what the campaign had been like. In the eighth century the bull's hide of Spain was thickly forested and largely without roads. The problems of communications and supplies for a tiny advancing army, let alone establishing and maintaining garrisons for a permanent colonization of the land, appear almost inconceivable now. The Moors solved them through a combination of religious fanaticism, long experience of surviving in almost desert conditions, ruthlessness, and political skills. Their fervour came from the prophet's message. They had a manifest destiny, they were marching on the road to paradise, and the proof, if it was needed, came when they penetrated Andalucía's golden triangle of water, wood and pasture, and found Granada. The plain round the city was so rich they decided it must be heaven's lower floor and that the chambers of paradise must be positioned in the sky directly above.

Their survival skills, honed in the barren Atlas mountains, made them exceptionally fast and self-sufficient travellers. They had no need for cumbersome supply columns. They were used to living off the land as they moved, and the Andalucian countryside was a constantly brimming larder. Where they met resistance whole communities were often summarily put to the sword. On the other hand if the local population sued for peace and the Moors saw advantage in a treaty, they struck shrewd but fair bargains and were able to press on, reasonably secure that an uprising behind them was unlikely. Their first real reverse came in 722 when they were defeated at Covadonga in the Asturias mountains. Ten years later Charles Martel beat them back from Poitiers. They retaliated by vanquishing Charlemagne at the wooded pass of Roncevalles in 778, but thirteen years afterwards Charlemagne hit back and returned to Spain to occupy Barcelona. About the same time the word *castilla*, to denote the precarious line of castles along the Moorish frontier, first appears in the Spanish language. Almost three centuries later the great warlord Rodrigo Diaz de Vivar, known as El Cid after the Arabs' respectful name for him, Sidi, 'My Lord', struck further south still and took Valencia. On his death the Moors recaptured his lands from his widow almost as a formality and without any real conviction. By then they had been in Andalucía for 400 years. After four centuries of Granada was there anywhere else on earth really worth the possessing?

Once we were settled in the valley we began to make a series of journeys which eventually took us over almost all Andalucía. Inevitably one of the first was to the fabled city which had cast its spell over both Moors and Christians equally. Granada stands 50 miles inland from the Mediterranean coast in the foothills of the Sierra Nevada beside the famous *vega*, the richest agricultural plain in Europe and the chief source of the city's wealth. The *vega* can yield three crops a year, ranging from wheat to tobacco to olives, and used to be known as *la tierra del ochario*, 'the land of the farthing', because of its extraordinarily low cost of living. There are several accounts of the city's foundation and naming. In one version it owes its existence to Grana, a daughter of Noah who has legendary associations with Andalucía; in another, to Granata, one of the daughters of Hercules who also has many mythical links with the region. In another still Granada was founded by the Jews who came to Spain with Nebuchadnezzar. Certainly when the Moors arrived in 711 the Jewish community was living in a quarter named Garnata. The Jews sided with the invaders against the ruling Christian Visigoths, and in due course the city, which for several centuries until then had used the Roman name of Illibria, became known by the name it bears today.

Built on and round the three hills of Albaicín, Sacromonte and Alhambra, Granada broadly divides into two parts. The modern town, which spreads out from the hills' feet, is prosperous, confident and a little bland, a city of plump and successful country bankers and lawyers with expensively but sensibly dressed wives. It has none of Sevilla's flamboyant cosmopolitan sparkle or Córdoba's dark and haunting melancholy. No anxieties or ambitions, apart from that of making money quickly and safely, seem to trouble modern Granada. As it always has been, it is a supremely comfortable place well fed in every way by the boundless riches of the surrounding plain. The three hills at the city's centre, and above all the Alhambra, in Arabic the 'red palace' after the hill's brick-red clay soil, are very different. Ancient, remote and in spite of their position stubbornly apart from the mainstream of Granada's life, they unfortunately pose an almost insuperable problem for anyone who wants to see them today.

Leafing through a guide-book to the city one evening I found a key at the back. The book was one of a series covering all Spain. The individual volumes were available in up to a dozen languages ranging from Swedish to Japanese, the number of different translations for any one place depending on different national tourist preferences. According to the key, only one site in Spain had proved itself saleable in every language the series offered. It was inevitably Granada. The city, more perhaps than anywhere else in the world, defines tourist pollution. For most of the year it is submerged beneath a tide of sweating, clamouring, tramping visitors and its air is blackened by the foul-smelling emissions of the cars, coaches, planes and trains that carry them there. Even the naturally courteous Grenadines, as the city's inhabitants are known, have been coarsened and hardened by the relentless impact of the foreign invasion, insulating themselves behind a barrier of rudeness and answering in an aggressive form of pidgin Spanish when spoken to.

The worst effects of all are on the Alhambra palace itself in high summer. At the very season for which it was chiefly created, the whole spirit and purpose of the building, tranquillity, fragrance, silence and coolness, are turned to a travesty by the press of the jostling shouting crowds thronging through it. After years of frustration and puzzlement in trying to see the palace clearly, I finally found the answer – the answer at least to experiencing a fragment of its magic. On certain nights between May and the end of October the Alhambra is floodlit. Granada is almost 3,000 feet above sea-level and its winters can be bitter. Arriving in the city one late autumn day as dusk was falling, we noticed that the palace's lights were on and streams of shivering tourists were heading away from the gates towards the warmth of their hotels. We went straight to the entrance and walked in. The palace was deserted. Even the guards had retired to their rooms. The moon was high and full. Starlight gleamed on the snowy-flanks of the Sierra Nevada. The night air carried the scents of flowers from the market gardens across the ravine of the Darro river, and rang with the sound of falling fountain water. For two hours we had the Alhambra to ourselves.

The Alhambra is the only medieval Arab palace left in the world. That it survives at all is due to chance and the speed of the Catholic Kings' campaign. Had they paused on the road to Granada and the city's youthful Moorish ruler, Boabdil, died, the palace would probably have been torn down by his successor and something else raised in its place. None of the traditionally 'noble' architectural materials such as stone or marble were used in its construction. The Arabs built out of whatever came to hand, in the Alhambra's case brick, stucco and above all rubble. It was never meant to last. It was simply a magnificent pavilion raised in sensuous delight to honour the ruler of the moment, the fourteenth-century Abul Hachach Yusuf and his son Muhammad who succeeded him. Ferdinand and Isabel were enchanted by it and undertook its restoration, but by the eighteenth century it had been entirely abandoned. It was vandalised by French troops during the Napoleonic wars, and two hundred years of abuse and neglect only ended in 1870 when it was belatedly declared a National Monument.

For someone brought up among the monuments of the northern architectural tradition there is something essentially frivolous about the Alhambra. The emblems of the northern past are massive and sturdy, hewn from stone and designed to outlast war, tempest and the passing years. The Alhambra in contrast is like a child's sandcastle, built for a day and waiting

Courtyard of the Lions, Alhambra

for the evening tide to sweep it away. Even the intricate stucco decoration resembles the shells a child uses, sticking them on by hand in elaborate patterns of fantasy. It is not so much a building as an astonishing celebration of the pleasures of life and of one in particular, water. Not long ago an Arab sheikh on a state visit to Britain asked to see Scotland. The Foreign Office took over the famous Gleneagles Hotel and despatched a senior official to accompany the sheikh's party. As soon as they arrived the rain started to pour down in impenetrable black torrents. The landscape was obliterated and sightseeing was impossible. While the official paced the lobby in frustration, the sheikh remained in his room. When the time came to leave, the official made a nervous apology for the British weather. The sheikh waved the apology away and smiled. 'I have had the happiest time of my life,' he said. 'For five whole days and nights I have been able to watch rain falling.'

The builders of the Alhambra would also have loved Gleneagles in a wet August. To the Moors then as now water was one of the earth's chief delights. Its viscosity, its capacity to refract and throw back light, the sounds it makes when it splashes, cascades or ripples, everything about it was studied and gloried in. They tapped and used it throughout Andalucía with a combination of subtlety and lavishness, and nowhere more so than in Granada. At times the whole city, as Théophile Gautier and many other visitors have noticed, gives the impression of having been built on water. Water wells up from the streets, spills along the pavements and tumbles down the steeply sloping alleyways, making the air even in summer moist and fresh. Its source is in the slopes of the Sierra Nevada from where, constantly replenished by melting snow, it pours into the city through an elaborate network of canals, channels and pipes. It pervades all of Granada's life but its presence is most vivid in the Alhambra and in the gardens of the summer palace above it, the Generalife.

In both palaces water has been used not merely for ornament. It has been employed as a noble building material of its own, as strong and elemental as the stone and marble they

Balcony above the Lindaraja garden, Alhambra

lack. Inside or out, water frames, echoes and locks together the
exuberant panels of construction and decoration, the halls and
courtyards, the arches, cloisters, bowers and scented banks of
flowers and shrubs. Without it, dominating the Court of the
Myrtles in a still silent lake, delicately veining the Court of the
Lions from the patterning fountain at its centre, churning and
pealing through the Generalife's gardens, Granada's Moorish
architecture would be sterile and even tawdry in spite of all its
gorgeously elaborate detail. As it is, the pavilions of the two
palaces, raised like a scattering of Bedouin tents embroidered

The Generalife, Alhambra

in silk and gold round a jade-green desert oasis, are quick and vibrant, sleekly muscled and alive. Walking slowly through them on that chill October night I understood the old proverbial Arab comment on a man sitting silently in deep melancholy: 'Leave him alone, for he is thinking of Granada'.

Although Granada today has become almost exclusively identified with the Alhambra, the city has many other splendid features and monuments. Right beside the Alhambra and looming heavily over it is the palace of the Emperor Charles v, a colossal stone Renaissance building which seems placed there deliberately to mock and intimidate the fragile Moorish palace below. Most commentators on Granada find it hideous, vulgar and intrusive. I like it greatly. It is bold, uncompromising and in spite of its bulk remarkably elegant – the circular internal courtyard is a triumph of sixteenth-century imperial design. It also houses an engaging and eccentric collection of paintings. In the town beneath the Alhambra hill at the side of Granada's cathedral is the Capilla Real, the royal chapel built at the order of the Catholic Monarchs as the resting-place for their bodies in the golden city which had obsessed them all their lives. The two, perhaps the most brilliant and energetic of all monarchs, lie side by side in simple lead coffins in a vault beneath the altar flanked by their daughter, the poor mad Juana, and her husband, Philip the Fair. The chapel above them is clean and shining. With none of the dust, dark and mustiness of most Spanish chapels, it always reminds me of one of the fenland churches – bold and bright and strong. Isabel's private collection of paintings, including some superb Memlings, van der Weydens and Bouts, hang in the sacristy. Together with the chapel itself, the banners, jewels and brilliantly painted carvings, they form a fine memorial to a passionate and stout-hearted lady and her equally resolute husband.

The year of Ferdinand and Isabel's reconquest of Granada, 1492, was also the year of Columbus' discovery of America. Columbus' epic voyage has tended to overshadow the events of the city's last days under Moorish rule and its eventual capitulation to the Christian Kings. As Ferdinand and Isabel's long and fluctuating campaign approached its end with their arrival near Granada, the city was ruled by the Caliph, Moulay Abdul Hassan. Hassan was married to Aicha, a queen by whom he had a young son and heir, Boabdil. The Catholic armies were encamped outside the city when a merchant, knowing the Caliph's eye for a pretty girl and hoping to curry favour with him, presented Hassan with a young Christian woman named Isabel de Solis. Hassan instantly fell in love with Isabel, who he named Zoraya, his 'morning star', and was soon speaking of leaving Aicha for her. Terrified that in his infatuation Hassan might decide to dispose of herself and her son by murdering them, the Queen fled from Granada with the little Boabdil. After they left, the besieged Hassan, spurred on by his new-found love Zoraya, set out to confront the enemy.

While he was away from Granada Aicha and Boabdil slipped back into the city, and the Queen had the boy proclaimed ruler. Hassan, having achieved nothing in his sortie against the Spanish, returned home to find Granada's gates barred in his face. Hassan was forced to retreat to Málaga where he took refuge with his enterprising brother, El Zagal, 'the valiant'. El Zagal was much more successful in his counter-attacks against the Catholics, and his victories prompted his sister-in-law Aicha to adopt the same tactics in the name of Boabdil from the fortress of Granada. It was a mistaken decision. Boabdil was promptly defeated and taken prisoner. After his capture a series of dynastic quarrels broke out among the Moors as they feuded over the title to Granada, quarrels which quickly led to the disintegration of the kingdom. Boabdil was then released by the Spanish in a calculated move to create further confusion and dissension, and he returned to the city to reclaim his inheritance. The attempt was doomed. Within a few years Boabdil was secretly negotiating with the Catholics to hand over the city in return for keeping the family's private fortune, and for being given large estates in the Alpujarras mountains to the south. The negotiations came to light, Granada's citizens rose in rebellion against him, and Boabdil was ignominiously forced to flee the city.

Accompanied by his mother Aicha, Boabdil took the road south towards Motril. Stopping at the crest of the pass before the road drops down towards the coast, Boabdil glanced back at Granada for the final time, muttered 'It is Allah's will', burst into tears, turned and galloped on. Kicking her horse after him, the ambitious and frustrated Aicha snapped contemptuously: 'You do well to weep like a woman for what you could not defend like a man.' As the two of them and their attendants disappeared on the far side of the Suspiro del Moro, 'the Moor's sigh' as the pass has been known ever since, eight centuries of Moorish domination of Andalucía came to an end. Boabdil did not last long in the Alpujarras where he had been promised sanctuary. Quickly tiring of falconry and coursing, he plotted a number of inept and utterly unsuccessful uprisings against his conquerors as a result of which an impatient Ferdinand exiled him to Morocco. Behind him the former Caliph of Granada left a large population of 'Moriscos', as the remnant Moors, converts by law to Christianity, were known. Some were assimilated into the emerging Spanish nation. Others, after further sporadic rebellions, were expelled too. Five hundred years later the Spanish, and particularly the Andaluz, continue to be haunted by them. They are literally in the Spanish blood – there can hardly be a Spaniard who does not carry some of their genes – and in Andalucía their mark on life and the land is everywhere. From the naming of its rivers, towns, villages and hills a map of Andalucía could equally well be a map of part of the Arab world. People like the old miller Fernando in the valley still use the Moors' constructions in their daily working lives. Notaries write their signatures with an Arabic device. Locally made pottery is always decorated with Moorish motifs. Like the Bedouins the country people cook outside their houses on little earthenware braziers filled with burning almond shells. Coriander and cumin are among their favourite herbs, and spiced kebabs, called *pinchitos*, are on sale in every town. When we first came to know Tarifa some of the older women still wore veils. Even today throughout Andalucía the women tie their scarfs in the distinctive Arab style so that if one end is thrown across the face, now normally only against wind or dust, it creates the hood of a chador. In some villages, like Almonte in the Guadalquivir marshes, the men too wear woollen scarfs even in high summer which are identical to the headdress of the Arab fedayeen.

The relationship between what the Andaluz sees as two separate cultures, the one inherited from the Moors and the other indigenous and his own, is wary and full of paradoxes. Old Fernando, who told me the Moors were the best thing that ever happened to Spain, had at the same time the common Andaluz prejudice against eating lamb on the grounds that it was 'Moors' food' and therefore not worthy of Christians. That coriander, cumin and kebabs were also Moors' food was either not recognised or for some reason considered of no importance. In the end I came to feel there were striking similarities between the Spanish attitude to the Arab empire and the attitude of the Latin Americans to the subsequent

Spanish empire. In succession both were dominated by what at the time was a richer, stronger, bolder and infinitely more vigorous civilisation. Both grew up in shadows and both eventually forged their own independence. Their feelings afterwards were like grown children towards strong-minded parents. Aware that in large part their parents have shaped and formed them, they can be at the same moment grudgingly grateful and deeply resentful. The Andaluz is like this, and the tensions over his inheritance from his Moorish past are still unresolved. I suspect they will remain so for many many years. According to a Masai proverb a child only achieves true maturity on his parents' death. Andalucía is a child of the Arab world and the Arab world will be with us for a long time to come.

I believe that what the Moors really left was what the Andaluz would most proudly and fiercely claim as his own creation – a powerful sense of identity and a shining rainbow of culture. When they arrived, remote agricultural hamlets scattered the countryside loosely united under the rule of the Visigoth kings but without any real feeling of kinship, shared experience or common tradition. On their departure eight centuries later, after the various caliphates and sultanates had flowered, fragmented and waned, the whole region had been endowed with music, song, poetry, story-telling, architecture that wasn't purely functional but used as a means of creating and expressing beauty, craft, learning, law, medicine, engineering, gardening – the idea of a cultivated garden is an entirely Arab concept – and a whole range of other skills, disciplines and callings. More than anything, the Moors gave the region's inhabitants a feeling of belonging to something larger than their immediate village or town, grand and prosperous as many of Andalucía's towns, virtual kingdoms in themselves, had become under Moorish rule. They were no longer merely dwellers in the Guadalquivir basin, the Ronda hills or the Málaga plain. They were all now Andaluz, citizens of the empire that occupied the golden triangle at the foot of the Iberian peninsula.

'For pity's sake, give alms!' the beggar's plea still rings out. 'For I am blind and in Granada.' Granada's citizens pause as they hear it. They may resent, despise and even fear the Moors, but better than anyone else in Andalucía they know the wonder the Arabs wrought. They know too that because of them they are called and are the Andaluz. Before they pass by they drop a coin in the beggar's palm. Walking on an icy October night through the silent courts and halls of the red castle of the Alhambra, sculpted in sand and water and decorated with a child's sea-shells, with a crescent moon above the Sierra Nevada's snows and the scent of jasmine in the air, it is not difficult to understand why.

ᚻᚷᚢ 9 ᚷᚢᚷ

Just below the upper square in Algeciras ran a narrow winding street that climbed up the hill from the market below. Midway along the street was a bright and bustling sweetshop, La Alicantina. There are Alicantinas in most Spanish towns. Named after the city of Alicante they sell the almonds, honey and above all *turron*, a rich sticky nougat made from the two, for which Alicante is famous. Turron is traditionally eaten at Christmas and in mid-December every year we'd make a ritual visit to the Alicantina, emerging half an hour later with a basket full of little packets, wrapped in silver paper and tied with pink ribbon, for the children's stockings.

As we came out one December I saw further up the street a shop I'd never noticed before. It was small, dimly lit and shabby. Peering through the dusty window I realized it was a toyshop. I went in and learned that the old lady who owned it was on the point of retiring. The shop was already sold and she was closing it the next day. Most of her stock had gone but on a shadowy shelf behind her head I could just make out some little figures half-covered in straw. I asked her what they were.

'*Belenes*,' she said taking them down and placing them on the counter. 'I've had them for years. They're the old-fashioned ones made out of clay. Nobody wants them now. People prefer the plastic ones. They're brighter, prettier and they last for ever.'

As in most Mediterranean Catholic countries every Spanish house at Christmas traditionally has its own crib, a miniature tableau depicting Christ's birth in the stable. Belen is the

Spanish name for Bethlehem and the crib's figures were called *belenes*. Certain figures were common to every crib: the infant Jesus in a cradle, the Virgin and Joseph, the three kings, a pair of shepherds, and usually an angel. In addition, depending on the area and the imagination of the local makers, the older cribs sometimes included models of the country people at work. As the old woman had said they had gone out of fashion. Modern *belenes* come in a standardised range. They are indestructible, garishly spray-painted, and made from injection-moulded plastic.

I examined the ones she'd put in front of me. I already had a few examples of country *belenes* for the Huerto's crib, but these were the finest I'd ever seen. Only a few inches high, modelled in clay and meticulously painted by hand, they'd been made by a craftsman with imagination and humour.

There was a street-vendor sitting asleep behind his table of wares, a boy fishing in a river with a trout on the end of his line, an old peasant woman scolding a cat who'd knocked over a pan above her fire, a girl carrying chickens to market, a farmer ploughing with two oxen, a herdsman skinning the carcass of a sheep. In a dozen vivid three-dimensional images they recreated a whole section of Andalucian country life.

I bought them all for a few *duros*. Then I told the old woman I'd like to get some more and asked her if she knew where they came from. She stared at me, puzzled, for a moment. Only an eccentric would buy these fragile figures with their already-fading colours in preference to the glittering plastic models in Algeciras' new supermarkets. Then she shook her head.

'I used to buy them from a travelling salesman,' she said. 'He passed by every autumn. I don't know where he came from, but it may have been Sevilla.'

I caught up with Elisabeth in the upper square. 'Tomorrow we're off to Sevilla,' I said.

There are two roads to Sevilla from the straits, the recently completed inland road that passes by Medina Sidonia and the older coastal highway. Both link up with the motorway just east of Cádiz, and both in quite different ways are equally beautiful. Inevitably I came to know the coastal road first and it remains my favourite. Angling away from the shore beyond the long white Atlantic beaches of Tarifa it climbs through a saddle and then falls abruptly. In the distance on one side are the western flanks of the sierras, green and flower-starred in spring, smoke-hazed and barred brown and gold as the summer dries. On the other is the rocky Atlantic coastline, winding to Cape Trafalgar and beyond until it dips towards Cádiz bay. Between the hills and the ocean lies the plain, a great flattened bowl of fertile earth across which the road presses arrow-straight.

It is farming country, cereal country, but most of all the land belongs to the bulls. The straggling complex of the Nuñez ranches, which produce one of the best known and most popular of the modern strains of the *toro bravo*, have their home pastures on the plain. The breeding of fighting bulls is largely confined to Andalucía, central Spain and Estremadura, and Salamanca, with Andalucía being the most important area. Other Andalucian ranches rear larger and more dangerous animals, the legendary 'bulls of death' of Don Eduardo Miura, which have killed more bullfighters than any other breed; the great Tulio Vazquez', or the strong and heavy Pablo Romeros'. The Nuñez bulls in contrast are relatively small and compact but for honesty, consistency and courage they are unrivalled, making them favourites with matadors and crowds alike. The Nuñez pastures border the Cádiz road. Often the ageing seed-bulls, massive creatures with grizzled noses and sweeping horns, would come up to the roadside fences and stand, fly-haloed and circled by white egrets, in wells of shadows beneath the trees. They looked so calm and stately they might almost have been confused with benign elderly cattle. Occasionally they were. About once a year I would stop on the Sevilla road and quietly warn a group of tourists, who'd clambered the fence to picnic on the far side, that they were eating in company with the most dangerous animals on earth. Fortunately the *sementales*, as the seed-bulls are known, seldom charged in the day's heat.

Further north the plain narrows, belts of woodland line the road, and the sky fills with birds. In the few miles before Vejer de la Frontera I have at one time or another seen in or above the trees every Andalucian bird of prey. Then, immediately ahead, Vejer itself comes into sight, a gleaming white little town perched on top of a steeply rising hill. Vejer was once described as the most beautiful town in Spain and from below it looks as if the inhabitants are determined to maintain its reputation. The walls of every house are so dazzlingly clean and bright they seem to have been painted afresh every morning. Vejer's position is unquestionably magnificent and the town is indeed very clean although no more so than most Andalucian *pueblos*; the brilliance of its whiteness comes from the fall of the light in the clear air on the hill's top, but there are other equally and even more dramatically set villages in many parts of the sierras. Beyond Vejer the road continues across rolling countryside until it reaches Chiclana de la Frontera.

Chiclana is a pleasant, casual and untidy place best known for its wine. The wine is a pale yellow-green in colour and slightly fortified, giving it an alcohol content somewhere between the ordinary country table wine and sherry. Drunk chilled on a hot summer day it is delicious, tangy, clear and fragrant, and for a time after we came to the valley I used to drive to Chiclana to buy it in great glass pitchers for the house. After a few months I stopped. Chiclana is a classic example of a wine that does not travel. Even a 60-mile journey in the back of a car seemed to change its character entirely. The clarity vanished and after a few days the pitchers were sour and harsh. As its lightness was also highly deceptive – people were drinking it as a table wine and suffering morose and painful consequences – I decided we were better off with much more expensive but reliable bottled sherries from Jerez and Sanlúcar.

Not long after Chiclana the road drops onto the marshy Cádiz salt flats, swings round the bay, and a few miles later joins the motorway. The motorway, one of Spain's first, was built to link the factories of Sevilla with the docks of Cádiz harbour, and so provide an outlet for the products of Sevillan industry to the sea. The planners counted on a system of tolls both to finance the motorway's construction and eventually to make it show a profit. They failed to take into account the Andaluz framework of values. The old road, narrow and bumpy but still perfectly serviceable, ran alongside the motorway. Faced with a choice between the two there was never any question. One was slow and free. The other fast and expensive. Time was a matter of no great importance and speed, furthermore, caused ulcers and coronaries. Container truck, fish lorry, family saloon and motorbicycle, everyone stuck firmly to the old road. For years the motorway proved a hugely expensive folly, a silent and empty lane of concrete running between Cádiz and Sevilla while beside it the dense traffic of the two cities bucketed contentedly on as before. Today as the congestion on the old road becomes almost intolerable vehicles are slowly beginning to use it, but the motorway remains one of the loneliest highways in Europe.

Like most of Andalucía's major cities Sevilla, the region's capital, consists of a tiny, succulent kernel encased in an immense, dark and brutally ugly shell. Only the approaches of Málaga are bleaker and more hideous. The motorway ends and for ten miles or more there is nothing on either side of the road except factories, cheap and tawdry housing developments with peeling paint and rusting windows, used car lots where derelict vans lie stripped and belly-up to the sky, metal silos and smoke-belching chimneys and pallisades of rattling corrugated-iron fences. The whole tarnished and corroding detritus of modern industrialisation seems to have been swept up like flotsam and deposited against the city walls. Then, abruptly, the road broadens. On one side, in place of grime, tenement and crumbling, blackened asbestos, there are avenues and trees, parks and squares, statues and soaring buildings in golden and smoke-grey stone. On the other, arced by bridges, the running waters of the Guadalquivir river with the lights of Triana leaping in reflection across the pulls and eddies.

Sevilla's early history is crisply summed up in the famous

lines engraved on the ancient stone of the Jerez gate. 'Hercules raised me. Caesar bound me with walls and towers. The Saintly King delivered me.' Hercules' contribution to the city's beginnings is lost, but as a human settlement Sevilla is certainly immensely old. As early as 1,000 BC it was already an important Phoenician trading centre. As Phoenician power waned it became in turn, in effect as well as often in title, the capital for five successive civilisations, Greek, Roman, Visigoth, Moorish, and Christian, and in addition for a time the capital of an entire continent, South America. Few other towns in the world can claim such a past. Under Moorish rule the name 'Hisaplis' was corrupted by the Arab tongue to 'Ixbilia'. After the reconquest – the city was taken from the Moors by the 'Saintly King', Ferdinand III of Castile in 1248 – Ixbilia became further corrupted in local speech during the Middle Ages to Sevilla.

Sevilla's golden age, which was also Spain's, started with Columbus' voyage to America in 1492. By 1503, only eleven years later, the city's sea-borne trade with the New World was expanding so fast the queen, Isabel, decided to create the Casa de Contratación, an exchange to regulate and stimulate trade even further. Sevilla was the obvious choice for the exchange's home. Already the seat of the royal court it had a fine sheltered harbour, swift access to the oceans down the Guadalquivir, and a long tradition of ship-building and sea-faring. Among the many expeditions which left the port in the wake of Columbus were those of Amerigo Vespucci, a Florentine convinced that Columbus had discovered not the Indies but a new continent and who eventually gave his name to it, and Magellan who left in 1519 determined to circumnavigate the globe. Magellan died during the voyage but the journey was completed by his companion, Juan Sebastian Elcano.

With the foundation of the Casa de Contratación Sevilla acquired a virtual monopoly of trade not only in the New World's riches, but as the years went by those of the Phillippines, India, and the Far East too. The wealth that poured into the city, the immense 'river of gold' that flowed upstream against the downward press of the Guadalquivir, was almost unimaginable. Contemporary accounts tell how the treasure ships would dock, the cargoes be unloaded, and then within a matter of hours how dazzling emeralds from Columbia and lustrous pearls from Darien would be displayed and traded in round the cathedral in the same great sacks that were used for chick-peas. The ultimate consequences for the national economy through inflation were devastating, but in Sevilla everyone, the nobility, the mercantile bourgeoisie and the people, seemed to benefit. God had placed the rainbow's foot in the city and the crocks of gold beneath it were real. The money was spent prodigally and exuberantly on palaces, churches, convents, parks, gardens and public buildings; and in fashioning a sumptuous way of life that proved remarkably durable.

Within two hundred years of Magellan's sailing the climate had changed and darkened. The seemingly inexhaustible flood of treasure had dwindled to a trickle, Spanish power had long since been on the retreat and, even more disturbingly for Sevilla, the Guadalquivir was silting up, making it difficult if not impossible for ships to use the port. In 1717 the Casa de Contratación was moved to Cádiz, whose deep-water harbour gave directly on to the Atlantic, and Sevilla appeared to be finished. Its obituaries were premature. Those who delivered them failed to recognize what the Phoenicians had shrewdly assessed 3,000 years earlier – its outstanding strategic position linking the soil wealth of the Guadalquivir valley with the sea. They also didn't count on the buoyant entrepreneurial spirit of the Sevillanos, or on the city's accumulated and underlying riches. Not all of the New World plunder had been dissipated. Much had been prudently invested by the citizens in buildings and land, both in Andalucía and throughout the recently joined Spains. Even in apparent decline Sevilla remained prosperous. Within forty years of losing the Contratación trading concession it was capable of building the Royal Tobacco Factory, at the time the largest building in Spain after Madrid's Escorial, the biggest single employer with a labour force of over 3,000, and amongst much else the inspiration for Bizet's *Carmen*. As late as 1929 the city fathers were still able to launch and complete an architectural under-taking on the scale of the Plaza de España, the monumental and engaging square designed to celebrate the city's ancient glories and provide it with a modern centre. Since then Sevilla has continued to thrive. The dredging of the river has opened its docks to shipping again. Industries have been developed, ore from the sierra mines and foodstuffs from the Guadal-quivir plains pour in to be processed, and the town now is as energetic and crackling with activity as ever.

Whenever we visited Sevilla, as we did that Christmas in search of *belenes*, we stayed at the Hotel Alfonso XIII. Opened in 1928 by Alfonso himself, and used by the king as a staging-post on his hunting trips to the Guadalquivir's marshes, the hotel is appropriately palatial, discreet, and opulently old-fashioned. Its rooms have mahogany doors and panelling. Its baths are great enamelled bowls with brass taps that unleash cascades of either steaming hot or glacially cold water. The pillows on its huge wicker-framed beds are so plump with down its guests can find themselves spending the night propped half upright. Along its corridors, their lofty ceilings lost in the dusky air, impeccably uniformed servants hurry silently and urgently as if travelling on royal errands. Inside the hotel everything is European and familiar, but the view from the upper windows is on to another continent – not Europe but Africa. Théophile Gautier found that of all the southern cities Córdoba gave him the most vivid reminder of the long Moorish presence in Andalucía. I always felt it keenest in Sevilla. Looking out from one of the Alfonso XIII's bed-rooms, with the fronds of the date palms rustling in the dry wind below, skeins of flamingoes crossing the sunset against the silhouette of the Giralda, and the last of the day's light shining off minarets and arches, it was difficult to believe I wasn't gazing down over an Arab town, over Tangier or old Casablanca, so strongly it seemed had the Moors put their print on the city.

The spell was quickly broken on the street outside. One of the Alfonso XIII's attractions is its position close to the river at the city's heart. Clustered within a few hundred yards are most of Sevilla's monuments, all of them framed and linked by the buildings and life of the modern town. The most imposing is the cathedral, a towering and emphatic fifteenth-century statement in smoke-darkened stone. The cathedral was raised on the site of the main Moorish mosque. In 1401, as they picked

The Giralda, Sevilla

their way through the mosque's rubble left by the battle for the town a hundred years earlier, the members of the chapter said: 'Let us build a church so enormous that everyone who looks at it will take us for madmen.' They were as good as their word. The building is cavernous, chill, misty and vast, ranking in size only after St Peter's in Rome and St Paul's in London. Not so much a church as an ecclesiastical fortress it evokes, like Albi in southern France, the sheer terror of the Almighty far more than any of the pleasures or rewards of faith.

Beside the cathedral rises Sevilla's best known landmark, the soaring tower of the Giralda, the 'weather-vane', a nickname acquired from the revolving bronze statue of Faith at the top. Originally a late twelfth-century minaret from where the muezzin called the faithful to prayer, the top storey, the lantern and the statue were added 400 years later, giving the tower a total height of almost 100 metres. Below it is the cool and lovely Patio de los Naranjos, the brick-paved Moorish courtyard of the orange trees. Built at the same time as the Giralda on the site of the ancient Arab scent, silk and jewellery market, it has a ceremonial fountain at the centre whose water is turned to gold each September by the tumbling oranges. Across the cathedral square is the Alcázar which although keeping the Moorish name for a fortified palace was in fact built by a Christian monarch, Peter the Cruel, a century after the Moors were expelled from Sevilla. Inspired by and drawing heavily for its detail on the Alhambra in Granada, Sevilla's Alcázar contains some of the purest examples of that remarkable blend of the Renaissance with Moorish traditions known as Mudejar architecture. Between the cathedral and the Alcázar is the Archivo General de Indias, the Indies Archives. Built in 1572 as an exchange it now contains a treasure-trove of maps, charts, books and documents relating to the discovery and plunder of the New World, including private papers of Columbus, Magellan and Cortés.

The catalogue of Sevilla's riches, reflecting a history that stretches back more than 3,000 years, is almost inexhaustible. From the Roman walls to the Torre del Oro, the riverside

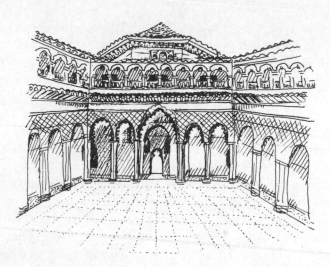

The Alcázar, Sevilla

tower of gold, built by the thirteenth-century Moorish governor, Abu-El-Ola, in 'whispers' in case the Spanish King Ferdinand heard of its glory and came to claim it, to the palaces of the Americas-enriched nobility to the noble tobacco factory, now the university, and the majestic Maestranza bullring, the list of the legacies of the city's past goes on and on. Every yard of the streets has been walked by a Hercules, a Caesar, a Columbus, an Isabel or a Velasquez. All of them, together with such lesser-known figures as Beethoven, Mozart and El Greco, have placed their mark on the town and their presence endures. Yet Sevilla is not only a city of obvious delights and easily recognized resonances. It is also packed with surprises, a fairground bran-tub of lucky dips where each plunge into the sawdust produces some new and astonishing prize.

One winter evening long after the *belenes* trip we arrived in Sevilla at dusk and as usual checked into the Alfonso XIII. At the hotel was a message inviting us for a drink with someone who'd left the name of Ignacio de Segorbé. I racked my brains trying to think who he was. Then I remembered. Ignacio was the nephew of one of our oldest friends in Andalucía, Paz, the Duchess of Lerma. Under the laws which govern Spanish inheritance, titles can be passed down through the female line. Paz, the younger of two daughters of a father without sons, had inherited the Dukedom of Lerma. Her elder sister had taken the family's senior title and become the Duchess of Medinaceli. Known as the world's most titled lady – she had inherited some twenty other dukedoms apart from Medinaceli – she had given her third son, Ignacio, one of the twenty, the Dukedom of Segorbé. Living close to the valley, Paz's children had been friends of ours for years, but for some reason we had never met her sister's family. Ignacio de Segorbé had left as his address the strangely named Casa de Pilatos, Pilate's House. The name was vaguely familiar to me, but I'd never been there and had no idea what it was.

The Casa de Pilatos turned out to be a ten-minute taxi ride from the hotel. We got out by a pair of wrought iron gates with a porter's lodge beyond. The night was starless and impenetrably black. The porter let us in from the street and said he'd take us up to Don Ignacio's apartment. He produced a tiny torch and we set off, following the pencil of wavering light generated by its almost flat batteries. The walk took longer than the taxi ride. Sometimes we climbed flights of steps, sometimes we seemed to be crossing halls and patios, sometimes puzzlingly we were in the open – I could feel the night air on my face and hear the splash of falling water – but the darkness was so intense it was almost impossible to be certain about anything. Finally we mounted some stairs, stopped at a door on the fourth floor, and Ignacio de Segorbé appeared to greet us. He turned out to be a delightful and erudite man in his thirties, who was both the family archivist and a successful businessman. His apartment, converted from a series of pigeon lofts, was airy and attractive but otherwise unremarkable.

After an hour or so we decided to go out to dinner together. As we got ready to leave Ignacio asked casually: 'Would you like to see the house on the way out?' A little surprised, I still didn't know what he meant by the 'house,' I said, 'Yes'. He turned on a battery of switches, opened a glass door on to a terrace, and beckoned me to step outside. I walked through and stopped in my tracks.

In the early sixteenth century one of the family's ancestors, the first Marquis of Tarifa, visited the Holy Land where he was struck by the resemblance between the hill of Golgotha and a hill outside Sevilla on which stood the Cruz del Campo, a cross erected in the countryside. The Marquis carefully measured the distance between Golgotha's summit and the site of Pontius Pilate's house in Jerusalem from which Christ set off along the Via Dolorosa. On his return to Sevilla the Marquis paced the same distance from the hill of the Cruz del Campo into the city. There he built what the locals inevitably named Pilate's House, although it is sometimes also referred to by its more formal name of the Palace of the Medinacelis.

Completed in 1540 and occupying several acres at the centre of Sevilla, the palace is Mudejar architecture's crowning glory. The ideas that inspired its design come from the flowering of the Renaissance; the hands and eyes that executed it were Moorish – Muslim craftsmen were largely responsible for the actual construction. The fusion of the two visions, European and Arabic, created something that was and remains magical. The palace's heart is an immense open courtyard with a great marble fountain in the middle. Running round the courtyard are two tiers of arches, the lower Moorish and the upper gothic. The ground floor walls and the walls of some of the chambers leading off behind are decorated with *azulejos*, glazed tiles set in intricate patterns which dazzle and glow like huge panels of jewels. Beyond the courtyard are the halls, gardens, rooms, chapels and libraries I had been dimly aware of passing through on our way up from the street.

Pilate's House is extraordinary enough by day and I went back often to visit in the light. But to see it for the first time at night, suddenly emerging in a blaze of luminescence from the darkness like a fairy castle swept through by the scents of jasmine and rose, was an experience without parallel. We walked slowly from room to room, hall to hall, patio to garden, as Ignacio talked about the building. He showed me

Pilate's House, Sevilla

the ceilings which the youthful Velasquez and his father-in-law, Pachecho, had painted, the tapestries from cartoons by Michelangelo, the marble statue of Pallas Athene by Phidias looted by the Romans from Athens and given by Pope Pius V to Pedro de Rivera, the viceroy of Naples. We looked at a Greek bas-relief of Leda being raped by the swan, the most graphic and erotic carving I have ever seen and probably the original for the copy of the same scene in the Emperor Charles v's palace in Granada. We stood in the muniments room surrounded by towering stacks of boxes or archives, each labelled with the name of one of the family's dukedoms and reaching back for more than a thousand years – Charlemagne's only known signature is in the family records. We studied the family portraits which include one of the Duke of Feria who was ambassador to the court of Queen Elizabeth I in 1588 at the time of the Spanish Armada. Not a notable success as a diplomat, the Duke's main claim to fame lies in fathering 250 children. He knew them all by name and provided for each one individually in his will.

Many of the individual works of art in Pilate's House, the paintings, tapestries and sculpture, would adorn any of the world's great national collections. More striking still, as I found that night and whenever I returned, is the house's own unity. It is by turn supple, austere and magnificent. An oak-raftered dining-hall, which might have come from some medieval northern castle, opens on to a garden of ferns, fountains and nightingales. A bare vaulted passage, stone-floored and uncompromising, leads into a tiled state chamber that vibrates with colour and splendour. Somehow all of the apparently disparate elements and styles fit perfectly together. And although the scale is vast, the house is utterly unpretentious. The sixteenth-century Marquis built not only in the grandest of Sevillan traditions, but with passionate concern and love. I can visualise him walking round the house when it was finished and saying quietly to himself at the end: 'It looks wonderful and it works.'

'I've visited houses all over the world,' Ignacio de Segorbé said as we reached the porter's lodge again. 'It's difficult for me to judge this one dispassionately, but I nonetheless believe it is the most beautiful building I have ever seen.'

Leda and the Swan, Pilate's House

He turned out the lights. As suddenly as it had leapt out from the darkness, the palace vanished. All I had left to remind me of it was the lingering smell of jasmine from its gardens, following us down the street on the air.

Revelations like discovering Pilate's House long after I first knew the city are typical of Sevilla. The oldest and richest of Andalucía's towns, it is also fundamentally different in character from the others. Córdoba, Granada, Málaga are all firmly rooted in Andalucian life and soil. They are, in the best sense, provincial. Sevilla is not. It is unremittingly chic and cosmopolitan, ranking alongside the focal-points for international café society with Venice, Paris and New York. Even Madrid cowers insecurely in its shadow. Elegant, expensive, and cynical, arrogantly confident of its aristocratic past and lavishly cushioned by its inherited or created wealth, Sevilla is a town which takes pride in glittering, above all during its famed Holy Week and the spring fair that follows. The hooded processions of the penitents, the shoulder-borne floats of the jewelled and garlanded Virgins, the anguished cries of the *saetas* – the improvised flamenco laments that arrow impulsively into the air above the pressing crowds as the floats pass and briefly silence the accompanying fifes and drums – the exuberance and glory of the Easter mass at the week's end, all combine to provide an unforgettable experience. Equally unforgettable is the fair the next week with its parades of carriages drawn by glossy high-stepping horses, its fireworks, feasting, music and dancing that lasts until dawn breaks over the Guadalquivir and the Torre del Oro lifts through the river mist into the sunrise.

Sevilla in *feria* is sumptuous and exhilarating. It can also be, for those outside the magic circle of the private *casetas* in the fairground, a little chilling and aloof. Ernest Hemingway and Orson Welles, Rita Hayworth and Jacqueline Kennedy, as ghosts or in person, can drink and dance the night away with the Sevillan aristocracy. Most visitors, their noses pressed like children's against a sweetshop window, have to watch from without. I enjoy the spring fair but I prefer the city in its other seasons, less ostentatious, less conspicuously extravagant, less flamboyant and self-conscious. Best of all I like it in winter. The tourist crowds have gone, the Alfonso XIII's corridors are silent and empty, the proud old town slumbers by the dark waters of the Guadalquivir.

All of Andalucía's cities have their own perfect day, each different, each shaped by their distinct climates, personalities and habits. Sevilla's starts on a December morning with a visit to the market where it is still possible with luck and patience to find the old-fashioned clay *belenes*, as I eventually did on that visit before Christmas. Afterwards one walks along the thronged and noisy pedestrian street Calle de las Sierpes, the city's main mercantile artery, crosses the bridge near the Torre del Oro, and enters the *barrio* of Triana on the other side of the river. Triana, the fabled breeding-ground of bullfighters and flamenco singers, is an abrasive working-class district, its houses hung with caged larks and goldfinches whose song fills the narrow streets. Triana is also famous for its brimming tankards of beer, the same clear gold in colour as the Moorish tower, and its platters of fresh shellfish, prawns, lobsters, crabs, clams, grilled razor shells, and spiny sea snails. After a long and leisurely lunch in the warm sunlight one recrosses the river and heads for the Maestranza bullring and a late-season festival, a charity bullfight. In winter the bullfight finishes at dusk. As darkness falls one joins the crowds streaming away from the ring towards the Barrio de Santa Cruz.

Lying just to the north of the cathedral square the Barrio de Santa Cruz, the ancient Jewish merchants' quarter, it is a tangled mosaic of cobbled alleys, lanes, patios, orange-tree planted squares, bars, restaurants, and seventeenth-century mansions, each with an arched gateway large enough to pass a four-in-hand. Its colours are ochre, bull's blood, and shining Andalucian white, and even in December the strong, fragrant scent of jasmine floods every passage just as it does in the Casa de Pilatos. Fountains play. Guitar-playing Sevilla university students run out from the trees' shadows to beg mischievously for their dinner money. Dark-haired and bright-eyed young Sevillan girls swirl and turn in private dances on the streets – no cars are allowed in the Barrio – as the dust coils up round their feet. Solemn and self-absorbed they ignore everyone, even the laughing groups of smartly uniformed sailors on a night out from the naval base. After dinner at one of the restaurants one sits out at a pavement bar, warmly wrapped against the crisp winter air, drinking *anís* or brandy and listening to the distant sounds of flamenco echoing down the alleys.

The poet Frederico Garcia Lorca, who died at the hands of the nationalists in the Civil War, once wrote of the city in a fragment that is more an incantation than a poem:

> *Sevilla es una torre*
> *llena de árqueros finos.*
> *Sevilla para herir*
> *Córdoba para morir.*

The lines are almost untranslatable. They say literally: 'Sevilla is a tower full of fine archers. Sevilla is a place in which to be hurt. Córdoba is where you go to die.' The grave city of Córdoba is certainly a suitable place in which to contemplate death. Sevilla's archers, by contrast, firing their arrows of loveliness, wound only with beauty. Sitting late at night in the Barrio de Santa Cruz watching the moon lift over the Giralda, Lorca's meaning is easy to understand.

༄ IO ༄

FOR A LONG time, of Andalucía's three greatest cities, Granada, Sevilla and Córdoba, the last seemed to me to be the most forbidding and least interesting. I'd known it at a remove from the start. Lying midway along the Guadalquivir river at the foot of the central plateau, it was the first major town one reached after winding down into Andalucía through the pass of Despeñaperros. On its outskirts the road first ran through the inevitable drear and grimy industrial suburbs. Then it swung round to follow the Guadalquivir through the city centre, crossed the river over the Roman bridge, and headed west towards the Atlantic across the undulating plain beyond. At the wheel of the car I would gratefully watch Córdoba disappear in the rear mirror. I was on my way home to the valley. I had no time to waste on the grim and scowling city behind me, over-hung with smoke and shadowed by the hills of the Sierra Morena. Then one day I decided to overcome my prejudice against its appearance from the car's windows and set off to explore it. I was glad ever afterwards that I did. Córdoba's great mosque, the Mesquita, is the most remarkable building, and at the same time the saddest one, that I have ever seen.

For half the journey the road to Córdoba was the same as the road to Sevilla. Clustered together an hour from the valley along it was a group of towns and ports which included Cádiz, Jerez, Puerto de Santa Maria and Sanlúcar de Barrameda. I always made a halt on the way at one of them and often visited them individually for other reasons.

Slender Cádiz, angling out into the ocean on a spit of wave-pounded rock, guards one of the oldest harbours in the world. The town was founded well over 1,000 years BC by Phoenician merchants from Tyre, and grew progressively richer under the Romans, Visigoths and Moors. The peak of its fortunes came in the wake of Columbus' voyages, when much of the river of gold flowing back from the New World passed through it. The gold proved a double-edged blessing. It also attracted north African pirates, whose swift and predatory corsairs made repeated raids on the town, and Spain's implacable enemy, the English, determined to destroy the fleets the gold had allowed Spain to build. In 1587 Sir Francis Drake sailed into the bay and, in the famous singeing of the King of Spain's beard, put torches to the anchored ships which Philip II had assembled to send as an Armada against England. Nine years later the Admirals Essex and Howard repeated the exercise, this time landing and sacking the town as well.

Rebuilt, Cádiz again became enormously wealthy when the silting up of the Guadalquivir in 1717 forced Sevilla to yield to it Sevilla's monopoly of trading rights with what by then had become Spanish America. Cádiz' most humiliating moment came at the peak of its fortunes just under a century later in 1805. After seven years intermittent blockading by the British, the French and Spanish fleets were once again bottled up in Cádiz Bay. Late on the night of 20 October the combined force, under the command of the French Admiral Villeneuve, managed to slip out of harbour. At dawn next morning they were sighted by Nelson off the Cape of Trafalgar a few miles to the south. After manoeuvring his ships for several hours Nelson hoisted his battle signal at 11.35 a.m. and fifteen minutes later the French opened fire. By mid-afternoon the engagement was over. Superior in numbers but badly equipped, poorly manned and brilliantly outsailed, the French and Spanish fleets had been routed. Napoleon's hopes of invading England had ended but Nelson was dead, felled by a sniper's bullet from high in the rigging of an enemy warship. The following day his body, carried by weeping sailors of his flagship *Victory*, was taken ashore at Gibraltar, an event still commemorated every year by a ceremony on the Rock.

On the coast south of Cádiz is a quiet little fishing village named Conil de la Frontera, whose broad beach stretches almost to the rocky point of Trafalgar. Among their other catches Conil's fishermen net the migrating tuna, and the village has a simple but excellent restaurant which serves fish collected only minutes before from boats still being hauled up on the sand. The restaurant was one of our favourite destinations on winter Sundays. We ate outside on the shore, played chess after lunch in the warm December sunlight, and then walked beside the grey Atlantic breakers towards the Cape surrounded by gulls and skimming flocks of waders. The villagers of Conil must have had a grandstand view of the epic battle – wreckage from the shattered French and Spanish warships drifted ashore for days – but their descendants view it today, if at all, as an insignificant moment in the country's past.

'Trafalgar?' the restaurant owner remarked to me once, scratching his head. 'I think I heard of a battle there once. Perhaps it was during the Movimiento. Smugglers and shoals off the headland, that's all it means to me.'

Modern Cádiz has become one of Spain's biggest shipyards and naval bases, but the old town on the isthmus is still leafy and quiet and filled with magnificent seventeenth- and eighteenth-century houses. Across the bay is the busy, noisy and cheerful port of Santa Maria which once indirectly provided me with an extraordinary experience. The theatre critic Kenneth Tynan was staying in the valley with his wife, Kathleen. Tynan was a dedicated follower of the bulls and the three of us decided to go to Santa Maria to watch the unpredictable matador, Curro Romero. Romero, his face a translucent and sweating grey-green with fear, was at his worst that day, and after a long dinner to compensate for the dismal *corrida* we set off for home.

We were travelling in the Tynans' rented car and as soon as we got in we discovered the headlamps had failed. As none of us were keen to spend the night in a hotel, I suggested we might be able to crawl back on the side-lights alone by using the lonely country roads through the hills instead of the crowded coastal highway. Kathleen sat in the back, I took the wheel, Tynan got in beside me, and we set off. It was midnight and the darkness was intense. As we reached the hills Tynan said, 'To make sure you don't fall asleep, I'm going to use the rusty instrument of my voice and sing to you.' He took a deep breath, and started. Travelling at a snail's pace the journey took over five hours. The entire way Tynan sang, in English, French and German, music hall and cabaret songs from the end of the nineteenth century up to the present day, the songs of everyone from Marie Lloyd to Piaf to Kurt Weill and Alan Jay Lerner. The moon rose and sank, the stars dimmed, the roadside owls fell silent, the sky began to grey with dawn, and still Tynan went on without ever once repeating himself. When we reached the valley at last in the early sun he was still, with the morning larks accompanying him now, in full chorus. It was an astonishing *tour de force*, witty and affectionate and moving, which turned a drive that would otherwise have been a nightmare into five hours of unforgettable pleasure.

Fifteen miles beyond Puerto de Santa Maria is another smaller port named Sanlúcar de Barremeda. Lying right at the mouth of the Guadalquivir, Sanlúcar is shabby, dirty, dust-filled and sun-baked, a straggle of dilapidated whitewashed buildings, some new, some immensely old, tossed out along the river's bank. Its roadways are lumpy and potholed, flies throng the streets, beggars, cripples and gypsies huddle in the alleyways, the air smells of stale wine and pungently of dried blood from the town's cockpit. Yet in spite of an appearance even less prepossessing at first sight than Algeciras, Sanlúcar is one of the finest towns in all Spain. It has palaces, libraries, churches, monasteries, cloisters and halls, the presence of the mighty Guadalquivir at its walls, the fecund and dreaming wilderness of the marshes on the far bank, the waters of the Atlantic lapping at its quays. Columbus sailed from its tiny harbour on his third voyage to the New World, so did Magellan when he set out to circumnavigate the globe, so have endless ships before and since, from Phoenician traders to the supply galleons of the Armada to refuelling German U-boats in the Second World War. Brave and boisterous, courteous, laughing and learned, a place of dance and song, letters and adventure, little tawdry Sanlúcar challenges even Ronda as the best and most expressive definition of the Andalucian spirit.

Sanlúcar has always been known for its eccentrics, but the strangest and most enigmatic person associated with it, the manic, white-haired Christopher Columbus, was not a son of the town and quite possibly not even Spanish, although the Spanish have long since appropriated him as one of their own. Born in Genoa, he arrived in Spain from Lisbon as a seafaring widower of 40 with a 5-year-old son and a fanatical obsession – to reach India by crossing the Atlantic. He'd already tried and failed to persuade the King of Portugal to back him. Now he was going to make a last attempt with Ferdinand and Isabel. He placed his son, Diego, in the care of the monks at the little monastery of La Rábida just south of Huelva, and set off inland for Sevilla where the court was based. His timing was hardly auspicious. Ferdinand and Isabel, both in the thrall of an equally powerful obsession, believed that now, after eight centuries, there was a real possibility of taking Granada. All their concentration and energies, not to mention the resources of their exchequer, were focussed on the struggle with the Moors. Columbus' manner and appearance were scarcely calculated to advance his cause either. Flamboyant, seedily grand and a compulsive talker with haunted eyes which convinced many people he was mad, he has been likened by Salvador de Madariaga to a pre-incarnation of Don Quixote.

Somehow he gained an audience with the monarchs who, to stop being pestered by him as much as anything, agreed to set up a commission to examine his proposals. Columbus was kept waiting for six years. When the commission finally made its report the verdict was damning. His scheme, they found, was 'vain and worthy of all rejection'. Dejected and bitter, Columbus went back to La Rábida to collect Diego, by then eleven, and prepare to leave Spain. In the little monastery, as H. V. Morton relates, the most extraordinary mystery of the entire Columbus saga took place. Columbus apparently revealed something to one of the friars, Juan Perez, something still quite unknown but so momentous that Perez promptly sat down and wrote a letter relaying it to the Queen. In spite of the fact that the struggle for Granada was approaching its climax, Isabel equally swiftly summoned the friar to the court. Within weeks Columbus was urgently called for too.

By then it was January 1492 and the Christian armies were at the gates of Granada. Columbus, wearing clothes and riding a mule which had been bought for him for the journey, arrived just in time to witness the capitulation of the Moors and the triumphal entry of Ferdinand and Isabel into the city. Seven months later his three ships, the *Santa Maria*, the *Niña* and the somewhat oddly-named *Pinta*, 'The Painted Lady', cast off from below the monastery – they had been outfitted in the little harbour of Palos beside it – and set out west across the Atlantic. In the end Columbus crossed the ocean four times. The voyages brought him the riches and status he'd always dreamed of – one of the provisions in his agreement with the Catholic Monarchs was that he should be ennobled on his return – but he died as he had lived, a lonely enigma who believed to the last his landfall had been in Asia.

Jerez, the fourth in the cluster of towns on the road to Córdoba, is the only one that is not a port. Lying 15 miles inland Jerez is rich, massively confident and a little smug. Its wealth comes from the apparently inexhaustible demand, until recently at least, for its wines: the sherries that are produced from grapes grown on the chalky soil of the vineyards that surround it. The word 'sherry' is an Anglicisation of the town's Moorish name of Xeres. Jerez's proud claim of having invented sherry is passionately disputed by Montilla, a much smaller town a hundred miles to the east where the same chalky earth, the Montillanos insist, was producing even better 'sherries' centuries earlier. I suspect the Montillanos may be right. In my experience their little-known wines are always the equal of and often better than the most famous of Jerez' sherries. What Jerez acquired, and Montilla missed out on, was the English connection – 'sherry', as a description of Jerez wines, was first used in England as early as 1608. The extent and age of the English penetration of southern Andalucía often surprises people who imagine it began a couple of decades ago with fish-and-chip stalls on the Costa del Sol. In reality its roots go back several centuries. One major influence was Gibraltar. An elderly British friend who lived near Algeciras told me of spending Christmas in Andalucía as a young man in the early 1920s with the parents of the present Duchess of Lerma.

Apart from the 60 servants in the house there were 40 Andalucian friends and relations staying as guests, all of whom spoke English interchangeably with Castilian. On Christmas Eve the family gathered to sing traditional English carols. Dinner on Christmas Day consisted of turkey, plum pudding and brandy butter. On Boxing Day everyone went out to a meet of the Mons Calpe hunt, where the pink-coated master and whippers-in hunted a pack of English foxhounds across the rolling Andaluz *campo*. Older and even more important than Gibraltar or Málaga as an instrument of mingling the English and the Andaluz was the wine trade, initially in Málaga, from where Falstaff's beloved sack was imported, and later in Jerez.

'I have made an interesting discovery,' Dominic Elwes once said to me, chuckling, on his return from Jerez' autumn wine festival. 'If you want to know whether a member of one of the Jerez sherry families is descended from the Andalucian or the English branch, make the following test. If they are tall, blond, blue-eyed, wear Old Etonian ties and talk in impeccable English about Lords and Wimbledon, then they've unquestionably been educated in Spain and come from the Spanish side. On the other hand if they talk like this . . .'

Elwes' voice slid into one of his brilliant impersonations of an Andalucian peasant struggling unsuccessfully in an almost impenetrable accent to grapple with the English language.

'And if they're small, shifty, sallow-skinned, smell like drains and wear old Córdoba hats and boots, then just as certainly they'll have been at Eton and Oxford, served in the Brigade of Guards, and be fully paid-up members of the English branch.' The paradox was typically mischievous, but as always with Elwes' falcon eye and bat-like ear for the idiosyncrasies and absurdities of human behaviour there was a large measure of truth in it. Jerez society is a blend of Andaluz and English mercantile families who, brought together by the sherry business, have married into each other again and again over the centuries. For some unaccountable reason the most distinctive characteristics of both nations, physical and cultural, seem to surface with equal regularity on the opposite side of each union.

So much has been written, at such length and so expertly, about the production of sherry that it is hard to add anything illuminating to the subject. There are four basic varieties of Jerez wine: the bone-dry finos with the paleness of sun-bleached sierra grass at an Andalucian summer's end, the deeper and fuller amontillados coloured like a moorland loch fed by peat streams, the rich-smelling amber olorosos, and the sugar-sweet slow-pouring dulces. Unlike the great French wines, none of the sherries depends on the year's 'vintage' – on rain, frost and sun and the individual personality they impose on a season's grapes. All sherries are mixed through the solera system under which the newest pressings are fed into the bottom of the 'ladder' and gradually mount its steps, mingling with and being strengthened by the older wines as they travel upwards, until the blend drawn off at the top has the same balance and character of those of its predecessors. There are no 'bad' sherry years. A warp in one season's harvest can always be compensated for by an infusion from a better year somewhere along the climb up the solera. When the wines emerge at the ladder's top they conform in taste, fragrance and colour to the stringent standards laid down in advance, and often long ago, by the bodega's masters.

In Britain, still the largest external market for Jerez wines

although it is rapidly being caught up by Germany and the Low Countries, sherry has become a polite occasional drink, the traditional glass to offer the local vicar before lunch on Sunday. In Andalucía it remains one of the region's glories, a drink like champagne to mark weddings, feast days and celebrations. Sherry, again like champagne, is by Andaluz wine-buying habits precious and expensive. Far from being an everyday social drink, poured out as an apértif in tiny glasses at a warm room's temperature, sherry is special and noble, a wine to be carefully chilled to enhance its flavour and drunk throughout the day and late into the night. Furthermore the Andaluz have a religious obligation to drink it. Why? '*Porque vinó del cielo.*'

As well as meaning wine, *vinó*, pronounced in much the same way but with an accent on the final letter, is the past tense of the verb to come. So in one of the many plays on words that delight the Andaluz, the saying means at the same time 'wine of the sky' and 'it came from the sky'. And because their priests have constantly told them they are duty bound to accept whatever God sends them from His home in the sky, the Andaluz are naturally obliged to drink wine.

Beyond Jerez, which the motorway bypasses, the road runs on to Sevilla, out along an escarpment above the plain of the Guadalquivir valley, and through yet another of Andalucía's immensely old little towns, Carmona. Beneath Carmona's walls in 206 BC Scipio defeated the combined armies of the Numidians and the Carthaginians, led by Hasdrubal. Carmona's Roman legacy includes a necropolis, one of whose tombs has a statue of an elephant at the entrance. Hannibal, best known of all Carthaginians, is probably most remembered for using elephants in crossing the Alps and Carmona's elephant must have been sculpted during the Carthaginian occupation of the town. Travelling often, when I lived in the Guadalmesi, between Andalucía and Africa – where I would watch the huge, immensely intelligent and devastatingly powerful animals wardened in their twentieth-century reserves by men with transceivers, guns and trucks – I used to wonder how more than 2,000 years ago they had been caught, 'tamed' and transported to Andalucía. However it was done, elephants had evidently reached the ferociously hot little town above the Guadalquivir well before the birth of Christ.

Further along the road to Córdoba, lying in a hollow, and hotter still, is Écija, the frying-pan of Andalucía. Écija, founded by the Greeks, is a bizarre, impacted and lonely town, once rich but long since in shabby decline. Its main square, the Plaza de España, is one of the strangest in Spain. The buildings, which incorporate the belfries of three ruined churches, all seem to have been built at a different time, in different styles and out of different materials, providing between them 1,000 years of Andalucian architectural history in a single sun-glazed little capsule. Écija is still a supply centre for the surrounding farms and for me its most attractive feature is its cluster of working craft shops: boot makers, saddle makers, basket and pannier makers, forges, and farriers. Forty miles beyond the town, the road finally runs into Córdoba.

Within fifty years of reaching Córdoba the Moors had made

it the capital of Muslim Spain. Over the next two centuries it became one of the richest, most brilliant and most exciting cities in the world, with a population of over a million, more than twice what it is today, at a time when London and Paris were little more than fortified villages. In 929 the ruler, Abdu'r-Rahman III, was so powerful he was able to proclaim himself Caliph and announce Spain's independence of Damascus. The glory lasted for only a century longer. By 1070 Al Andalus had fragmented into an ant's heap of warring *taifas*, little Moorish kingdoms, and Córdoba had surrendered its independence to Sevilla. Less than two centuries later still, it fell to the Christian reconquest. With one exception, only odds and ends survive from Córdoba's years of splendour, but that exception, the great mosque, is so magnificent, so bold and powerful and intricate, it not only stands in itself as one of the greatest

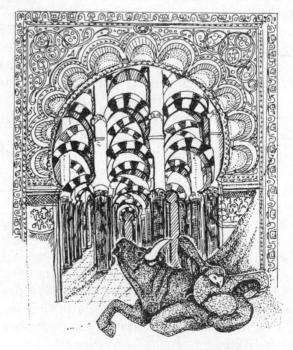

The mihrab in the Mesquita, Córdoba

The Mesquita, Córdoba

achievements of the human imagination, it evokes Córdoba's entire lost world of Arab intellect, art and faith.

Started in 785 and progressively enlarged over the next 200 years, the basic concept of the Mesquita is simplicity itself: a vast single-storey rectangle, 200 yards in length and 150 yards in width, roofed, pillared, and arched, and set with the shining jewel of its *mihrab*, the prayer alcove, facing Mecca, of filigree and Byzantine mosaic. Within that bare framework what the Moorish vision created is breath-taking in its suppleness, scale and beauty. From the outside the Mesquita resembles an old and sinewy fortress watchfully gazing down on the Guadalquivir. Entering it is like suddenly walking into a forest of petrified tree trunks. In the cool and darkened air line upon line of pillars stretch away on every side apparently to the edge of the world. Lifting above them are rows of double arches, painted in bands of white and bull's-blood red and retreating until they seem to vanish in distant mist. One walks, and it appears to be for miles, through the silent trees until a cascade of shimmering light pours out from the three chapels of the *mihrab* like a secret fountain in the middle of a dark wood.

149

Then turning away the light vanishes and the austere forest envelops one again.

Originally the outside walls were open and the whole mosque, although cool even then because of its immense size, was filled with the scent of orange blossom from the trees outside and glittered with bars of sunlight. The bricking up of the walls was a fearful error, but nothing compared to the terrible humiliation inflicted on the noble building in the mid-sixteenth century when the canons of Córdoba ripped out its heart to build a Christian cathedral. Even the devout Emperor Charles v was appalled when he learned what they had done. 'You have destroyed something unique,' he said in fury and anguish, 'to build something trivial.' Inside the cathedral, which squats in the middle of the mosque, is a curious marble carving of a bull expiring from a ruptured stomach. The official church explanation is that the bull was so moved by his contribution to God's temple in hauling stone to the site, his innards erupted in delight. It has never struck me as a very plausible story. I think it much more likely the wretched animal died of shock when he saw the grotesque act of vandalism the canons had committed.

It says much for the Mesquita that in spite of lodging a hideous swollen cuckoo at the centre of its nest its presence is still so awesome and majestic. Like the Alhambra its survival in any form is due to chance and fortune. The two buildings, totally different in design and purpose, make fine complements to each other. One a sumptuous palace of delight, the other a huge and audacious act of faith, together they reflect perfectly the two dominating strands of the Moorish *duende*, the playful spirit and the driving daemon of the Andalucian Arabs. The Mesquita inevitably dominates the city but Córdoba has many other attractions, packed close together as always in Andalucía's great towns at its centre. The Judería, the old Jewish quarter, is an enchanting network of narrow lanes, little tree-filled squares, and shining white houses whose gates open onto the prettiest gardens in Andalucía, brimming over with flowers and ferns, vines and creepers, urns and fountains. It has one of Spain's only two ancient synagogues, a tiny four-teenth-century hall with an even smaller balcony overlooking it where the women worshipped; a collection of fine museums including one devoted to bullfighting in the house where Maimonides, the codifier of Jewish law, once lived; and for me most memorable of all the constant sound of flamenco, spilling out from windows and doors, rising from patios, pealing over roofs and tumbling down streets. Paradoxically for such a grave and reserved city which believes in hard work and early nights – Garcia Lorca called it the most melancholy city in Spain – Córdoba to the ear is perpetually in musical *fiesta*, in flamenco *fiesta*.

There are as many explanations of the origins of flamenco – in Castilian the word means flamingo – as there are for the derivation of Andalucía. One popular theory has it coming to Spain from Flanders, whose exotic songs and dances performed by the Flemish at court reminded the Spanish of the flamingo's courtship displays. Another, which is my favourite and as persuasive as any of the others, was given to the writer, Madeleine Duke, by an old Andalucian musician and historian. 'It was a Persian called Ali ben Zeryab who brought this music to Andalucía in the first half of the ninth century,' he told her. 'Zeryab had been a pupil of the famous Baghdad musician, Isaac the Moselite. One day when both of them were performing before the Caliph, Harun al Raschid, Zeryab's songs surpassed his master's. Isaac became extremely jealous and angry, and gave Zeryab the choice between death or exile. So Zeryab left his country and became a wanderer. He took his songs to many countries. I have heard that to this day they are sung in the north of India just as we sing them in Andalucía. It was in Córdoba that Zeryab finally settled down. Abdu'r-Rahman II, the Sultan, was a man of great culture; he was delighted with Zeryab's talents and showered him with gifts. Zeryab became the Sultan's constant companion and in this favoured position his gifts ripened, and he became an arbiter of civilised pleasure. An Arab writer of those days said Zeryab knew more than a thousand songs by heart, each with its own music. Zeryab claimed he learned them from the spirits of the air. He added a fifth string to the lute and developed a style of playing unlike any other musician. He evolved a blend of Arab, Persian and Sindhi songs into *cante jondo*, our present-day flamenco.'

While loving flamenco and having listened and danced to it many many times over the years, I cannot in any sense claim to be an authority on its music. Unquestionably flamenco during this century has been bedevilled as an art-form by two opposing influences, both of them foreign and both equally degrading. On one side, tourism has cheapened and trivialised flamenco into banal but accessible melodies accompanied by snapping castanets. On the other, the economic patronage of a few solemn and self-appointed experts has made it knowing and self-conscious. True flamenco, *cante jondo* or deep song in its proper name, is neither trivial nor solemn. Reaching beyond the ordinary rhythms of words or music like the piercing *saetas* of the Holy Week processions, it is a call from the depths of the soul that charts the farthest shores of joy or grief, love or longing, soaring hope or plunging despair. It cannot be ordered or bought. It has its own spirit and comes of its own accord, often only after long hours of being teased out from the hidden place where it uneasily rests.

The best *cante jondo* is never performed. It erupts spontaneously in unexpected places and on unlikely occasions: towards dawn after a night's drinking in a small, bare room, in the midday heat of a countryside *romería*, at evening on the sea's shore by the flames of a fire that has burnt all day.

Flamenco's other expression, dancing, has two main forms which spring from a common source. One, the accompaniment to *cante jondo*, is as vivid, improvised, subtle and flexible as deep song itself. The other, a river of movement that has divided over the centuries into endless regional channels, is more formal and structured, an infinity of swirling dance patterns like Sevillanas and pasadobles which every Andaluz is expected to know and perform as one of the most basic of social graces.

Apart from the Mesquita and the songs and dances which cascade over the city, Córdoba has one other and even more potent attribute – the wealth of the Guadalquivir plain lapping against its walls. The *vega* round Granada made the kingdom of Granada rich. The Guadalquivir made all Andalucía rich. I have travelled the valley of the Guadalquivir, from its high and foaming start as an icy stream in the Cazorla hills to its muddy, rippling slide into the Atlantic below Sevilla, at almost every season of the year. After all those many journeys I believe the best time to see the great river and the countryside through which it flows is in late autumn. The crops are home, the air is clear and fresh, the texture and contours of the ground stand out clean in the late sun.

ONE OF ANDALUCÍA'S greatest glories is its food. While the region doesn't have a long and sophisticated culinary tradition like France, it more than compensates by having one of the finest, freshest and broadest ranges of raw materials in the world, from both the land and the sea. They are seen at their best in Andalucía's markets.

The market stands at the heart of every Spanish *pueblo*, even in cities as big as Madrid and Barcelona. If the town is old and hasn't been redeveloped it is often next to the church, occupying a large warehouse-like building with its floor-space divided by wooden partitions into little booths. The larger towns and cities have daily markets on several different sites. Algeciras has four while the much smaller Tarifa has only one. A village like Pelayo doesn't have one at all, depending instead on a couple of shops and daily visits from a fishvan. Not long ago fish vendors would travel high into the sierras carrying fresh sardines and anchovies in ice-panniers on donkeys. On the return journey they transported local produce down to the markets in the towns, making crops like chestnuts, almonds and olives an economic proposition for the small hill-farmer. The arrival of the truck followed by soaring petrol prices changed the traditional pattern. Fish was no longer a worthwhile commodity to take up to the sierras. Transport down to the coast or the plains disappeared, many of the scattered crops went unharvested, and the villages became more and more isolated.

The markets below were largely unaffected. They found

other sources for the hills' produce and went on with their business as before. The Andaluz is not an early shopper and the markets open today as they have always done at about 9.00 a.m. Well before then the cafés and *churrerías* in the near-by streets will have opened for business. The market cafés specialize in thick pale coffee made with condensed milk and stiffened with a dram of sticky *anís* to fortify the stall-holders for the morning ahead. The *churrerías* provide the staple for a breakfast that can be eaten at any time until the stalls close at midday. *Churros* are a variety of doughnut, piped through a funnel into boiling oil in short lengths if they are potato-based, or the same way in big swirling circles if they are made from the alternative and lighter flour-based mixture. In the north of Spain *churros* are coated in sugar, in the south salted. Sold hot from the scalding oil, the shoppers take them to the cafés wrapped in greased paper and dunk them in their coffee or hot chocolate, the women gossiping and the men debating local politics or chewing silently on tooth-picks. Travelling slowly between them round the pavement tables there is invariably a blind man selling state lottery tickets. Sometimes he falls ill. When that happens a member of his family takes his place, a wife, daughter or son who disconcertingly use his white stick and blackened glasses, tapping like him along the street but staring out from behind the glasses with bright seeing eyes.

In spite of the arrival of cold storage, Andalucian food preparation is still dominated by the hot climate and the lack of refrigeration facilities in the past. Preserving in salt or oil, by smoking or drying, spicing or pickling, is one of its major features. Where foods are not preserved they are always fresh and in season. The markets, which provide an instant picture of what is happening week by week in the surrounding country-side, sell both. There are small regional variations between different markets, but their general pattern and the range of produce for sale is the same all over Andalucía. Algeciras' market, housed beneath its splendid concrete canopy, is a typical example.

The stalls are grouped together more or less according to the

types of food they offer. Close to the entrance are the butchers
who supply kid meat, young beef, chickens, rabbits, pork,
occasional game birds like partridges and lapwings, and a
selection of spiced dried pork sausages and blood puddings.
The meat hangs from hooks across the front of the stalls,
roughly carved into large boneless lumps which follow the
lines of the muscle. Most of it is sold either as *filete*, sliced into
thin steaks and priced according to its tenderness and position
on the carass, or in lumps for stewing. Pork fillet is often
available marinated in paprika, garlic and salt, a mixture
called *escabeche* which with vinegar and lemon or marjoram is
also a favourite way of preserving fish. The butchers may also
have trays of strange-looking little yellow lumps which are
unborn chickens' eggs to be put in stews, and bulls' testicles
hanging in bunches of forlorn rubbery bags.

The next group of stalls belong to the fish merchants.
Depending on the season and what the boats have brought in,
their counters will be piled with different types of clam, some
finer and more expensive than others, razorshells, sea snails,
rape, tuna and swordfish steaks, sardines and anchovies,
shrimps and prawns, langoustines, cod, mackerel, *salmonete*

or red mullet, sole, and tiny and delicious flatfish called *chanquetes* which have to be floured in a sieve with a delicate hand before being fried. Then there will also be octopus, squid, sea urchins, mussels, occasionally much-prized little elvers known as *angulas*, which are eaten piping hot in garlic sauce with a wooden fork, and sometimes, too, *percebes*, curious anenome-like creatures from the Atlantic coasts. Finally for brief periods there are wooden boxes of oysters, lobsters, several varieties of crab, Saint Pierre, and rascasse for soup.

Beyond the fish stalls are the delicatessens and grocers with cheeses, York and smoked hams, olives, dried chickpeas, lentils, beans, salted pork, sausages preserved in lard, lengths of smoked ham-bone to flavour stews, big circular drums of salted sardines, and *bacalao*, a strong-smelling salt cod eaten everywhere in Andalucía. Then there are the vegetable and fruit stalls. Many of them deal in only three or four varieties, huge bunches of carrots with their fronds still attached to show their freshness, lettuces tied with grass strings from the fields, waxy sand-covered potatoes, and big misshapen tomatoes which are sliced and served uncooked with olive oil, chopped garlic and rough salt. Others sell everything in season. The vegetable merchants may have broad beans, green beans and

peas, cabbage and chard in winter, dark curling spinach, little tender-skinned marrows, green and red peppers, aubergines, orange chunks of pumpkin, yams, cucumbers, and large purple onions, mild-flavoured and sweet. In the fruiterers there will be oranges and lemons all year round and then, depending on the season, apples, pears, strawberries, cherries, melons, custard apples, grenadines, quinces and pomegranites, together with pineapples and bananas from Morocco. Figs are laid out on their own leaves, first the green with their honey-sweet centres, then the black with vivid scarlet flesh inside. Grapes are the final treat of the year before olives and nuts announce the arrival of winter.

Clustered round the market's walls outside are the smaller dealers whose stalls often consist of no more than a stool and an upturned barrel. Peasant farmers offer the produce of their tiny *huertos*, or live chickens, rabbits and quail in cages. Gypsies sell country-harvested snails from sacks, black or pink-gilled mushrooms, and bunches of the two varieties of wild asparagus, the bitter for soups and stews, the sweet for omelettes. The spice lady, an essential figure in every Andalucian market whatever its size, has a wooden trestle table brimming over with sacks of herbs. Coriander, marjoram, fennel, black peppercorns, cumin, thyme, rosemary, lavender, bay leaves, rough salt, sticks of cinnamon, expensive cloves, dried red peppers threaded on twine for flavouring stews, nutmeg and mace, shelled amonds for sweets, verbena for tea, liquorice sticks for children to chew, tiny boxes of precious saffron to colour *paella*, and a whole variety of plants to cure disorders from poppy seeds to induce sleep to *abrotonomacho* to halt baldness. The spice lady is not only a merchant. She is also a consultant and advisor who can provide from her stock anything from a suitable love potion to a remedy for a donkey's flatulence.

Since Roman times Andalucia has been famous for its bread. Its quality came, the Romans believed, from the special sweetness and fatness the Andalucian sun gave to the ears of wheat. There were bread stalls in both Algeciras and Tarifa markets, as there are everywhere in Andalucía, but we usually bought our bread direct from the little local baker in Pelayo, the village over the ridge where the children first went to school. The price of bread in Spain has been regulated by the government for several hundred years, and there has been a bakery in Pelayo since records were first kept. The present baker inherited it from his father who in turn inherited it from his father who also inherited it from his father.

'Beyond that I don't know,' he told me once when we were discussing its history. 'The papers don't say who owned it before, they just list the price to be charged. But I believe it has been in my family for many, many generations. People have always needed bread and we Andaluz don't like to leave our *pueblo*, least of all when we have a good place and job there.'

The bakery was a long, dusky and cave-like building, arched in the middle and with the ovens at one end. The loaves were put in and taken out with long-handled wooden paddles which had turned dark mahogany in colour over the years from the oven's heat. The flour was a coarse-ground mix, fed with a shovel-full of lime and leavened by sourdough – dough containing living yeast kept over from the previous day's baking whose ancestry must have stretched back years or even centuries. The blend produced a bread which dried out but never went mouldy. It could be kept for a week or more without changing noticeably in flavour or texture.

Everyday loaves weighed either a kilo or half a kilo and were round or shaped like a double-pointed tear-drop. But huge four-kilo loaves were baked on order for the local charcoal-burners and cork-strippers who needed them to last two weeks in the hills. Before our first visit to the Coto Doñana reserve in the Guadalquivir marshes, Elisabeth stopped off at the bakery to buy some bread to take with us on the expedition. The baker accidentally learned what the bread was needed for and looked at her shocked.

'You can't take ordinary loaves with you for that,' he said. 'You need bread that will stand up to the *marismas*, absorb the heat and damp, last, and still taste good. I will design a special Coto Doñana loaf for you, *señora*, something I think between one for a mule train to Ronda and a three-day sardine-fishing trip.'

The loaf was designed and baked that night, and ready for collection in a limited edition of a dozen when we left at dawn next morning. On our return the baker asked anxiously how the bread had fared in the marshes. It was excellent, Elisabeth told him, crisp and firm and delicious to the end, as indeed it was. He beamed happily.

'I was sure it would be,' he said. 'I even felt confident enough to stamp the loaves with my initials. From now on that is what you will always take with you on your journeys, and I will always sign the bread myself.'

Although Pelayo bread, whether as ordinary loaves or in the signed Coto Doñana limited edition, lasted for up to two weeks, it was at its best eaten hot and fresh with butter and honey. Butter in Andalucía is an expensive luxury sold in tiny packets. The peasant Andaluz usually spreads his bread with dripping or a trickle of green olive oil, rubbed in either case with a clove of fresh garlic. But whenever we had honey in the house we always indulged in butter. The honey came from Ana's uncle who had hives, fashioned out of gnarled grey cork stripped from the oak trees, in the clover and buttercup meadows behind Algeciras. It was laid down like wine every year until it had turned to a dark, cloudy and crusted gold. Then he would bring it to the house in thick green bottles and wait apprehensively until it had been tasted and pronounced, as it always was, magnificent.

In the Guadalmesi most of our food came from the local markets, our wine from Jerez, Sanlúcar and the north, our honey from the lower slopes of the sierras behind Algeciras, and our bread from Pelayo, but our cheeses came from the valley itself. They were made by José's aunt at his little family farm on the spur below the house. She was famous for her cheeses along the straits. They were made in spring from goats' milk from the valley's flocks and coagulated from the stomach of a new-born kid, killed after its first suckling. The little dried bag of the stomach hung from a rafter in the stone cottage and she broke off a tiny nut from the curd every day to add to the flocks' morning yield. When the mixture was ready she would plunge her hands into the bucket and knead the spring curds until the whey had separated. Then she would pat and shape handfuls of the cheese on a straw mat, squeezing out the whey until she was left with a solid stem-patterned cake. The cake would be dried for a couple of weeks; after this it was stored in olive oil in urns until it was ready to be eaten. One of her trade-marks was to pat the rind first with dried *pimento*, ground sweet red peppers, so that it acquired an aromatic scarlet crust.

The only animal more prized in Andalucía than the goat is the pig. Goats produce milk and meat. Pigs yield no milk but, in terms of being converted into protein, they leave goats far behind. Every part of a pig – head, ears, back, flanks, haunches, and even trotters – can be turned into food. It wasn't long after Ana moved into the Huerto Perdido before she insisted we acquired one. Her peasant instincts about waste were affronted by the disposal of the house's scraps into an unproductive dustbin. Manolo the dustman, the Guadalmesi's champion pig-breeder, was called in, and soon afterwards a very small pig with a ring through its nose arrived.

Manolo kept a daily eye on the pig's progress and several months later as it approached maturity he decided it should be castrated. This posed a problem. Castrating pigs was a professional job and the local castrator lived between the valley and Tarifa. Unfortunately he had a girl-friend in the town who he visited regularly. As everyone knew, if a castrator slept with a woman on the night before he did his work, the pigs would catch fever and die. This was what had happened the year before when most of the Guadalmesi's pigs had been lost and the castrator had almost been lynched. He was reluctant to come back to the valley, its inhabitants were determined to keep him away, and Manolo was nervous in any event that even if he came he might have been up to no good during the night and our pig would be the unfortunate casualty. Nonetheless it had to be done and eventually Manolo hit on the answer.

'All is well, Don Nicholas,' he said as he arrived smiling one morning. 'I have asked him to a *fiesta* at my house tomorrow. By the end of the evening I will make sure he is too drunk to find his way home. He will have to stay the night and I can keep an eye on him. I will bring him straight down the next day.'

Forty-eight hours later Manolo appeared with the castrator stumbling wearily beside him. The man had dark shadows under his eyes and reeked of stale wine, but he managed to perform his operation and the pig suffered no ill effects.

Not long afterwards autumn arrived and it was time for the animal to be killed so that its meat could be salted down for the winter. The whole business was as complicated as securing the uncontaminated services of the castrator. The *matanza*, the killing, had to take place at dawn after a night when the moon was waxing and the dew was light. If the moon was on the wane the pig's blood would fail to flow properly, reducing the amount of black pudding it yielded, and if the dew was heavy, heralding a hot day, some of the meat might become rotten before it was preserved. After consultations with Curra the witch, a morning in early October was chosen.

The killing itself was a man's job and two of José's cousins from the valley, Juan and Juanito, volunteered to do it. The rest of the work was the responsibility of the women, and Ana arranged for her sister, her aunt and two of her nieces to be on hand to help. Everyone involved, as at all country *matanzas*, would be rewarded by a share in the result. Juan and Juanito arrived at 4.00 a.m. while it was still dark in the forest. By daylight they had built a fire under the cork oaks, heated a vast cauldron of water over the flames, and honed their knives on whetstones. As the sun came up the women appeared and a few minutes later the wretched animal met its end in a brief, bloody and hideously noisy execution.

Its body was scalded over the boiling cauldron, scraped clean of bristles, nailed to a cross-bar on a tree in the glade, and swiftly and expertly gutted. Hanging there in the early light it looked exactly like an image from *Les Très Riches Heures du Duc de Berry*, spoils from a hunting trip in a medieval forest. The men's work was over but just before they left Juanito blew up a pale yellow tubular balloon and handed it to Elisabeth smiling.

'For the children, *señora*,' he said.

The balloon was the pig's bladder. It also appears in the pages of the old Duke's book which was compiled and illustrated over six centuries before. With the men gone the women took over and the real business of the day started. The first step was to wash all of the pig's intestines over and over again in running water, either in the Huerto Perdido's stream or under the kitchen taps, and then soak them in vinegar until they were ready to be stuffed with black pudding or sausage. Ana's aunt had brought huge bunches of parsley and marjoram. In the house already were stocks of rough salt, peppercorns, bay leaves, and dried red peppers which had been turned almost black by the sun. All else that was needed were wooden boxes and a number of tall earthenware crocks, both of which were also to hand. The black pudding, made out of the pig's carefully gathered blood, chopped up pieces of its back fat and *pimentón*, powdered dry red peppers known in Hungary as paprika, was prepared first.

'How do you know when it's ready?' I asked Ana as I

watched the mixture, stuffed into the cleaned intestines which had then been cut and knotted into lengths of sausages, simmer in the cauldron beneath the trees.

'Don't be stupid, Don Nicholas,' she answered sharply. 'It's ready when it sings, of course.'

Ana was right. Black pudding does indeed sing at the right moment, whistling and bubbling through the tiny airholes that long boiling in the cauldron produces in its skin. Like almost everything else from a pig, Andalucian black pudding is put by for the winter, when it is either sliced into stews or eaten fried with thick slices of country bread.

After the black pudding had been dealt with the shoulder meat was minced, chopped, mixed with spices, herbs and garlic and pressed into sausages too. The pig's belly, together with its tail, trotters and ears, were laid in the wooden boxes and heaped with salt from the Cádiz salt flats. The salt from Cádiz was unrefined and so still contained saltpetre which, as the winter months went by, gave the raw bacon a faint pink tinge. The meat needed to be turned in the salt once a week but provided it was, it would keep until spring. The pig's hams were put aside to be sent up to the sierras to be cured in the cold dry mountain air. Andalucía has a number of sierra villages known all over Spain for their *jamón serrano*, but the best and sweetest of all come from Jabugo in the Sierra Morena where the altitude, breezes, sun and temperature combine to create perfect conditions for curing hams all year apart from high summer. Our hams were destined for Jabugo.

Most of the rest of the meat was chopped, spiced and made into sausages too. The lard and back fat were rendered until all the solids were crisp and brown and had become *chicharros*, a treat for children often sold in Spanish corner shops. The remaining lard was then extracted, coloured red with peppers, scented with herbs, garlic and cumin seed, and used to preserve the final chunks of pork in the same way as the French store goose for the winter in its own fat. When the last of the meat had been cooked it was tipped into one of the earthenware crocks, the aromatic liquid mixture was poured over it, the contents were allowed to set, and a wooden lid was placed on top. Afterwards the crock would be dipped into as the winter months went by, the meat being scooped out for stews and the fat being spread on bread.

By the end of the day of the *matanza* almost all of the pig had vanished into crocks, boxes, trays, jugs and the long plump loops of the intestinal sausage skins. All that was left unpreserved were its liver and kidneys, which had been put aside since the animal was gutted at dawn. As dusk fell everyone involved, including Juan and Juanito who had finished their day's work, reassembled by the fire. There the lights were skewered, roasted over the embers, and eaten as supper with bread, wine and lengthy reminiscences of *matanzas* past. Finally everyone collected their share of the pig and left for home under the stars.

'Excellent,' Ana said contentedly as she stood surveying the laden tables in the kitchen after they'd gone, her hands on her hips and her apron dark with dried blood. 'Tomorrow, Don Nicholas, I want you to get another. It's time we started again.'

As well as being the time for slaughtering pigs, autumn is also the season for olives. The market olive sellers always have at least a dozen varieties, each flavoured in a diffent way or of a different degree of ripeness or size, but once again Ana insisted we prepared our own. Unlike the French, Italians and Greeks, the Andaluz do not preserve their olives in oil. They use brine instead and although regional tastes differ, almost all Andalucian olives are preserved green and young rather than black and ripe. To rid the freshly picked green fruit of its natural bitterness, the olives are first cracked with a mallet or rolling-pin to break the skin and then soaked for a week in water which has to be changed every day. When the bitterness has been washed out they are put in an earthenware crock filled with a strongly salted and acidulated liquid. The acid can be provided by vinegar, quartered lemons, or, as in Sevilla, by bitter oranges. Then a number of herbs are added. Again, local preferences dictate which ones. Round Tarifa and Algeciras sticks of fennel, together with thyme, marjoram and rosemary, were favoured. In another *pueblos* chillies and heads of garlic, roasted lightly over an open flame, were considered equally important.

Two weeks later the olives are ready. Like the pieces of pork preserved in crocks of lard they keep their goodness throughout the winter, needing only to have the liquid in which they're steeped skimmed from time to time. Not unlike olives in their preparation although appearing earlier in the year are another of the Andalucian countryside delicacies, snails. Snails are a summer crop. They come in two varieties, large and small, but the most prized are the small which, eaten in their own clear soup accompanied by a tankard of beer, are the traditional preparation for a long night at a town's *feria*. Unlike the well-known huge and dark species of Burgundian France, Andalucian snails tend to be tiny and pale with translucent sepia-veined shells. As soon as the winter rains end and the *campo* dries out in the heat, they oestivate by climbing the tall thistles and anchoring themselves under the protective spikes.

They are harvested by women and children who go out into the fields with sticks and buckets and rattle the stems until the snails fall off. In recent years roadside fence-posts and electricity pylons have been adopted by the snails as roosts, but in spite of the tempting clusters they acquire the Andaluz have learned to leave them alone. Ingested lead paint and the absorbed discharge from petrol and diesel engines make the snails unappetising and dangerous. After being gathered the snails are placed in a covered bucket with a bunch of pennyroyal, which always grows close to their roosts, and left for two or three days to evacuate themselves. Then they are washed seven times in salt and running water, at the end of which all their foam will have disappeared. Finally they are placed in a huge pot, flavoured with coriander, peppercorns, cumin, dried chillies, and another sprig of pennyroyal, brought gently to the boil, and simmered for an hour. After being skimmed with pennyroyal once more, the snails are ready. The pot remains on the stove, heated up for anyone who wants to dip into it, until the snails, which keep clean, fresh and spiced to the end, are finished.

As well as being served at meals, snails like so much else from the Andalucian table are also eaten as *tapas*. In English a *tapa* is literally a snack, but the translation does no justice at all to the wide and delicious range of dishes the word represents in Spanish. *Tapas* are served in every bar with all but the cheapest drinks. They range from a couple of olives on a little glass saucer to a portion of expensive sierra-cured ham or a platter of hot prawns in garlic. The basic *tapas* are provided free as the normal accompaniment to a drink, the more elaborate ones have to be ordered and paid for. Visitors to Andalucía who come across them often believe *tapas* are no more than hors d'oeuvres, a prelude to a proper meal. In fact to many Andaluz *tapas* make up the day's meals both at lunch and in the evening. A busy man like Juan Carlos Barbadillo, the sherry sales man from Sanlúcar, often goes for days away from home without sitting down at a table and existing entirely on *tapas*.

'They are light and healthy,' he explained to me once as we stopped yet again at a sierra bar and crunched some sea snails brought up that morning from the coast. 'They are always fresh and they change with the seasons. Why should I sit down to bloat and harm myself on huge set meals? Eating *tapas* I can travel, talk and drink all day, and my stomach gets nothing but the best and most digestible of what it needs. To get your food from *tapas* is the finest and most enjoyable way to eat in all the world. Where else does a meal last for eighteen hours and yet the dishes taste as good at the end as when you started – and you're still sober enough to take pleasure in them?'

Andalucía has ocean, sea and river, mountain, valley and plain. It harvests them all, in the wild and under cultivation. The food it gathers, from mushrooms, nuts and wild aspar- agus, to beef, ham and cereals, pomegranites, cheese, elvers, lobsters and swordfish, is prepared and served in almost every way known to cookery. Andalucian cuisine draws on many traditions. But its emphasis is always not on complexity or ostentation but on the virtues of its raw materials, on their cleanness, freshness and their individual tastes. Preserved or raw, in *tapas* or as formal meals, in rich, carefully prepared country stews or as rapidly chopped salads sprinkled with Cádiz sea-salt and tossed with the first pressing of green olive oil, it invariably reflects the region's prodigal bounty.

ᘓᕬ 12 ᕬᘓ

TRAVELLING BY CAR from the valley to Madrid, as we occasionally needed to do, there seemed to be only two feasible
ways to get to the pass of Despeñaperros and so up to the
central plateau. One was to curve west and take the road that
ran through Sevilla and Córdoba. The other was to swing east,
follow the coastal highway to Málaga, and then turn inland
towards Granada. The roads finally came together just below
the pass, but to take either was like travelling half-way round a
circle to reach a point immediately on the opposite side.
Looking at a map it always seemed to me it should have been
possible to cut straight across and avoid the time-consuming
detours.

For a long while I was assured by people who made the
journey from the area round the valley, even by those who had
made it often, that it wasn't possible. Across the direct route
lay the sierras. The sierra maps were notoriously unreliable.
Many of the roads they showed didn't exist or were no more
than tracks. Where they did exist and were passable by car,
they frequently didn't link up with the next section. Like every
other sensible person I should stick to the normal routes to
Despeñaperros. Then one evening I met someone who'd lived
near Algeciras on and off for over forty years. He was English
and during all his years in southern Andalucía he'd been a
passionate explorer and traveller in the hills.

He agreed the maps were unreliable, but said they were
equally unreliable in the opposite way. They failed to record
many perfectly adequate sierra roads, built for a variety of

reasons, which did exist. He always travelled to Madrid through the hills, and he showed me half a dozen ways of crossing them so that one eventually reached the pass. I tried several later. His routes weren't any faster than the two main roads, in fact they were probably even slower, but they were certainly far more attractive to drive. Several had a further great advantage. At one stage or another they touched on the sierra town of Ronda, not that the town ever needed an excuse to pass through it. Ronda, which has one of the most spectacular settings in Andalucía, was reason enough on its own.

Most people who visit Ronda now start on the coast, and for speed and convenience use the new highway that winds and climbs precipitously up through the mountains from its start near the sea at San Pedro de Alcántara. From time to time there are lofty views through the pines of some plunging ravine, but I always found it a cheerless and intimidating approach. There are many other approaches, each with its own attractions, but the loveliest of all, particularly in spring, was along the road we took from our valley. Rising from the sea-level to a pass above the town, over 3,000 feet, the road traversed a complete cross-section of the sierras from its enveloping plains and foothills to its barren mountain peaks.

The journey started just east of Algeciras where a narrow road turned inland off the coastal highway. A moment later the roar of the trucks heading for Málaga and Cádiz faded, and on either side there was only the green and silent cork forests and sunlit glades of Almoreima. Until recently Almoreima was the largest single estate in Europe remaining in private hands. Its forests were famous for fallow deer and for the hunts organized each autumn, as they had been for hundreds of years, for the owner and his guests. As on all privately owned land in Andalucía which supported game, Almoreima's deer were fiercely protected against poachers and every few hundred yards there were warning notices nailed to the roadside trees.

Midway through the forest was a peasant *venta* which specialised in venison. Beside it were two corrals containing six captive deer which, the *venta*'s owner insisted, came from '*muy lejos*', from far away. Slaughtered in turn and replaced by others from equally far away, they were the source of the meat on sale inside. Every time we visited the *venta* I examined the deer carefully. For years they never changed. One had a distinctive nick in its ear, another a slight limp, a third an unmistakable cast in its eye. The quality of the venison never changed either. It was always excellent. But its taste owed more, I suspect, to a shotgun, a moonless night, and the Almoreima herds than to those amiable and ageing creatures in the corrals. Whatever Almoreima's gamekeepers knew or guessed, there was nothing they could prove or do. The estate was just too big to patrol effectively.

It was in the *venta* that I learned about Pepe *el Penitente*. Each time we drove through the forest we passed a stocky man trudging alongside the road with his head lowered and his hands crossed behind his back. His feet were bare and all he wore was a black beret and a tattered pair of trousers. Winter or summer, in storm, rain, sun or darkness, he was always there. One day, intrigued, I stopped the car and greeted him. Usually Andalucian country people return any greeting with a smile and are happy to break off from whatever they are doing for a talk. Not this one. He didn't even glance at me. He simply continued on his way, frowning and purposeful.

His name was Pepe, the owner of the *venta* told me, and he came from the local hamlet of Estación de San Roque. When the railway came to Andalucía the rugged character of the countryside meant that the track often had to be laid several miles from the towns the trains were designed to serve. Whenever that happened settlements grew up round the station halt. In time several of the settlements developed into substantial independent villages, but they always kept the name of their parent town. San Roque was built on a hill at the junction of the Gibraltar isthmus with the mainland, and its station, where Pepe lived, was 8 miles away at the start of the Almoreima forest. Pepe earned his living as a casual labourer. A quiet, reflective man, he'd been pondering the

crucifixion one day when he had a vision. The people of
Andalucía, it came to him, as representatives of the human
race had not done enough to atone for Christ's death on the
cross. It was up to him to make good their failure.
The way Pepe decided to do it was to walk in penance. He
chose a stretch of the forest road which he calculated was the
same distance as the Via Dolorosa and set out. That was
twenty years before I first saw him. Since then he'd trudged up
and down the same stretch every hour of the day and night
when he wasn't working, eating or sleeping. It was a fearsome
burden he carried but Pepe was implacable. As far as anyone
knew he hadn't missed a day since he started. After I discovered what he was doing I always pulled into the side of the
road and waited respectfully until he had passed so that he
wasn't enveloped in dust from the car. When I last drove
through the forest Pepe had been undergoing his elected
penance for almost forty years. In that time he must have
walked over 100,000 miles. For all I know he is walking
still, head bowed, back mahogany-coloured from the sun and
the wind, eyes gazing at the forest but seeing not Almoreima's
oaks and deer and drifts of golden-rod, but a figure turning in
agony on a cross.

As the forest starts to thin out, a steep hill rises abruptly
from the plain like an isolated watch-tower a few miles to the
east of the road. The hill is crowned by a ruined fortress with a
tiny village, Castellar de la Frontera, huddled round its walls.
Castellar was originally a Moorish stronghold. When the
Spaniards captured it during the reconquest they decided it
was too remote to garrison. To prevent the Moors from using
it against them if Castellar changed hands again, as happened
to so many other frontier castles, they set it on fire. The Moors
were great falconers and Castellar had a renowned mews
where the finest hawks taken in the sierra were kept. When the
flames burned through the wooden cage-bars the birds took to
the air. They circled the burning castle until the fire died down.
Then they returned and started to nest in the cavities and edges
of the now deserted battlements. The hawks and falcons flying

Castellar

round Castellar today are the direct descendants of the hooded birds with their bells and jewelled jesses flown from the wrist on horseback by the Arabs over six hundred years ago.

That at least is the unshakeable conviction of Castellar's present-day historian, a retired customs clerk with gout and a fondness for brandy. Every Andalucian village has a chronicler of its past, always self-appointed and often with a startlingly unconventional interpretation of historical events, and Castellar was no exception. Although the only hawks I ever saw flying round the castle were groups of lovely slate and chestnut-coloured lesser kestrels which hunted the evening air, he insisted peregrines and other falcons he couldn't name nested there too. He may well have been right. Castellar was a strange and haunted place. Just before we came to live in the valley the provincial authorities with support from Madrid decided to convert the castle into a parador, one of the network of state-run hotels. A brand new village was built near the foot of the hill, the entire population was moved, and then funds ran out, leaving the original Castellar and its fortress abandoned and silent once more.

The only person who stayed behind was a crabbed and hunchbacked old woman who'd taken up quarters in the castle. She wore a black shawl over her head, grew mandragora and yellow devil's apples round the great Moorish door, and was known to be a *bruja*, a witch. She occupied a single room on the top floor. The door had long since rotted and fallen off, the wind moaned through the unglazed windows, and all the room contained was a filthy straw mattress, a charcoal brazier, some bundles of drying herbs, and a dark brooding painting of Our Lady of the Sorrows. The room was bitterly cold in winter, the stairs up to it were steep and dangerous with rotting floorboards, the brazier was a permanent fire hazard, and she had to draw her water from a well a hundred yards away, but the old woman adamantly refused to move. She was offered a cottage with every modern facility in the new village and several times the police were sent to drag her screaming down the hill to instal her in it. Always, as soon as they'd gone, she'd hobble back up to the castle and return to her garret like some broken-winged crow flapping painfully back to its roost in the crags.

Eventually the authorities gave up. They allowed her to stay and gave her a tiny pension as the castle's door-keeper. The castle was officially closed but the old woman regarded the building as entirely her own property. When the rare visitor arrived she'd carefully scrutinise their face. Then, if she approved what she saw, for a few pesetas she'd allow them inside as if she was letting them into her home. Once she let me in as dusk was falling. I climbed to the flat herring-bone brick roof at the castle's top. Far below the battlements, the forest and pastures of the plain stretched away towards the distant rim of hills. The landscape's texture, its colours, sounds and smells, had barely changed in the six centuries since the Moors had been driven out. The evening wind was scented with wild lavender. Kestrels wheeled and called. Whisps of mist were rising from the river. The peal of goat bells floated upwards, plumes of smoke circled over clearings in the trees, and oil lamps flickered from little hamlets hidden in the dense wildwood. As the stars came out I felt I was seeing the Andalucian countryside exactly as it had appeared at that hour to the Moorish sentinels, gazing north for the pillars of flame against the sky that would signal the approach of the armies of the Catholic Kings.

Beyond Castellar the plain gradually narrowed until it came to a point at the base of the sierra foothills. Draped like a white lace bedcover over the first of the hills round which the road curved as it started to climb was another and larger frontier village, Jimena de la Frontera. Outwardly a typical Andalucian *pueblo* and many miles from the Costa del Sol, Jimena on acquaintance proved to have a distinctly cosmopolitan character. Just outside the village lived a Texan entrepreneur who sold the 'Pope's Bible' – every copy carried the Holy Father's personal signature or at least a very passable facsimile – on an instalment plan to recently converted Brazilian Indians. The former colonel of an English cavalry regiment had settled on a nearby farm with his horses, his gun-dogs, and his wife. Inside the village one could hear Dutch, Hungarian and Norwegian spoken; a delicatessen sold roll-mops and Hellman's mayonnaise; and an authentic trattoria offered home-made pasta. Meanwhile the village's other life, the life of the Andalucian merchants, farmers and peasants, continued as before.

On the Costa del Sol in a single generation mass tourism and foreign settlement have destroyed a social framework, an economy and an entire way of life. Whole villages and their communities have simply disappeared, swallowed up in one vast and constantly expanding concrete ghetto threaded by neon-lit highways. But in places like Jimena, where the foreign impact was limited, there was no tension or even incongruity in two quite different cultures existing side by side. As flexible as they are resilient, the Andalucian *pueblos* have never found any difficulty in absorbing people and customs from other countries, which in the past as often as not meant the other Spains. The process has been part of their evolution from the start. Someone from the outside world moves in. After a while they acquire *vecindad*, the right of 'belonging' and taking part in local affairs. If they behave fairly and decently they soon become accepted as full members of the community. In time the two, outsider and native, fuse into one and both are the richer. It is of course a process that operates to a greater or lesser extent in every human community. What makes the Andalucian variety so sane and attractive is its utter lack of xenophobia or prejudice. A newcomer carries no baggage from the past. He is received without any assumptions about his race, religion, class or colour. From the moment he sets foot in a village he is treated solely for what he is – a man equal to any other. From then on it is up to him alone to prove his mettle and his worth. Judging by the brisk business among the locals, Jimena's trattoria owner hadn't been found wanting.

For a while after Jimena the pastures and cereal fields of the plain were replaced by orange and lemon groves. Then the countryside became wilder and more rocky and the road began to climb in earnest, spiralling upwards through woods that now included chestnut, pine, poplar and the occasional grove of olives as well as the dominant cork oak. Throughout Andalucía the earth beneath olive trees was always cleared and tilled to improve the trees' yield, and also to make the task of gathering the olives easier. Olive-picking was traditionally women's work. Lengths of cloth were laid out beneath the trees and depending on local custom, the branches were either shaken or beaten with sticks until the crop had fallen; the olives were then collected and carried away in huge red baskets. To clear the higher branches the women often had to climb up into the trees. Whenever a man appeared, everyone would scramble down to the ground and stand shouting and abusing him until he was driven away. As every Andalucian activity was governed by ritual or ceremony, for a long time I assumed it must be some ancient superstition to do with the flavour of the oil or the trees' fertility next year. Then I learned from a giggling Ana that the country women never wore underclothes.

Outside the olive groves the roadside undergrowth was dense and spiny, and in summer the banks blazed yellow with gorse blossom. From time to time the road levelled out and ran along a hog's back ridge. On either side the landscape fell away into deep gorges and valleys where little, apparently inaccessible villages shone like sunlit drifts of snow among the dark woods. The Ronda road was an artery for the produce of the surrounding valleys and the villages were linked to it by tracks hidden beneath the trees. At intervals along the road itself were other villages which acted as way-stations and collecting-points. A farmer would ride through the forest with a mule-load of vegetables, leave it to be taken by truck to market, and return home with supplies he might have ordered a month earlier. The first of the way-station villages, 25 miles up in the sierra beyond Jimena, was Gáucin.

Some time between the end of the Napoleonic wars and the mid-nineteenth century, Ronda was 'discovered' by the officers of the British garrison at Gibraltar. Some young lieutenant of hussars, I imagine, with a week's furlough in front of him and a volume of Wordsworth in his saddle-bag set off on horseback into the sierras. He reached and explored the dramatically-set mountain town and then, tingling with the new awareness generated by the Romantic revolution, he hurried back to tell his comrades in the candle-lit mess about the splendours he'd found. However it happened, Ronda became the favourite goal for expeditions into Spain from Gibraltar. It was the one sight every newcomer to the garrison had to see and many of them went back there again and again. The journey was two days' hard riding and Gáucin at the midway point was the logical place for an overnight stop. The

Gáucin

village had an inn which catered for travellers with horses and the expeditions soon adopted it as their almost private halfway base. The inn was originally known as Don Pedro's *Posada* after its owner, an energetic and efficient Gáucin peasant, but within a few years the name had been changed to the Posada Inglés – the Inn of the English – in honour of the new clientele.

In 1863 Don Pedro acquired, or perhaps was given by one of his guests, a visitors' book, a sturdy volume half-bound in leather with marbled endpapers and blank pages. Afterwards, every officer from Gibraltar who made the Ronda journey was asked to sign his name before he mounted his horse to leave in the morning. Most of them felt obliged to add a comment praising Don Pedro's hospitality; although I doubt whether their host could read Castilian let alone English. Typical of the comments was one I found in the book on my first visit to Gáucin, a tart observation written with a quill pen in fading ink by one of my own ancestors, a Captain A. D. Luard, who spent the night at the inn in the spring of 1876. 'People are (what an abominable pen) apparently in the habit of writing a good deal of nonsense & rubbish in this book. I would merely observe that I arrived here anticipating an Andaluz *venta*, but that I found it very superior to others, except in such cities as Seville. In fact it is an Hotel.' Before and after him come battalions of names and regiments which read like a lost roll-call of British imperial might: Sanderson of the Grenadier Guards, Perkins of the Rifle Brigade, Hunter-Marshall of the 9th Lancers, Cameron and Sinclair of the 93rd Highlanders. Among them is an entry in Arabic by the explorer Sir Richard Burton, and another by the great Victorian botanist A. H. Wolley-Dodd. Then in the 1890s Ronda was linked to Algeciras by rail. The demanding two-day journey could be made in a couple of hours in a comfortable train, and the Posada Inglés lost its profitable military connection.

Until quite recently Andalucía had two types of resting-places for travellers, *posadas* for those on horseback and simpler *fondas* for those on foot. With the arrival of cars and metalled roads the traditional *fonda* largely disappeared, being replaced where necessary by small, cheap and generally ugly modern commercial hotels. But a number of *posadas* continued to survive virtually unchanged in design and management since their foundation in the eighteenth century or even earlier. The Posada Inglés, even after its abandonment by the British, was one of them. Don Pedro's establishment was built against a hill slope in the middle of the village. On the lower ground floor were the stables. Above, and reached from a cobbled alleyway on the other side, were a kitchen and a communal dining-room. Higher still, up the stairs, there were a number of spotlessly clean little bedrooms with tiled floors and severe oak-framed beds. It was the individual bedrooms, combined no doubt with the host's character and table, which made the Posada Inglés stand out from other sierra inns. Elsewhere it was normal to eat and then wrap oneself in a blanket to sleep on the floor with the other guests in the same room. At Don Pedro's, the officers from Gibraltar could retire to bed and write their diaries in privacy.

The reason for the inn's survival after the officers left was the same as had created it in the first place – the Andaluz' abiding passion for the horse. In common with the rest of Europe before the train and the car, horses had always been the fastest and most efficient form of transport in Andalucía. Rail and motor should have dispossessed them entirely as they did virtually everywhere else. They did not. Andalucía was different. The hills were too rugged, the dividing ravines too sheer, the plains too quixotically meandering, the towns and villages, tossed over the landscape like a spray of white confetti, too randomly scattered. In any event as the poorest region of one of Europe's poorest countries, Andalucía's economy was too fragile to provide the investment needed for a modern communications system even if the terrain had been suitable. In many places the horse, together with the mule and the donkey, remained not only the best but often the only means of transport.

The importance to Andalucía of its bloodstock was recognized by the government in Madrid. One day as I passed through San Roque, the little town at the head of the isthmus of Gibraltar, I saw an army groom leading a magnificent bay stallion into a yard. I stopped and got out to look at it. Inside the yard were two more stallions, a grey and a chestnut. All three were in the same superb condition with coats that gleamed like sunlit water, tossing heads and manes and bright, intelligent eyes. As I stood watching them a uniformed captain appeared. He was in charge of the stallions and he explained what they were doing. The bay was a Spanish pure-blood, I learned, the grey an Arab, and the chestnut an Anglo-Arab.

'We take them round the Andalucian cavalry bases to service the army mares,' he went on. 'Originally it was just for the military. Then Madrid decided they could help improve the privately owned stock. Now anyone can bring us a mare. I choose the right stallion to cover it. If the mare foals, we brand the foal and give the owner a certificate. It costs the owner nothing, the foal's worth considerably more, and pedigree blood's introduced into the local breed. Of course mares can only be really successfully covered at full moon. As the army mares take precedence, it limits the number of private ones we can service.'

As I discovered that day it wasn't only the Andalucian peasant who knew the full moon determined fertility, as it did so much else. Madrid, which gave the captain his orders, held the same view.

While horses in Andalucía were essential transport for a variety of journeys and activities – a bull-rancher for example could only tend his herds on horseback – the Andaluz attitude to them was deeper and more complicated than a simple dependence on the function they performed. Horses were often an integral part of Andalucian ritual and ceremony. Several of the ancient annual pilgrimages, most notably the *romería* of the Rocío, depended in large part on horses for their very existence. Nothing else could have carried the pilgrims across the marshes to the Virgin's shrine. More than anything, a good horse was a living expression of its master's achievements, of his power, authority, and wealth. From time to time when I was sitting in some isolated sierra *venta* there would be a clatter of hoofs on the road outside, and a local landowner, with his agent riding behind, would dismount from a glossy high-mettled thoroughbred. He would stride into the bar and a few moments later ride away again, the great shining horse moving in a slow controlled canter and its shoes striking sparks from the roadway.

Ostensibly the landowner had stopped off to make some trivial purchase, to buy a pack of cigarettes or a box of matches. In reality his visit was a gesture, a demonstration to everyone in the *venta* – several there probably worked for him either directly or indirectly – of his *categoriá*. He was a man of substance, a man to be held in respect and obeyed without question. He showed it by the quality of the horse he rode and his effortless control over the handsome, powerful animal. Once after a day's coursing on a ranch near Medina Sidonia I watched the owner ride back to the *cortijo* in the gathering dusk. His horse, a young pedigree stallion, was highly-strung, wayward, and nervous. He rode it deliberately and theatrically along a ridge against the setting sun, making it in turn gallop, canter, high-step, and then pirouette in slow rearing circles. It was a remarkable display of horsemanship. The stallion's eyes rolled wildly, white foam over its flanks, and it whinnied as the spurs pricked into its ribs, but it never once challenged its rider. His authority was absolute. As they reached the *cortijo* the ranch-owner glanced up and laughed in pleasure at the farm foreman who was waiting to take the horse from him. The foreman smiled back, nodded, and lowered his eyes. It was a token of submission just as eloquent as the drooping head of the tired and sweating horse.

Although the Andalucians were brilliant horsemen, certainly the most skilful in Europe and probably in the world, they seldom made any mark in the international riding arenas. At events like the Olympic Games showjumping, the Mexicans excelled, but the Spanish team – which usually consisted of a group of Andalucians – often failed to qualify for the final. It took me some time to work out why a race so extraordinarily proficient at home seemed quite unable to compete with other countries abroad. In the end I realized there was a simple explanation. Elsewhere, having lost its original function, the horse had become a toy for which a whole range of artificial activities had been developed, and which a number of people had enough time and money to make themselves specialists in. In Andalucía the horse remained a working animal. Andalucian life left no time to indulge in pursuits like showjumping. The horse was a source of pride and a symbol of power, but ultimately every animal however impeccably thoroughbred was kept for a purpose – to pull a cart, to draw a carriage, to carry herdsmen across the huge bull pastures and, of course, as the survival of the *posadas* like the Posada Inglés demonstrated, to bear travellers as they had always done through the sierras.

Above Gáucin was a ruined castle to which Guzman the Good, the Tarifa commander who sacrificed his son to the Moors, retired after being ennobled by his grateful king, and where he was buried. Then on the far side of the village the road wound higher and higher. Occasionally looking down I would see griffon vultures, red and black kites and short-toed eagles wheeling over the gorges far below. There were blue rock-thrushes in the gullies, dazzling banks of wild lupin and antirrhinum, and clumps of orchids on the verges. In the sierras orchids grew almost up to the snowline, but they were at their most spectacular lower down. Hidden in a bowl in the hills behind Jimena de la Frontera was a 30-acre pasture on a limestone base. Briefly every spring the entire pasture was covered from end to end in an unbroken sheet of bee orchids, turning it for a week into a true field of the cloth of gold.

One of the roadside villages beyond Gáucin was named Benadalid. Set on a spur below the village was a Moorish watch-tower which the local priest had commandeered as a cemetery. As the road circled upwards, the tower, with the coffins neatly stacked on its roof and the parapets bright with bunches of flowers, looked like a gaily-decorated doll's house. Throughout Andalucía the dead were honoured for a while in cemeteries like Benadalid's, although few communities made such enterprising use of an ancient watch-tower. Then after a decent interval the coffins were removed, interred communally, and the vacant space occupied by the next to depart. The Andalucian attitude to death, the only certainty in a life where even taxes weren't inevitable, was pragmatic. A man died, he was put in a wooden box, the proper respects were paid, and the matter ended. As a race they tended to be short and their coffins were carpentered to a standard size. Not long after we came to live in the valley the husband of an English couple, who'd settled locally, died. His widow summoned the village undertakers who dealt with the matter with typical Andalucian courtesy, delivering the body to the church for the funeral service as they would have with one of their own. Just before the service the widow decided to have a final look at her late husband. He had been an imposing man well over six feet in height. When she opened the coffin she discovered outraged that in order to fit him inside, the undertakers had carefully

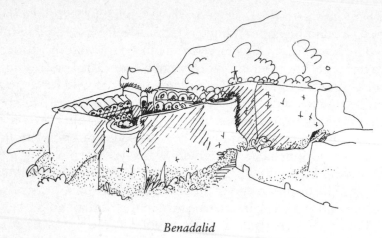

Benadalid

sawn off his feet at the ankles and placed them together, still
encased in their sturdy British shoes, by his head.

As the road climbed still higher after Benadalid the trees
disappeared, the vegetation became sparse, wiry and stunted,
and the rich forest landscape turned into a wilderness of
windswept boulder and scree. In winter the hillsides were
driven by rain, mist and snow, in summer reflected heat
blazed off the stone and the air was arid and glaring. It was
Ronda moon country, desolate and pitiless, where the mag-
netic content of the barren rock was so strong that in places
parked trucks were reputed to have been pulled up the inclines
as their bemused drivers sat by the road watching the empty
cabins. Then the twisting road crested the pass, plunged
abruptly down and finally into Ronda itself.

Ronda was built along the top of a cliff that rears above the
huddled plain below like an immense Atlantic breaker. Midway along its length the cliff is slashed through by a chasm
known as the *tajo*, through the base of which runs the Guadalquivir river. The plunging cut of the *tajo* divides the town in
two. In Roman times – Ronda was originally a Roman settlement – the two sides were spanned low down at the town's
sloping rear by a still-existing stone bridge. Much later when

the old city, the Ciudad, leapt the gorge and began to spread out on the western rim of the cliff as a trading centre known as the Mercadillo, a new and loftier bridge was thrown across the ravine at the breaker's crest. The Mercadillo came into being in the late eighteenth century. A hundred years afterwards, the new bridge was replaced by a broader and more elegant construction, a bridge which could accommodate four-in-hand carriages as well as laden mules and peasants on foot. Its unfortunate architect fell to his death in the gorge from a viewing platform on his last tour of inspection before the bridge was declared open.

Like a cluster of martins' nests along the cliff's edge, Ronda still straddles the ravine. On one side by tradition live the town's gentry, on the other its merchants and traders. Beneath them both the cliff falls sheer to the plain where the land levels out before rising again into a crescent of jagged, dark and mist-hazed hills. The plain, like Granada's *vega* although much smaller, is rich and fertile, a little scoop of inland delta fed by the mountain streams and rivers. Perched in its eyrie above, Ronda, linked both to the coast and to Andalucía's inland cities, is a crossroads, a robust trading centre, a gateway to the sierra villages and a funnel for their produce. The Moors recognised its importance better than the Romans or the Visigoths before them. They gave the town fortifications, an impressive mosque, now the church of Santa Maria la Major, and a number of palatial houses. Ferdinand and Isabel regarded the mountain-bound fortress city as no more than a stepping-stone on the path to the treasure trove of Granada, and hurried on. Ronda's citizens saw their town very differently. In the sierras Ronda was a kingdom all of its own. It always had been and, come Arab or Papist, it always would be. The town's dour, independent spirit took a fearsome battering during the Civil War – Hemingway's account of republican atrocities in For Whom the Bell Tolls was drawn from stories of what had happened there – but Ronda endured. As so often before, it patched together the brutally riven fragments of its past, struck a new peace, and set about its business again – the business of an almost magical focus for barter and exchange, like Bokhara or Samarkand, for the people of the uplands.

One of Ronda's proudest claims is that its lovely bullring, with its pale tiled roof above the stands and its slender columns of stone supporting the tiers, is the oldest in Spain. In fact it is

Ronda gorge

not. Sevilla's famous Maestranza, built in 1761, is older, and there were other permanent rings, now demolished, in towns like Madrid and Saragossa before then. Nor is it really a bullring at all. Ronda is the home of the royal Maestranza de Ronda, an organization formed in 1707 which claims descent from a much older chivalric order, the Brotherhood of the Holy Spirit, founded by Philip II in the late sixteenth century. The purpose of the Maestranza was to encourage the practice of horsemanship and martial arts among the local nobility, and the main function of the ring, which the order built in 1784, was as a large riding school. By royal charter the Maestranza was allowed to put on bullfights too, but there was a limit of four a year and all the proceeds had to go to charity – a form of *corrida* now staged in many other towns and known as a *festival*.

While Ronda may not have the oldest bullring in the country it undoubtedly has the oldest, and the smallest, bullring guide. He is called Luigi and he was born in 1896 in Bologna in Italy. Wizened and a little frail now, he stands smartly to attention in the centre of the ring with his chest thrown out like a bantam cock and his eyes fixed on the gate. When someone enters he calls out, beckons them imperiously over to him, and offers to tell them the ring's history in Spanish, English, German, French, or Italian – according to Luigi it is built on the site of a Roman amphitheatre. I once persuaded him to tell me his own story.

'I was a great singer,' Luigi said. 'I was famous all over Europe. One night in 1921 I was engaged to sing in Circe's nightclub in the Strand in London. After my performance the English press milord, Lord Beaverbrook, invited me to drink champagne at his table with his good friend, Signor Marconi. Lord Beaverbrook had been astonished by my art and Signor Marconi, as you must know, came from Bologna as I do. So we all had much in common. Lord Beaverbrook and Signor Marconi owned the Reina Victoria Hotel here in Ronda in partnership. Lord Beaverbrook said although I was a great artist, my talents were being wasted in a career as a famous

Ronda bullring

singer. Instead he and Signor Marconi offered me the job of head porter at the Reina Victoria. I left for Spain the same week.'

Whether the Canadian newspaper tycoon and the Italian inventor really were close friends and in the Andalucian hotel business together, I never established. Luigi had no doubt about it. The memory of that evening at Circe's nightclub in the twenties, of the champagne, the applause and the remarkable offer, was as vivid to him as if it had happened yesterday.

'I was at the hotel for over forty years,' Luigi finished. 'In that time I saw many thousands of scandals. There are secrets I could tell you which would make your hair turn white. But I will not say a word. All my life I am famous for being discreet. I will take what I know unspoken to my grave. When I retired I was made the official guide because I was famous for my knowledge of the city. I will now tell you about the oldest bullring in Spain.'

The hotel where Luigi had been employed, the Reina Victoria, was on the rim of the cliff in the Mercadillo. A solid late-nineteenth century building with magnificent views from its rooms and terraces, its clientele came from all over Europe drawn to Ronda often to convalesce after illness or in search of a cure for asthma in the high, clear sierra air. One of its guests was the poet Rainer Maria Rilke whose full board in 1913 cost 7.50 pesetas a day, and whose room has now been turned into a tiny Rilke museum. The Reina Victoria had what was effectively a sister hotel in Algeciras, the Reina Cristina, another sombre and even more imposing nineteenth-century edifice which became a favourite wintering-place for the rich and elderly British until well into the 1960s. Between the two world wars the fabulously wealthy Bendor, Duke of Westminster, following the trail of the officers from Gibraltar, used to bring house-parties out to see Ronda. The parties would travel from England on his private yacht, which anchored in Algeciras bay. In place of the Posada Inglés the Duke rented both the Reina Cristina and the Reina Victoria in their entirety. Then, to make the journey between them, instead of horses he chartered the local train and all its passenger rolling-stock. By all accounts his guests enjoyed the trip, but I doubt whether they experienced the same exhilarating shock of surprise and delight on first seeing the town as the young ensigns and subalterns toiling up through the forest two generations earlier.

Of all Andalucian cities that I came to know, from the very start Ronda was my favourite. Even the journey to it from the valley had a rare and perfect balance. For once, to arrive was as satisfying as to travel. Ronda gathered together and held out in open hands almost all that was best in Andalucía. Its people were shrewd, tough-minded, friendly and open. Long familiar with visitors from other countries they had little of the tunnel-vision, the complete and suffocating self-absorption, of the smaller sierra communities. They knew a world existed beyond the *tajo*'s cleft and they were ready to discuss it with a warm if sometimes naïve enthusiasm. The naïveté was unimportant. What crackled was the gusto of their interest. They practised fine crafts – Bernardo's bright and meticulously-woven harness came originally, I discovered, from a workshop set into the bullring's outer wall. Their shops were welcoming and well stocked. Their houses were clean and fragrant in winter with the herbal scents from *bolinas*, little matted cushions of dry rosemary, lavender, rock-rose and gorse used to kindle the open fires. Their market, perched like so many other of Ronda's buildings on the cliff edge, was a shadowy Aladdin's Cave of the sierra's natural riches which Ferdinand and Isabel, had they but known, would surely have stopped to savour before pressing on to their rainbow's end in Granada.

Bearded soldiers of Spain's foreign legion, dressed in crisp apple-green combat uniforms, thronged the bars and eyed the tantalisingly pretty local girls. The streets were always charged with a sense of excitement. Someone rich, celebrated, and mysterious was always arriving at or leaving the Reina Victoria. A *corrida*, perhaps featuring Pablo Romero bulls and the legendary Ronda hero, Antonio Ordoñez, always seemed to be imminent. An arts festival of dancing, painting and *cante jondo*, the guitar-accompanied 'deep song' of Andalucía, was always about to begin or already in full swing with the brilliantly lit Mercadillo alive and throbbing with music until the early hours. At whatever season, under winter snow or in the torrid heat of summer, Ronda was always bold, gay and vital, a town that didn't tolerate fools – one had to keep one's wits about one on Ronda's cobbled alleyways – loved music, words, dance and the drama of the bulls, and above all celebrated beauty both in itself and in its majestic surroundings. I loved it at every time of the year but most of all, like the valley, in early autumn. Looking down from the cliff across the plain on a still and translucent October day, poised somewhere in the sunlight between earth and sky with late-migrating swifts arrowing over the roofs and the call of bells drifting up from the village below, was to be as close to heaven as anyone can reasonably require.

Trips to Ronda from the Guadalmesi valley had one additional delight. The day's business finished we drove back at dusk. The route of the journey home lay directly westwards across the hills. All the long drive we were accompanied by an apparently endless rolling sunset, the sun lowering with us peak by descending peak as the road wound down to the straits. Only when we reached the sea, the stars came out, and the sleeping lion of Gibraltar reared up against the African hills, did the sun drop below the horizon and night fall.

FROM TIME TO time as we travelled the country roads of Andalucía during the summer months, a solitary car would appear on the horizon ahead of us. As often as not the car would be an ancient black saloon with a load wrapped in grey canvas on its roof. As it sped by in a cloud of dust we would glimpse the driver and four passengers inside, three of them pressed tightly together and drowsing on the back seat. All five were men. They all wore the same dark glasses, drab suits and highly polished shoes, but the passenger in front was always slighter and younger than the others. Unlike the others, too, he never seemed to sleep.

Occasionally one of the cars stopped beside us at a roadside *venta* and the occupants came into the bar. The men's faces were pinched with exhaustion, and their skin had the same colour and texture as the canvas covering the load on the car's top. They stood together in a group apart, speaking little, drinking quickly, in a hurry to be on their way again. As they left, someone else at the bar might glance round and call out, '*Suerte, hombre!*' Good luck! Then the youngest of the five, the passenger in the front seat, would turn, force a weary smile, and lift his hand in acknowledgment. Moments later the car would be gone.

The old black saloons were what I named '*corrida* cars'. Criss-crossing not only Andalucía but all of Spain during the bullfight season, they carry young and aspiring matadors from one engagement to the next. The matador's companions, the four older and heavier men, are what the horse-racing world would call his connections, his manager, advisers, and confidants, while the canvas-wrapped load contains the swords, capes, and clothes that are the tools of his trade. For me the shabby *corrida* cars, speeding along some lonely sierra road in the midday heat, and the listless groups of wan-faced men inside them, are as potent and evocative an image of the bullfight as any trumpet call or flash of gold and scarlet on the sand of a ring. Like so much else that the outside world regards as being quintessentially Spanish, the bullfight in fact belongs to Andalucía, as the Spaniards themselves acknowledge.

'So you come from Andalucía!' a voice in the crowd will shout as a matador from the south steps into a northern ring. 'Then show us how to fight bulls!'

More nonsense and rubbish, in the irritably apt phrase in the Gaucin visitors' book, has been spoken and written about the bullfight than about almost any other aspect of Spanish life. Ranging from the portentously solemn to the mindlessly banal and hostile, it has bedevilled the spectacle for foreigners for generations. Even the English term 'bullfight', first listed in a 1753 supplement to Chambers' popular encyclopedia, is a mis-translation. The word has become so familiar it is inescapable, but in Spanish it doesn't exist for the simple reason that as no contest is involved, it would obviously be incorrect to describe the spectacle as a 'fight'.

To the Spanish the bullfight is the *fiesta brava*, the noble festival, and its staging a *corrida de toros* – a running of the bulls, often shortened to a *corrida* or simply *los toros*. The *corrida*'s origins are so ancient as to be entirely unknown. Some of the world's oldest cave paintings have been interpreted to suggest that challenging and running bulls may have been one of the earliest organized human activities. Bullfights of some sort unquestionably took place in Crete round 3,000 BC – Pliny notes the horsemen of Thessaly honed their skills through games with bulls – and by the eleventh century AD the practice was well-established in Spain. The heroic El Cid was famous for his exploits in killing wild bulls with a lance from his horse. From then on, the bullfight has been an

193

integral part of Iberian life and history. Two sixteenth-century popes, Pius v and Gregory xiii, chose respectively to ban it and then restore it, the first on the grounds of the appalling injuries bullfights were causing, the second because he acknowledged the habit of running bulls was so deeply ingrained that the papal decree was being ignored and the Holy See's authority undermined. In 1702 the Bourbon monarch Philip v made another attempt to ban the practice. His decree too was flouted in the countryside and on his return to power in 1725, after being deposed, his first act in an attempt to curry public favour was to reverse his prohibition. Since Philip v's day the *corrida* has flourished largely unchallenged although considerably changed.

Early Spanish bullfights were conducted from horseback and the sport, as it was then considered, inevitably became the prerogative of the gentry and nobility. Its survival through its various repressions was left in the hands of the peasants. Passionate enthusiasts of the *corrida*, much readier than their betters to disregard papal and regal commands but unable to afford a horse, they took to running the bulls on foot. The peasant takeover of bullfighting was effectively recognized and accepted in the early eighteenth century when the great Romero family of Ronda expanded and modified the new techniques.

By then a chivalric pastime had become a popular entertainment. The Romero dynasty's founding father, Francisco, pioneered the use of the *muleta*, the scarlet square of cloth guided by a stick. His son, Juan, initiated the concept of a team of professional bullfighters guiding, helping, and watching over the matador, literally the 'killer' of the bulls and also known as the *espada*, the swordsman of the ring. Juan's own sons Pedro and José both became famous bullfighters in their turn, Pedro the best-known in the country. On his retirement in 1830 Pedro Romero established the Royal School of Tauromachy (the art of running bulls) in Sevilla, and from there sent a stream of youthful matadors to the Spanish rings.

Today's bullfight, in spite of having been modified at intervals since the eighteenth century, notably by the innovating Cuchares, a matador of the early 1800s, still owes its form, structure, and most of its conventions to the Romeros. It is not a contest and least of all a sport. The *corrida* is an elaborate, formal, stylized, and intensely dangerous ritual, an improvised act of theatre in which only one thing, the bull's death, is certain. The rest is left to the afternoon, the animal, and the man. The preparations for any bullfight start long before the day when the *corrida* takes place. Months or even years in advance an impresario will contract to hire the ring. With the ring secured he will approach the owner of a bull-ranch, and negotiate to buy a string of eight fighting bulls, six to be run and two to be held in reserve in case of accidents. Finally he will contact the managers of three matadors chosen much as a producer selects actors for a theatrical production – a star to head the bill, a reliable performer in second place, and a promising newcomer to complete the cast. All will have their prices. The impresario will have his budget. Between them they will juggle and balance the financial equation.

Two days before the *corrida* the bulls are trucked in from their ranch and unloaded in corrals beside the ring. The following night the three matadors and their supporting teams, the *cuadrillas* employed by each, arrive in town and check into local hotels. Next morning the six favoured bulls are sorted into pairs, the best as gauged by the eye with the worst, the second best with the second worst, and the middle two together. When the pairing has been agreed by the matadors' representative, one from each *cuadrilla* attends the *sorteo*, the drawing of lots from a hat, and the representatives go back to tell the matadors what, in their assessment, the pairs they have drawn are like.

At the advertised time, normally 6.00 p.m., the matadors enter the arena – traditionally the bullfight is the only event in Spanish life which never starts late. They march in line abreast, the most senior on the right, the second in rank on the left, and the third in the centre. Seniority in the *corrida* is decided not by age but by the date on which the matador took his *alternativa*, a short ceremony confirming him as a fully-qualified bull-fighter. It also decides the order in which the three will run the bulls. The most experienced takes the first and fourth, the second and fifth go to the next in rank, and the remaining two to the third. Behind all three walk their teams including the mounted picadors. Anyone directly involved in the business of running bulls is known generally as a *torero*, including the matador himself, but all the *cuadrilla* also have other names according to their specific function. Depending on the individual matador's status and earnings, some of them will be a permanent part of his entourage, others will have been engaged for the afternoon.

For the next two hours – each bull takes about twenty minutes to run and be killed – everyone is answerable to the president of the *corrida*. Normally a local dignitary, the president sits in a box in the stands flanked by two advisers, often retired bullfighters, who guide him on the events taking place below. Although in part purely ceremonial, the president's role is also practical. He can award trophies for successful performances, determine to some extent the rhythm of each bull's running by deciding how long the various acts of the bullfight should last, and in the rare event of a physically defective bull refusing to charge he can order it to be taken from the arena and be replaced by one of the substitutes. More than that he has considerable powers under Spanish law.

It comes as a considerable surprise to many people to learn that the *corrida*, quite apart from its own long-established form and conventions, is regulated by a section of Spain's criminal code. The code covers a huge range of aspects of the bullfight from the size and age of the bulls to be fought to the health of the horses used by the picadors. Inevitably from time to time it is abused, as in the intermittent scandals when the bull's horns are shaved to make it less dangerous. But when violations are detected punishment can be swift and severe. The code also extends to the performers themselves, the matadors. If a matador, contracted to appear, arrives at a ring, decides for some reason or other that a certain bull looks too dangerous, and refuses to fight, by dusk he can well find himself in prison. If he does, the decision will have been the president's who, invoking his statutory powers, will have instructed the police to arrest him.

Within a few minutes of the president signalling the start of the *corrida*, a broad and heavy wooden door swings open and the first of the six bulls gallops into the arena. To watch the next twenty minutes, and the rest of the afternoon, without some idea of what's happening is like trying to understand a complicated play in an unknown language without a synopsis of the story or a list of the characters. The *plaza* is a constantly-shaken kaleidoscope of scarlet, gold, and plunging black, of music and cheers, blood and flaring capes, racing figures and the occasional sculptured pattern created by the fusion of a man and a charging animal. None of the other performing arts, and the *corrida* belongs here with dance, music and theatre, depends so much for its enjoyment on sheer technical knowledge of its challenges and possibilities – and the means used to explore and solve them.

Very broadly, within the allocated twenty minutes the matador has to learn how to read and understand the bull, to control and dominate it in an aesthetically satisfying series of passes, showing grace, courage and virtuosity, and finally to kill it with a slender sword which he has to place in the animal's back by diving in over the horns. When the bull first gallops into the ring the matador and his assistants test and examine it using their large pink and gold capes as lures. Every bull is different. All they have in common is furious aggression and an almost limitless capacity to maim or kill. At that early stage the matador wants to know how fast the bull runs, the angle it favours in charging, from which side it prefers to hook, and a whole range of other information about its nature as a fighting animal.

He has three or four minutes to find out. Then the president signals, the trumpet sounds, the horsemen enter the ring, and the second phase of the bullfight starts. It was quickly discovered when bullfighting changed from a horseback activity to one on foot that a bull could not be run and killed while it retained the capacity to carry its head high. The raised horns, supported by the massive mount of muscle on its back, cut down anyone who opposed it. The answer was to attack the muscle and force the bull to lower its head. As a result the picadors, the burly armoured horsemen, became part of the *corrida*. Often loathed by the audience, but skilful and much-respected by those who work with them, their job, using their strength and the steel-tipped lances, is to bring down the bull's horns so that the matador can run and kill the animal in the *corrida*'s final act.

After the picadors have done their work, three sets of *banderillas*, heavy barbed darts mounted on wooden shafts, are placed in the bull's back. Their purpose is usually explained in books about the *corrida* as being to correct a bull's natural tendency to hook right or left when it tosses its head. In fact they very seldom if ever have this effect. Placed by a member of the *cuadrilla*, or occasionally the matador himself, after a swerving run, they lock into the bull at random, catching arbitrarily in the flesh on either side of the spine. What they do instead is slow the animal still further. When the darts have been placed the matador picks up the small red square of the *muleta*, perhaps dedicates the bull to the audience or to a friend in the crowd, and walks forward to confront the animal.

In the ten minutes or so that remain the matador has to do his *faena*, his bluntly-named 'job'. He starts by testing the bull again to see how it is running now after the punishment of the lances and the darts. Then he begins to pass the animal, changing the cloth from hand to hand, winding the bull round him, guiding it away, altering the angle from which he cites it again, trying all the time to link the different passes together so each in a series blends into the next. The bullfight has an extensive literature, in English as well as Spanish, and volumes have been written on the *faena* alone, but the *faena*'s object is quite straightforward — to show conclusively that the matador, and not the bull, is dictating what happens. In the *plaza* the

bull becomes the embodiment of danger and imminent death. Unarmed the matador offers himself to it again and again. By dominating and then defeating it with a single sword-thrust in a final gesture of daring, the matador triumphs on behalf of himself and the entire crowd.

That certainly is what should happen and what the crowd goes to the *plaza* to see. In practice the *corrida* all too seldom finishes that way. Far more often the wind is blowing, the bulls are wayward and unpredictable, the matadors are tired, frightened or inept, and the risks are too high. In any of those circumstances, and they seem to occur in well over three-quarters of all *corridas*, the spectacle disintegrates. Instead of a proper *faena* the matador nervously flaps the scarlet cloth once or twice, stabs ineffectually at the bull from a prudent distance with the sword, takes the *descabello*, a specially adapted weapon designed to kill the animal by severing its spinal column, and having failed with that too orders one of his *cuadrilla* to end the business with a *puntilla*, a dagger stabbed into the base of the bull's skull. On those sadly frequent occasions the *plaza*'s status as a theatre of conflict, courage, and art, is reduced to the level of a knacker's yard.

A successful *corrida* needs brave and accomplished matadors. Almost more important it needs brave and appropriate bulls. The Spanish fighting bull is not, as many people believe, a wild animal. It never existed in nature. A creature as artificial in its way as a poodle, the fighting bull is man-made, a product of selective breeding. Its original genetic inheritance comes from two sources: the native bovine stock of the Iberian peninsula and the bulls imported by the Carthaginians. By the sixteenth century, and probably well before, the crossbreeds of the two races were being kept or culled according to the characteristics they showed, the most important being aggression. Like all animals a bull is at its most aggressive in defending territory. The early breeders, like their successors today, retained only those few individuals which exhibited almost psychopathic aggression over their territories.

The result is an animal programmed to do nothing but attack. In the past bulls have been matched with lions, tigers and even elephants. The result has always been a fiasco. The bull has destroyed every animal put before it, even an elephant ten times its weight. No other creature on earth can match its speed, its strength or the lethal weapons it carries in its horns. Almost as formidable is its intelligence. When a bull is loosed from the *toril*, the bullpen, it will never have seen a man on foot before. Initially it charges the cape because the cape is moving. Twenty minutes later it will have learned that the man and not the cloth is its proper target. From then on it becomes unfightable, no longer a participant in the *corrida* but an executioner. By law every bull that has appeared in a ring must die, either during the *corrida* or immediately afterwards outside. At the end of those twenty minutes it has become too dangerous to live.

One can watch a thousand *corridas* and learn every nuance of the bullfight's arcane and complex vocabulary, but there is in the end only one way to appreciate what a fighting bull is really like – to go out and face the charge of one oneself. Every year the *ganaderias*, the bull-breeding ranches, hold *tientas*, testings of the quality of the young stock. In small private rings the immature cows and bulls are exposed to men on horses and examined for their courage and determination. Those which perform well are kept. The others are separated and castrated to be raised as steers for beef. Most *tientas* include the running of one or two young and proven bulls which for some reason or other are not destined for the ring. They are normally brought in to allow novice matadors to try their skills in private without the pressure of a watching crowd.

One of my close Andalucian friends was the matador Miguel Mateo, known as 'Miguelin', who like a number of successful matadors has his own bull-ranch. It was at a *tienta* there that I first got into the ring with a bull. Although I'd seen many bullfights by then, I found that at eye-level on the sand everything was different. Although by *corrida* standards the bull was tiny it appeared immense, a dark menacing presence carrying its head high and its horns level with my face. I walked forward and cited with the cape. The bull didn't so much charge as explode forward. One instant it was motionless on the far side of the ring. The next it was on me, gouging and stabbing and hooking. Following the cape it hurtled by me, but before I had even begun to swing round it had turned like a cat and was coming back. Its speed was breath-taking. I managed to scramble another pass, the bull savaged the cape, smashed through it, and then mercifully lost me for a moment from its vision. Sweating and panting I stepped back behind the protection of the wooden *burladero*.

Since then I have caped bulls at *tientas* on many occasions. Coached by Miguelin I have learned the basics of handling a cape, and once or twice I've even managed to make an almost respectable pass. But even now, every time I step into a ring and see the bull start to move, I still get the same sense of shock and disbelief I felt the first time that any animal could be quite so fast, so powerful and so blindly dedicated to doing nothing except remove me from its territory.

Paradoxically the campaign to save the fighting bull by ending the *corrida* would, if successful, have only one certain result – the bull's extinction. It is not an efficient converter of grass into protein. Other modern strains of cattle can do the job better and more economically. Theoretically, with the bullring lost as a market, the ranch-owners would replace their *corrida* herds with one of these new strains. In practice they would almost certainly make a different choice. The way bulls feed allows their pastures to be shared by a host of other plants and creatures – the orchids, wild flowers, birds, butterflies and animals. However, modern technology has shown that almost any space of Andalucian land can be exploited much more profitably than through beef production by methods like hydroponics. The intensity of the new methods excludes any competitors. There is literally no living-room under a plastic canopy for an otter, a nightingale, a swallow-tail butterfly or a wild hyacinth. So if the *corrida* disappeared not only would the fighting bulls vanish, but great tracts of ancient countryside and the communities of wildlife they have supported for hundreds of thousands of years would be lost too.

For anyone going to a bullfight for the first time there is no substitute for taking a companion who knows the *corrida*. If one isn't available, I would single out just two of the many factors involved in the relationship between the bull and the matador to concentrate on. Both concern the bull's physical make-up. The first is its sight. Apart from a cone of binocular vision in front, a bull has monocular vision to the sides and to some degree behind. The rear monocular 'window' slants away quite sharply from its horns, leaving an area of blindness behind its shoulder. This blind terrain is often exploited by meretricious and showy matadors who step inside it as the bull passes and press themselves to the animal's flank, apparently exposing themselves to immense danger but in reality staying relatively safe.

The second point concerns the way a bull charges. A bull can only launch itself forward in attack with its spinal column in a straight line. This again allows a showy matador to cite a bull from apparently suicidal positions, secure in the knowledge that the animal will have to adjust its posture and so change the direction of its charge before it moves. Equally, the great matadors will genuinely expose themselves by citing from angles where their own bodies are already part of the target; they have to depend on their skill with the cloth to guide the slashing horns away.

The greatest matador of the modern era, and in the view of many the greatest of all matadors, is Antonio Ordoñez. Now retired, Ordoñez came appropriately like his father, the Niño de la Palma, from the cradle of bullfighting, the city of Ronda. Immensely knowledgeable about fighting bulls, which in his own words he loves almost as much as his children, Ordoñez in the ring personified all that was best in the ancient Ronda style of *tauromaquia*. He was consistently brave, intelligent, graceful and above all honest. In every *corrida* he crossed from his own territory into that of the bulls, and faced them on their own terms there. The price he paid for doing so over the years was horrific. Once, going up to have a drink in his hotel room, I walked in as he emerged naked from the shower. Above the ribs his body was supple and balanced and muscular. Below it was a pocked and cratered landscape of scar tissue, stitch marks, and the dark ugly punctures of over twenty major horn wounds.

Ordoñez saw me staring at his legs and laughed. 'I was drunk,' he said. 'Other men get drunk on wine. I get drunk on bulls. The consequences are even worse.'

The nature of the bullfight is at best elusive and more probably indefinable. A *corrida* is an act of theatre improvised by a cast that changes with every performance. During the past twenty-five years I have seen over 500. Every one was utterly different from all the others, reflecting the day, the weather, the bulls, the men, the crowd, the season, the place, even the changing social climate of the times. Of them all I would pick out two which seem to me in their totally contrasting ways to best express what the bullfight is and what it means to the Spanish, or more particularly to the Andaluz to whom it belongs. Both inevitably featured Antonio Ordoñez.

The first took place in Ordoñez' home town of Ronda. In September every year Ronda mounts a charity bullfight, a *festival*, known as the Goyesca, when in honour of the painter everyone taking part dresses in the costume of Goya's time. During the Ordoñez years the annual Goyescas became the best-known bullfights in Spain, eclipsing even the great *corridas* of Madrid, Pamplona, and Sevilla. The audience was international. People came to Ronda from all over the world just to be present in the little ring for two hours on an autumn afternoon. The pageantry of the occasion was spectacular, the atmosphere in the sierra town was warm and happy, but most of all there was Ordoñez, and with him on the bill the country's finest matadors, running bulls in front of his own people.

In 1975 Ordoñez' second bull was a *manso*, a difficult and nervous animal reluctant to charge. He did what he could with it – being Ordoñez he got more out of the bull than any other *torero* alive would have been able to – but when he walked back to the *barrera* after finally killing it his normally smiling face was grim and angry. He had only two chances to perform and one of them, through no fault of his own, had been wasted. Ordoñez waited while the afternoon's remaining two bulls were run. Then he walked into the ring, bowed to the president, and asked for the substitute bull. He had no right to do so. Under Spanish law when the announced six bulls have been killed, the *corrida* is over and it is illegal for another animal to be fought. But from Ordoñez in Ronda it was not so much a request as a command. The president prudently nodded.

Ordoñez then went over to the main gates and ordered them to be opened. Waiting outside were hundreds of Ronda's poor, its cripples, its beggars, its unemployed, who had been listening to the sounds of the *corrida* beyond the walls of the ring. Ordoñez was their brother and their hero, almost their god. If they couldn't afford to watch him at least they could be close to him as he demonstrated his art, an art that because of him had made Ronda and themselves famous throughout the world. Ordoñez told them to fill the *callejón*, the narrow pasageway between the fonce and the stands. His instructions once again were illegal. By law the *callejón* must remain empty. On that day not even the Guardia Civil would have challenged

Ordoñez' command. With the *callejón* filled to bursting he ordered the substitute bull to be released in the ring.

The bull, unlike its *manso* predecessor, was bold and aggressive. When the time came for the *faena* Ordoñez collected the animal, drew it to the edge of the ring, and systematically ran it in groups of passes round the entire circumference of the plaza, showing it in turn to each segment of the tumultuously applauding crowds. Finally he led the bull into the ring's centre and killed it with the classic single sword-thrust. As the bull fell, the crowds erupted over the wooden *barrera*, hurled away their crutches and sticks, seized Ordoñez, hoisted him into the air, and carried him away through the gates in a triumph that was as much theirs as his.

The second *corrida*, which was also a *festival*, took place out of season in Tarifa in January. The little port is fortunate in having Ordoñez as its patron and whenever he could he headed the bill for the annual charity bullfight to raise funds for local medical services. To run the bulls with him that afternoon he had invited two of his greatest contemporaries, Antonio Bienvenida and Curro Romero, and also his son-in-law Paquirri. It was rather as if Laurence Olivier had decided to perform at a village hall accompanied by Sir John Gielgud, Sir Ralph Richardson, and the young Richard Burton. Instead of the costumes of the Goyesca the four matadors and their teams wore the traditional *festival* dress of *traje corto*, the grey trousers, dark jacket, and flat black Sevillan hat.

Tarifa's bullring is tiny, wood-framed and only fifty yards from the sea. An hour before the fight started it was packed. Unlike Ronda there were no international celebrities in the little bare stands, only the town's fishermen and the peasant farmers from nearby. The winter sunlight was bright and clear, and the air smelt of salt and was full of the sound of breaking waves; gulls wheeled overhead and the red and gold bars of the Spanish banner snapped against the sky. The day proved to be one of those rare occasions when the bulls are flawless and the men match them. In turn the four matadors gave performances that would have won them accolades in Madrid. Then

Ordoñez' second bull galloped into the ring – he and Bien-venida were taking two each, and Romero and Paquirri one. The bull was small with a partridge-wing hide, broad, well balanced horns, and bright, intelligent eyes. Ordoñez decided to run it himself from the start with the cape. At the end of the first pass the animal turned on him and charged again without being cited. It did the same eleven times in succession. As he walked away at the end of a dazzling series of *veronicas* Ordoñez was frowning, not out of worry but with the intent clouded expression of someone aware something rare is hap-pening. The horses entered the ring, the bull without any provocation hurled itself at the nearest, and the *picador* lowered his lance. As he was about to plunge it into the bull's back Ordoñez suddenly shouted at him not to touch it. The horsemen left and the *banderilleros* started to take their place on the sand. Again Ordoñez waved them away before a dart could be placed.

Puzzled and anxious, his entire *cuadrilla* clustered round and began to plead with him. The first two acts of the bullfight had passed without anything having been done to make the animal ready for the *faena*. The bull was as strong and dangerous as when it had come into the ring. Ordoñez ordered them all to get behind the fonce, picked up the scarlet cloth, and walked forward. He had barely come within the animal's range of vision when the bull charged again. The next fifteen minutes were the most remarkable in my entire experience of the bullfight. The bull was dauntless. Its concentration never wavering, it charged again and again and again. Ordoñez would link pass after pass, swing the animal away from him, and turn to cite it again – and there would be no need. Running true and straight the bull was already hurling itself at him again of its own accord.

Finally when both had run each other into the ground, when the bull's head was sagging with exhaustion and Ordoñez' face was sheeted in sweat, Ordoñez came back to the *barrera*. He tossed away the stick that had helped stiffen the cloth and took the tempered steel sword needed for the kill. Then he returned to the centre of the ring. He lined the bull up, sighted down the blade, crossed the cloth lure in front of his stomach, and plunged between the horns as the animal attacked him for the final time. The bull burst through the cloth, but the sword didn't enter its back. At the last moment Ordoñez let it fall harmlessly onto the sand. As the animal passed he touched it lightly with his hand at the point where the blade would have speared in. Then he swivelled away. Moments afterwards, using only his hand as a lure, he guided it back into the *toril* to the same tumultuous applause that had sounded unbroken since he'd first walked out to confront the bull.

The grant of an *indulto*, or reprieve, to a fighting bull is extremely rare. It happens only when an animal shows such extraordinary qualities of courage and nobility in the ring that the president, in response to the request of the matador and the audience, decides the law requiring it to be killed should be waived. Instead he returns the bull to its breeder who normally takes the animal back to his ranch and keeps it there, carefully isolated from man, as a seed-bull for future generations of *toros bravos*. I have witnessed it only three times in twenty-five years of watching *corridas*. Only once have I seen it happen to a bull which, like Ordoñez' that afternoon, left the ring untouched. I doubt it has happened before or since.

The applause for Ordoñez had rung out tumultuous and unbroken from the moment he walked forward to test the bull at the start of the fight. When he returned at the end it continued for minute after minute, the cheers even longer and more rapturous than the ones which had saluted him at Ronda. Death is normally an inescapable part of the *corrida*. It is never its reason or what the Andalucian crowds go to the ring to see. They go to see one of their own confront death and triumph over it on their behalf. Ordoñez had done that for them. In Tarifa that night the bars stayed open longer and the celebrations went on later even than during *feria*.

14

ONE NOVEMBER NIGHT a car drew up in front of the Huerto Perdido and a few moments later my friend Juan Carlos Barbadillo walked into the house. He embraced me, smiling, and then announced dramatically, 'I have finally decided to forgive you.'

It was several months since I'd seen him and his remark was only partly in jest. Quite unintentionally I'd given poor Juan Carlos a fright which, as he said afterwards, might well have cost a lesser man his life through a heart attack. Travelling Andalucía as a salesman for the family's sherries, Juan Carlos sometimes found himself on the road late at night with the Huerto close at hand and home in Sanlúcar still two hours driving away. As his job required him to be what might be called convivial during business hours, whenever his day ended close to the house Juan Carlos prudently spent the night with us and finished his journey next morning. One night he arrived very late after what had obviously been an exhausting series of professional appointments. We had a final glass together and he headed off for bed in the guest room he used on his visits which by then he knew so well I didn't need show him to it. Shortly afterwards in bed myself I heard a terrified scream and the patter of racing footsteps.

I ran out to find Juan Carlos slumped trembling and speechless in a chair in the living-room. It was several minutes before I gathered what had happened. Then I found out. Since his last visit a wounded eagle owl had arrived at the house. Owing to the lateness of the hour I'd quite forgotten to warn Juan Carlos

I'd installed the bird in the towering guest bedroom cupboard, whose clothes rail I'd lowered three feet to provide a perch. Juan Carlos had opened the cupboard door to hang up his jacket and suddenly like an avenging angel the immense creature had erupted out of the darkness, talons slashing, orange eyes blazing and beak snapping like rifle fire. Juan Carlos had understandably reeled back in shock, fled from the room and collapsed. I explained, apologised, tried to calm him, and offered him the other bedroom instead. Juan Carlos refused. However late it was, he insisted, and whatever the distance in front of him, for once he was going straight home. Still ashen-faced and shaking but sober as a judge after the encounter, he walked with dignity out into the night.

'I shall search the room first for any hidden devils,' he now went on. 'But assuming I don't find any, I shall stay the night. Tomorrow I'm taking you up into the sierras for a few days. I'm going to show you some true mountain *pueblos* in the Ronda *serranía*.'

In most foreigners' minds the word *pueblo* evokes an image of a little white-walled village, as evocative of Andalucía as a Sevillana dress or a bullfight poster. A *pueblo* is indeed a village but the word's meaning is considerably more complex than that. First, it can be applied equally to a town or city or any permanent human settlement. Madrid is just as much a *pueblo* as any little hamlet in the sierras. Next, it represents the people as well as the place, meaning in that sense a community. Thirdly it can be applied to an entire nation. The 'Pueblo Inglés' is a common way of describing the British. Finally, the word has a fourth dimension which embraces all the others. Sometimes, trying to find an analogy for the Andalucian social system, it has occurred to me that the clan structure of the Scottish highlands is the closest.

When one Andaluz asks another where is his *pueblo*, he is not only enquiring where the other comes from geographically. He is asking which clan he belongs to. If the *pueblo* turns out to be near his own he will instantly be able to put his companion in a context. Every *pueblo* has its own widely

Sierra pueblo

known and unchanging characteristics. The inhabitants of
Aculla are mean; those of San Andres avaricious and untrust-
worthy in business. People who come from Benalaura have
cross-eyed daughters, those of Santa Maria are idle and poor
farmers. Men from El Burgo are always cuckolded by their
wives, and the women of La Brena are notorious for their bad
breath. The judgements are not teasing banter. They spring
from iron certainties. The *pueblo* is both home and family and
by definition better than anyone else's. So the competitiveness
between neighbouring *pueblos*, and the denigration of one by
another, is intense. More than once in the most fervently

Catholic country in Europe men from one *pueblo*, jealous of another's Virgin, have raided the other village and destroyed the Mother of God herself.

There is inevitably a tension between the traditions and values of the self-enclosed world of the *pueblo* and the requirements of a national government. This was vividly illustrated for me in the case of a man named Ramón Cuellas. For years Cuellas was the chief of the secret police in Algeciras. He was a textbook fascist. He was small, stocky, sallow, and wore heavy dark glasses. He drank with the local army colonels, told dirty stories, idolised Franco, held political opinions well to the right of Ghenghis Khan's, was cheerfully corrupt and reputed to be a skilled torturer. One day he went to lunch, as he often did, with a group of like-minded cronies at the Reina Cristina Hotel. Midway through the meal he stood up and tapped on the table for silence. Somewhat puzzled, everyone in the dining-room fell silent and turned to look at him.

'There is something I wish to say,' Cuellas announced. He paused. Then he added with dignity, 'Fuck Franco.'

Afterwards he walked from the room. The following day Cuellas had vanished from Algeciras. Three months later I learned he'd been transferred to a small sierra village where he was checking alfafa quotas. He was extremely fortunate not to be in prison – publicly insulting the head of state was a serious offence – but his career was over.

Why did this exemplary secret policeman, Franco's apparently fanatical disciple, turn on his idol and sacrifice everything in that brief and extraordinary remark? Speculation in the town rumbled on for weeks. There were suggestions Cuellas was drunk, that he'd had a nervous breakdown, that he'd been frustrated over promotion and the outburst was an impulsive protest. None, to me, was convincing. Cuellas was a modest drinker with an equable temperament who had a powerful and interesting job – the nearness of Gibraltar meant he was in constant contact with Madrid. Something else had impelled him to destroy his life. I finally learned what it was late one night in a conversation with one of Cuellas' friends.

'Ramon was torn in two,' his friend told me. 'He believes utterly in Franco and the Movimiento, but he believes just as deeply in his *pueblo*. In the end his feelings for the *pueblo* proved stronger. He could not denounce them, as he was required to do, any longer.'

The pull of different allegiances between the state and the local, which Cuellas eventually found unendurable, has bedevilled Spanish history. It is an extension of the ancient problem of the different Spains, or what Franco called the 'fissipariousness' of Spanish society – the inherent inclination of the country to divide. Franco, like every Spaniard a son of the *pueblo* himself, came to see it as the most subversive force in Spanish life. It had to be overcome because destiny had given the country a unique and heroic role. The Spanish people are God's army on earth. If the army mutinies and splits into warring factions, it naturally becomes a spent and useless instrument. Spain must therefore remain united. Franco's answer was to contain the *pueblo*'s power, he knew he could never eliminate it, by force. Under his régime the police was largely successful, although the price the country paid was fearsome.

Another striking feature of the Andalucian *pueblo* which it shares with the Scottish clans is that in spite of the vast differences in wealth between rich and poor, the *pueblo* is almost entirely classless. In a well-known story two British girls visiting Sevilla some years ago during the spring fair went out on their first morning to see the city and do some shopping. In the street they hailed one of Sevilla's horse-drawn cabs and spent the next two hours exploring the town. When they returned to the hotel they were unable to understand why the cab-driver refused payment. As he drove away the hotel concierge appeared. He saluted the man smartly and explained to the young women he wasn't a cab-driver at all, but a Sevillan nobleman who had been on his way to the fair driving his own carriage and pair. Looking after him astounded one of the girls remarked, 'How astonishing for someone like that to do what he did.' The concierge laughed. 'Not at all, senorita,' he said.

'It is exactly because he is a nobleman that he did it. In Andalucía if a beggar had the carriage and horses, he would have done the same.'

The knowledge that every Andaluz is equal, and capable of the same chivalrous behaviour as the Sevillan marquis, lies at the heart of the *pueblo* concept. Like the clan the *pueblo* is an extended family and in any family every member ultimately has the same social status, whatever their gifts, achievements or failings. In Andalucía the instinctive *pueblo* sense of equality has three powerful reinforcements. The first comes from the church. Every Andaluz is constantly reminded that in the eyes of God all men are level. It happens not only in church but much more potently in the fairs, festivals, pilgrimages and celebrations that thread daily life. They belong to and are attended by the entire community, they give Andalucian existence its meaning, and they are egalitarian.

'How can I think any *gran señor* is better than I am?' the moon-tormented Domingo said to me when we were discussing the Rocio pilgrimage. 'We walk in penance together, we enter the Virgin's shrine together, we kneel and confess the same sins, we take the same bread and the same wine. How can the man at my side who goes with women as I do if I have the chance, gets drunk from the same bottle, maybe tells a few small lies, cheats a little in business, uses bad language in anger, does all we are told not to do and yet, like me, is forgiven for doing it, how can such a man be any different?'

Domingo shook his head. 'No, Don Nicholas. Maybe in your *pueblo* you see things differently. But I tell you, here in Andalucía I and the *duque* are equals. We both have land and we both have pride. He has more money than me, that is the only difference. Money comes and goes – look at the sadness of Benalmin. But land and pride last for ever.'

Land, if not pride, is the second factor that unifies Andalucian society. Whatever has happened by way of industrial development in cities like Sevilla, Córdoba and Huelva, the Andalucian *pueblo* remains essentially agrarian. The earth supports the people, and not only the poor but the rich. The millionaire nobleman is just as dependent on the land as the most impoverished share-cropper. It gives them both, it gives every member of the *pueblo* family, a binding common interest. The third cohesive force is Andalucian culture. Every Andaluz, whatever his station in life, speaks the same and often highly sophisticated cultural vocabulary.

Walking up the valley from the sea one evening I heard music coming from a little wooden forester's hut. As I passed, a washing girl from the Mesón de Sancho roadhouse ran out and pulled me inside. She, another washing girl and two peasants from the Guadalmesi were holding an impromptu party. A candle had been lit, a bottle of Jerez wine produced, a little cassette recorder was playing, and dancing was in progress. I could only stay thirty minutes as we had been invited out that night. In those thirty minutes I danced Sevillanas, drank wine, listened to songs being sung, and discussed the forthcoming Algeciras *feria*. Later in the evening we arrived at another party. At first glance the two occasions belonged to different worlds. The second party was set in a large and beautiful hacienda. There were 200 guests instead of five. The women were dressed in elegant Sevillana dresses and the men were wearing dinner jackets. In place of the cassette player the music came from a group of guitarists accompanied by flamenco singers.

In reality the differences between the two parties were non-existent. The songs and dances were identical. The Jerez wine came from the very same vineyards. The same topics, the Algeciras *feria*, the countryside, the weather, the prospects for the bullfights, dominated the conversation. A guest at either party could have walked into the other and been entirely at home. Both groups had the same social graces, sung the same songs, and told the same jokes. They were all Andaluz. It would be wrong to portray Andalucía as a completely classless Eden. While no Andaluz ever considers himself inferior to anyone else, a handful consider themselves superior. Almost every little *pueblo* has someone who believes himself to be above his fellows, endowed by nature with a keener intellect, finer sensibilities, or a more acute judgement. Invariably the conviction turns the person into a malcontent, scorned as much by the other villagers as he scorns them. But in the main in the *pueblo*, very much as in the clan, kinship, faith, the land and the shared culture far outweigh any imagined distinctions conferred by birth, upbringing or education.

Juan Carlos and I left for the sierras on a dank autumn morning with the skies dark and the rain streaming down over the Guadalmesi. We drove through Algeciras and turned inland beyond on the road that we always took to Ronda. As we came into the Jimena valley the sun broke through the thick clouds, the early mist began to lift, and flocks of dazzling white cattle egrets flapped round us in the wake of the grazing herds in the roadside pastures. We made our first stop of the day in Jimena at 10.00 a.m. It set the pattern for the journey. Juan Carlos was travelling the Barbadillo sherries. His job was to check how the bar-owners of the sierra *pueblos* were doing with the family wines, to take their orders for further stocks, to meet the company's local agents in the larger villages, and generally to create goodwill for the Barbadillo name. The work mainly involved sitting in bars, drinking, telling the latest ribald joke, and above all exchanging news and views about Andalucian life, about horses, crops, weather, women, game-bird shooting, *ferias*, local politics, and very occasionally the bizarre activities of the remote central government in Madrid.

Jimena de la Frontera

It was a job at which Juan Carlos excelled. Like the writer Luis Berenguer, he had known the country people all his life. He understood their ways, shared their interests, and enjoyed their company as much as they did his.

'When I go to work I'm on holiday,' Juan Carlos said to me as we came out of the Jimena bar with an order for a dozen bottles of wine, two promotional posters of the Jerez horse fair, and a packet of paper napkins over-printed with the Barbadillo name. 'What is the point of business if it isn't fun?'

The direct road to Ronda bypasses Jimena at the foot of the hill. This time we took the much narrower road that runs through the village and out to the north on the far side. Soon we were climbing steeply into the sierras through forests of scented eucalyptus and groves of poplars, shining like candles in their brilliant yellow autumn foliage. Beneath them the undergrowth was bright with the scarlet berries of rosehips, wild cherry and *modroño*, the strawberry tree whose branches the sierra gypsies pick and sell in the markets as Christmas decorations. Because of the height and the season there were relatively few wild flowers, but the day before on a journey to Sevilla I found snowdrops, crocuses and bluebells all flowering by the roadside within a few yards of each other. Occasionally we passed a little whitewashed cottage. Hanging from nails round the door were baskets of country produce for sale – brown eggs, pale forest mushrooms, red and yellow apples, glittering pomegranites, and glossy-skinned chestnuts. Beside us trout rose in the shining pools of the Hozgarganta river and the high air was clear and still in the sunlight.

At least once an hour throughout the day we stopped at a bar or a *venta*. From the number of bars we passed which carried the Barbadillo sign we could have stopped every ten minutes. Although the Barbadillo bodega is small it produces some of the region's finest sherries and one, the fino Solear, which is matchless. A dry pale amber wine with a fleeting scent of camomile, it has the same pre-eminent standing among the wines of the Jerez region as the Macallan among Scottish single malt whiskies. At each halt we drank a couple of *copas*,

Sierra pueblo

chatted to the owner, and ate a few *tapas* of smoked mountain ham or perhaps some grapes pickled in *aguardiente* before heading on. Late in the afternoon we came to our destination for the day, the little mountain town of Ubrique. Half an hour earlier the coastal storms had overtaken us again. The sky blackened and the rain deluged down in driving sheets that turned the afternoon air to darkness. As we crested the ridge before Ubrique the storm whirled away and the sun cut through the massed clouds. The town suddenly appeared in front of us, a cluster of radiantly white houses cradled by the jagged hills with the foot of an immense glistening rainbow resting on its roof.

Some of the sierra towns and villages are relatively new settlements, founded a few centuries ago or even less. Most, particularly the larger ones, in spite of their isolation and apparent inaccessibility are extremely old, dating back before the Moors to Roman, Phoenician or even remoter times. At some stage in Andalucía's distant history its early inhabitants must have rippled up from the coastal plains, discovered a workable niche in the high hills, and colonised the upland woods and meadows. Ubrique, a natural fortress, is typical of the sites they must have chosen. A republican stronghold during the Civil War, it proved so difficult for the beseiging nationalists to take they eventually called up a plane from Sevilla to fly over the town and drop leaflets carrying the message: 'Ubrique, if in five minutes from now all your arms are not piled in a visible place in front of the Guardia Civil post and the roofs and terraces of your houses are not covered in white sheets, the town will be devastated by the bombs in this plane.' The threat was effective, although not quite in the way the nationalists had intended. Without spreading out a single white sheet or leaving a gun behind them Ubrique's citizens promptly abandoned the town and took to the hills behind.

A number of the sierra communities still follow the medieval tradition of guild towns, each specialising in a different craft In Ubrique's case the craft is leather-work, which employs almost everyone in the town and is carried on through concerns ranging from small family businesses, where the leather is still worked by hand, through co-operatives to companies owning mechanized workshops. Originally the raw materials of the hides and skins were supplied locally. Now they come from all over the world, reaching the little sierra town in high-smelling blood-stained bundles and leaving it as elegant wallets, cigar cases, handbags, belts, shoes, and suitcases. The increasing demand for good leather-work has not only made Ubrique rich, but uniquely in the sierras has caused a rise in the town's population over the past twenty years. From dawn to dusk and often beyond into the night, every street echoes to the tap of the *petacabras*, the tools used to beat out and soften the untreated leather.

Although Ubrique's wealth sets it apart from its neighbours, the daily life of all the sierra settlements has much the same pattern. Early every morning, as happens all over Andalucía, the casual workers and the unemployed gather in the main square to try to hire themselves out to any employer needing labour. If they fail, with nothing else to do they often remain talking and smoking in the square for most of the day. Meanwhile the town is about its business. The buoyancy of Ubrique's economy means that the town can provide work for women. By day they work alongside the men at the leathercraft tables, but as soon as the day ends the sexes separate. The women go home to deal with the household chores and prepare the evening meal, while the men repair to the bars or, if there is one and the men have sufficient status to be members, to the Circolo de Artistas. Universally known as the Casino, the Circolo de Artistas is the club in every prosperous Andalucian town patronized by the local businessmen and bourgeoisie. One of the traditions of the Casino is that foreign visitors to the town are welcomed as honorary members.

In spite of its riches Ubrique is too small for a Casino, so Juan Carlos and I spent the evening moving from bar to bar discussing the town's affairs with his many friends over endless glasses of Barbadillo and *tapas*. A favourite autumn *tapa* in the sierras is acorns. Every few minutes someone would reach into his pocket, pull out a handful and offer them round. With its skin peeled away the flesh of the cork oak's acorn is sweet and delicious, tasting rather like a plump hazel nut. At 10.30 p.m. there was a short break while the men returned home to eat their wives' meals. Then an hour later everyone assembled again and the talk and the drinking continued. I retired to bed soon after midnight but Juan Carlos was up for another three hours.

'The day is for working and drinking,' he said as we drove on early next morning. 'The night is for drinking and talking. Life's too brief itself to cut either of them short.'

There are in Andalucía about 700 little towns and villages. Ranging in size from Ubrique with a population of some 10,000 down to tiny hamlets with a couple of hundred inhabitants, every one of them has some distinctive point of interest, some particular festival or *romería* or historical claim to fame. We visited perhaps a dozen during that trip and I explored many more afterwards, but as Juan Carlos said it would take a lifetime to do justice to them all. Our next stop was at Grazalema, perched like a wind-blown and cloud-swept bird's nest higher still in the hills. Much older even than Ubrique, it was used by the Visigoths, the Romans and thousands of years before them by Andalucía's first hunter-gatherers; and part of the town was razed by Napoleonic troops in Spain's early nineteenth-century war of independence. Grazalema's traditional craft was glove-making, but unlike Ubrique the demand for its gloves has dried up and the town's population has fallen by over a half since the war to little more than 2,500 today. Rearing up behind it to the north is the peak of San Cristobal, the first glimpse of Spain caught on the horizon by the laden treasure galleons returning from the New World.

Much lower, in the valleys beyond Grazalema, is the village of El Gastor. El Gastor is smaller and poorer than Grazalema, and its women still cook on the pavement outside their houses over clay braziers fuelled with burning almond shells, filling the few streets with the scents of herbs and making them at night look lined with glow-worms. Juan Carlos insisted we went there because he'd heard a country veterinary surgeon, who'd retired to the village, was creating a little private museum of rural tools and artefacts. We found the old man and he showed us the collection he was assembling with evident love, learning and an immense pride in the knowledge and skills of the Andalucian country people he'd worked among all his life. Fifteen miles to the west of El Gastor is Setenil. Built partly round a hill and partly along the ravine of the little Guadalcorcun river, half of Setenil's houses are made of whitewashed brick and half are troglodyte dwellings, hollowed out of the sandstone cliff that overhangs the ravine. Like the troglodyte caves at Gaudix to the east of Granada, Setenil's subterranean houses are extremely practical, remaining cool in summer and conserving heat in winter.

Following the winding track beneath the overhang of the cliff, with the river tumbling on one side and the shadowed cave houses opening on the other, we stopped to ask if there was too much autumn water for us to cross the river at the ford ahead. An old and toothless gypsy woman began to answer when she was silenced by a powerful blow across her ears from her middle-aged daughter.

'Blessed Miracle of Our Lady's Immaculate Conception!' her daughter bellowed. 'Shut your face!'

It was several moments before I realized the daughter hadn't been invoking the virgin birth as part of some fearful gypsy curse. She was simply addressing her mother by her christian name.

We forded the river, continued to the west and, climbing high into the hills again, we came to Carratraca. A spa renowned for its sulphur springs as early as the Roman occupation of the sierras, Carratraca's waters are still used during the summer season today. The village, whose visitors within living memory were rich and numerous enough to support three gaming casinos for relaxation after the baths, has a small and clean *hostería* which proudly lists the distinguished clients who have lodged there. At the end of the list, and it includes Napoleon III's wife, the Empress Eugénie, Rilke, Lord Byron and Gustav Doré, is a gentleman with the wonderful and unlikely name of Mr Trinidad Grunt. I have never been able to find out who Mr Grunt was or why he merited a place on Carratraca's roll of honour, but there he is, commemorated in the lonely village in the hills along with the most splendid names in Europe.

Not far from Carratraca is a high and fertile little plateau called after the village of Teba which sits, like a saddle slung over a horse's back, on the steep ridge above. In winter the oval plain below the ridge is stained purple with rain. In spring it blazes with incandescent veins of yellow, as gorse and broom

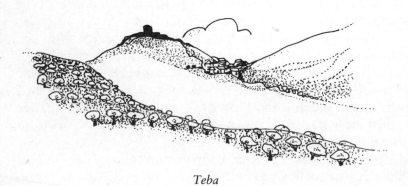

Teba

blossom along its watercourses. In summer a haze of chalky dust stirs like mist over the red earth beneath. During the Moorish occupation Teba was a small but important fortress outpost on the western approaches to Granada. On his death-bed in 1329 the Scottish king, Robert the Bruce, summoned James Douglas, his old friend and long-time companion in arms, and instructed him to bury his heart in the Holy Land, which Bruce had never been able to visit during his life. Tears streaming down his face the older warrior promised to do as his king asked. Within hours of Bruce's death that night, Douglas cut out the king's heart and placed it in a silver casket. Soon afterwards he set sail from Aberdeen with a small company of his bravest knights and their squires.

Douglas's ship put in for supplies at Sevilla. As he docked he learned the Spanish king, Alfonso XI, was harrying the Moor-ish garrisons along the frontier on the road to Granada, but the Christians were in danger of being thrown back. Douglas instantly volunteered his men in their support. He hired horses, rode out from Sevilla and caught up with Alfonso XI's troops on the Teba plain. What happened then, across a divide of almost eight centuries, is impossible to establish. The Moors certainly had a well-supplied castle in the village above. They knew the contours of the little plateau, they brought their cavalry down from the hill, they formed up in deceptively fragile-looking crescents. Alfonso XI, leading his army in person, was still studying their battle formation when the Scots' contingent suddenly broke ranks and charged, possibly out of sheer impetuousness, more likely as a result of a breakdown in communication between two bodies of soldiers without a common language.

Douglas inevitably led his men. Within moments of launching the assault he must have known the little group of Scots was doomed. Bruce's heart was hanging in its silver casket round his neck. As the Moorish cavalry enveloped him he broke its chain and hurled the casket in front of him, shouting, 'Onward as thou wert wont, Douglas will follow thee.' Seconds afterwards, as the casket vanished amid the clashing spears, he was cut down by the Moors. According to Scottish legend the casket was found by the victorious Christian forces on the battlefield at the end of the day and sent back to be buried in Scotland. Teba remained under Spanish control from then on but near-by Canete, which was also captured during the same campaign, changed hands on six further occasions before the reconquest was over. Teba celebrates the festival of San Isidro on 15 May with a procession down to the river Guadalteba, which ends with a *corrida* fought in open country on the river banks.

Nearer Ronda the village of Montejaque also holds a *romería* in mid-May to commemorate an attempt the villagers once made to save Ronda from the plague. Montejaque's Virgin was famously powerful and the villagers tried to drag her to Ronda to heal the city. The further they took her from home the heavier the Virgin became until they were eventually forced to turn back, when she got progressively lighter as she approached the village again. The citizens of Ronda watched her retreat in despair, but all was well. Her presence even a mile outside the walls had proved effective enough, and the following day Ronda sent word to Montejaque that the plague was over. Casabermeja, not far away, has a *romería* in April which ends with an open-air picnic for the whole village, during which the young have to tie the 'devil's tail' by knotting two ears of corn together without pulling them from the ground, an achievement which guarantees them good luck for the year. At Jubrique the feast of Santa Cruz is celebrated by filling the streets with flowered altars, while Benadalid marks its August festival with two days of re-enacted battles between the Moors and the Christians. 'Ben', the prefix to the names of many sierra villages, is a corruption of the Arabic word *banu* meaning 'sons'. Benadalid was so named because in Moorish times the village was occupied by the sons, or more broadly the tribe, of Jalid.

Apart from their place four-square at the centre of every Andaluz' existence, defining his very being, the most striking feature of the *pueblos*, and particularly those of the sierras, is their extraordinary diversity and richness of interest and culture. From an aeroplane or a distant road they look identical, little tightly clustered huddles of uniform white houses roofed with the same ochre tiles. But walking through them, exploring them, talking to their inhabitants, the rareness and singular character of each blazes into life. One still uses the aquaducts and fountains built by the Romans, another the engineering bequeathed by some Moorish caliphate, a third has glorious Renaissance doors and balconies, in a fourth the bullet holes and burn marks left by Napoleon's troops still puncture and scar the walls. Their physical texture is wonderfully dense and varied. So is the stuff of their lives. The *pueblos* speak with different accents, tell different stories and jokes, follow different traditions, practise different customs and crafts, celebrate different festivals in different ways, rise and go to bed at different hours. Every one is a packed and private little world of its own. Together their separate bands of colour and vitality form a rainbow of Andalucian life as shining as the one which broke through the storm as Juan Carlos and I crested the ridge before Ubrique.

≈≈ 15 ≈≈

JUST TO THE west of Algeciras is a little bay with a track leading up from it into the hilly coastline at the start of the straits. The track passes an abandoned whaling station and then comes out on the crest of a ridge. The whole area is considered of strategic importance to Spain's defences, and the outward flank of the ridge is lined with rows of two-man concrete gun emplacements, built years ago and facing out to sea ready to repulse the long feared second Moorish invasion. The invasion hasn't so far come, the emplacements have never been used, and the little concrete boxes are as neat and unmarked as when they were erected.

On the other side of the ridge the ground falls into a little ravine through which a stream runs in winter, and where in summer dry white boulders and pink oleander blooms shine in the sun. Damsel flies flash gunmetal green over the rocks and lizards soak up the sun, but few people go there: the occasional Guardia Civil patrol, a child wandering up from the bay, a goatherd following his flocks. Midway down the slope is another military installation facing the opposite way from the gun emplacements, not over the sea but inland towards Andalucía. A series of linked fortifications, it looks quite different from the untouched bunkers only a few hundred yards away. Its concrete walls have been blasted and shattered by shells. The iron rods that reinforced them stick up like grotesquely bent and rusting pins. Crumbling blocks of mortar are scattered everywhere. Even the earth round the building is pitted with craters. In spring the craters are briefly hidden by papery white narcissus, but as soon as the flowers die the scars show up again. The two sets of fortifications always struck me as a poignant reminder that the worst wounds inflicted on Spain are not by its enemies but by itself.

No one really knows how many people died in the Civil War. (In just one of its countless battles, the inland building was destroyed and five of the six brothers who lived in the farm beyond were killed.) The accepted figure is one million, but how many were really buried in the cemetery at Granada, how many were really slaughtered in the streets of Ronda, Cádiz, Almería and a thousand other towns and villages, how many really died of disease and starvation, is quite impossible to calculate. The horror of that terrible family blood feud remains so vivid and numbing that more than forty years later the survivors will still rarely talk about it.

The war lasted two and a half years, starting in the summer of 1936 and ending in the early spring of 1939. It was the culmination of almost two decades of turbulence and unrest, which were ignited by the revolutionary general strike of 1917. In 1923 General Miguel Primo de Rivera, with the support of the king, Alfonso XIII, established a dictatorship to try to subdue the increasingly militant working classes. Seven years later, publicly reviled, Primo de Rivera was forced into exile, to be followed soon afterwards by the king himself. In 1933 the former dictator's son, José Antonio Primo de Rivera, founded the deeply conservative Falange movement in an attempt to stem the tide of republicanism sweeping the country which was leading to the break-up of the nation into different Spains once more. The military found common cause with the Falange and in July 1936, as national life in the military's view became threatened with anarchy, they announced the formation of a Movimiento Nacional, a national movement to save Spain. Less than a month later General Franco, the army's chief of staff, flew from Morocco to Sevilla, assumed command of the nationalist forces, and with the support of the Church embarked on what was effectively a holy crusade.

Nothing and no one was spared by either side in the brutal

227

clash over the thirty months that followed. The collision was in part economic, between labour and capital, in part philosophical, between communism and fascism, in part religious, between atheists and the army of God. But most of all it was a Spanish quarrel. All wars, as the poet Christopher Logue has pointed out, are civil wars, but a war within a family provokes more passion, more violence, more hatred and bitterness than even the worst of conflicts between strangers. Spain, in spite of the existence of the different Spains, is a family, having more in common than that which divides it, and what it did to itself then was horrific. If the figure of a million dead is correct, one in thirty of the whole population died at the hands of a fellow countryman. Scores that had nothing to do with the war were settled in blood. Brother turned against brother, father against son, mother against child. Old and loving friends infected by the frenzy found themselves confronting each other guns in hand. Whole regions savaged their neighbours and then, with nothing left to destroy, turned inwards to mutilate themselves.

Eventually on 30 March 1939 the last republican stronghold Valencia surrendered to the nationalists, the guns were silenced, and those who were left of the stunned and bleeding Spanish people began to stare round at what they had done to themselves. From the nationalist perspective the forces of Satan had been routed, the soul and unity of Spain had been saved, and freedom, dignity and peace had been justly restored to the land. On the crushed republican side a dream had ended. Liberty had been exiled from Spain; and so had half a million of its best and bravest citizens. The armies of bigotry and repression had triumphed, the proud regions had been humiliated, and all over the country the working man had been reduced once more to a status little better than a slave's. Spain had been pitched back into the Dark Ages.

There were a considerable number of survivors of the Movimiento both in the Guadalmesi and at La Ahumada, but I never asked them what years later they felt about it. The wounds were still too raw and I knew they seldom spoke about it even among themselves. But I did discuss it on several occasions with the master-carpenter from Tarifa, Ramón Sosa, a brave and educated man and a dedicated republican who'd been captured by the nationalists, put to forced work as a prisoner in the Spanish enclave of Ceuta, and finally escaped to Morocco by climbing the barbed wire fence under gunfire from the camp guards.

Had the war, I asked him once, been worth fighting? He thought for a long time. Then he sorrowfully shook his head. 'No, it wasn't,' he said. 'I was a socialist then, I still am one, I will be a socialist all my life. But nothing was worth the tragedies the Movimiento brought. Not socialism, not justice, not even freedom. What separates us from the nationalists is we now know that and they still do not, The terrorists have joined the side of the fascists. They believe death is a price worth paying. No, *señor*. Because the price is not paid by them. It's paid by the children, the women, the old, the innocent. There are other ways to win what we want. But through war again, never.'

Andalucía, with its tradition of anarchist and syndicalist thought, was inevitably a bastion of republicanism. Virtually none of its cities, towns or even tiny *pueblos* escaped the war's ravages, but for me Málaga more than anywhere else epitomised the suffering that seared the region. By 1963, when I first visited Málaga, the war-mutilated had been given official permission to sell cigarettes and matches on the streets. Every doorway and passage-opening along the length of the broad Avenida del Generalissimo Franco was clogged by a grey or black bundle tied up with string. The bundles were people and the string held their clothes round their shattered bodies. The grey wrapped the men, the peasant grey of dark striped trousers and paler shirts. The black belonged to the women who wore it draped from head to hem. Many of either sex, with both of their legs amputated, perched knee-high to the passer-by on little wheeled sleds. Others, the luckier ones who'd lost only one limb, rested their crutches against the wall and leant beside them. They were not beggars or gypsies or *Moros*. They were simply the Andaluz who, innocent or complicit, had been crippled alike in the country's orgy of insanity.

A few still haunt the streets today but most of them have disappeared, tidied away by the aid programmes of an increasingly ashamed and affluent society or vanishing of their own accord into the *pueblos* and *barrios* that originally reared them. They have not left without trace. The passageways the cripples blocked now open onto Málaga's flea markets where tourists and antique-dealers still haggle over the war's debris: the painted Madonnas and children, the gilded altar candlesticks, the broken carvings from the caskets that held the remains of saints, the prayer stools and the fragments of ecclesiastical cloaks embroidered in gold and silver thread. Forty years on the church, one of the strongest metals in the alloy of the war's hatred and violence, remains even in its plundered relics a force in Andalucian life.

Málaga itself is an attractive and prosperous port which like Andalucía's other main cities huddles at the centre of sprawling rings of modern industrial and housing development. Sixty

Málaga castle

Fortress near Málaga

years ago it was a favourite winter resort for rich Madrileños
escaping the icy cold of the capital, and the front was lined
with elegant and imposing villas. Today the winter visitors
have moved west along the coast to Marbella, but by day the
town still has a stately old-fashioned feel. Horse-drawn carriages clop slowly in the shadow along the broad leafy boule-
vardes, and jacarandas blossom violet against crumbling
facades with windows covered by ornate wrought-iron grilles.
At night Málaga changes and becomes a brassy and noisy
sailors' town. Prostitutes patrol the streets, and the bars,
together with the little satellite businesses that circle round
them, the boot-blacks, lottery ticket sellers, cigarette ladies and
pinchito stalls, stay open until the early hours.

East of Málaga the road runs for one hundred and fifty miles
along the coast to Almería, passing on the way the inland hills
and mountains of the Alpujarras. Under the Moors Málaga
was a great pottery centre but at the same time Almería was
more prosperous still, ranking for a while as the richest city in
Europe after Constantinople. Its wealth came from the silk
trade. The climate and soil of the Alpujarras was discovered to
be ideal for both silk-worms and their food plant, the mulberry
tree. Silk had one striking advantage over other valuable
commodities. The cocoons were so light huge quantities could
be carried by a single mule across even the most difficult
terrain. The raw silk was brought down from the mountains,
woven into damask, cicaltoun, sendal, georgian, camlet and
turaz, and exported all over the known world. The trade and
the city collapsed after the reconquest. Modern Almería is a
solid provincial town dealing in the fruits and vegetables of the

surrounding countryside, and increasingly in tourism as more and more of the coastal villages on either side are developed.

Eastwards of Almería the terrain becomes increasingly barren and flat, a sterile wasteland of sand dunes and dry water-courses punctuated here and there near the shore by idiosyncratic little towns like Mojacar. To the north-west the landscape is almost as monotonous, although undulating and fertile as it rises through the Andarax depression. The area is Almería's market garden, bearing oranges, lemons, vegetables and above all a vine which produces large and sweet white grapes. In Andalucía as in southern France the New Year is traditionally ushered in by eating one grape at every chime of midnight. Almería's vines fruit long after those of the region's other vineyards have been harvested during the autumn. When the markets open after Christmas almost every town has one little stall selling the last of Almería's grapes, sweet and slightly wrinkled by then, for the New Year celebrations.

Baeza

One hundred miles to the north of Almería are two little towns separated by only a few miles, Ubeda and Baeza. There is no reason at all to approach them from Almería. They are just as accessible from almost anywhere else in Andalucía, but it was after a journey to Almería that I saw them first and somehow I still remember them most vividly in association with the ancient silk capital of Europe. Both are set close to the upper reaches of the Guadalquivir and surrounded by olive groves. Both date in their modern appearance from the early Renaissance. Both are encircled by white Andalucian houses but where the heart of Ubeda, the larger, is dark, that of Baeza, little more than a village, is golden. The dark and the gold come from the stone used in their construction and the way it has weathered over the centuries.

Each is crammed with buildings of nobility and beauty, palaces, churches, chapels, seigneurial mansions, court houses, squares, even, in Baeza's case, an abattoir which could well have been the living quarters of a prince. In turn they were visited and adorned by the Catholic Kings, by their daughter the mad Juana and her husband Philip the Fair, by the Emperor Charles v on his way to his marriage in Sevilla with Isabel of Portugal, and by many other of Spain's monarchs. Today the two little towns stand side by side, black and gold, lonely and remote from Andalucía's highways, each in their different colours a memorial to the glories of the country's past.

From time to time an ancient station waggon would draw up in front of the Huerto Perdido, and what appeared to be a school would tumble out. The car belonged to a man named Luis Berenguer who would eventually emerge with his wife in the wake of their ten children. Berenguer was an ebullient and cynical employee of the Spanish customs service in Cádiz. He was also a wit, an intellectual, a very considerable and successful novelist, and that rare creature among the Andaluz – a sharp-eyed observer and critic of Andalucian life and society.

Spain has been likened to an oyster that constantly spits out pieces of apparent grit which are in fact its pearls. Over the centuries Jews, Arabs, gypsies, nonconformists and thinkers, have all felt the lash of intolerance and nationalism and been forced to leave. From Maimonides to Picasso and Madariaga the roll-call of the country's exiles is a sorry record of waste and loss. Berenguer was a piece of grit who tried to spit himself out and failed. Leaving Andalucía as a young man he entered the merchant marine, travelled to the USA and Canada, learnt English, and spent several years voyaging round the world. Finally, unable to stay away any longer, he came back. He had always been determined to become a writer, but the size of his growing family forced him to take a supplementary job with the customs. As soon as he came off duty every day he poured out his scorn for and even deeper love of Andalucía in a series of books, perhaps finest of which is *El Mundo de Juan Lobon*, 'The World of Juan Lobon'.

'We Andaluz are besotted with ourselves,' he would say striding up and down the Huerto's living-room. 'Compared to us a blind crofter on the most remote Hebridean island has a positively global vision. We think nowhere else exists on earth. We have an immense amount to give, and we give it generously, but we can neither take nor learn anything. Did you know the wheel came to Andalucía 10,000 years after the rest of the world started using it? It's true. We were offered it by some neolithic haulier but we told him we did things here in the superior Andalucian way – on foot. We'd still be without it if someone hadn't told us the wheel was invented by an Andaluz. That made it acceptable.'

Berenguer would clench his hands in despair and shake his head.

'If you can understand Andalucía you will make yourself a fortune and be able to rule the world. Why? Because you will have discovered the secret of how human stupidity functions at its purest.'

'Why then, Luis,' I would ask him, 'do you go on living here?'

Berenguer would chuckle. 'Very simple. Life here is sweeter than anywhere else on earth. That is the pain of being a thinking Andaluz.'

Sometimes Berenguer's judgements on Andalucía seemed to me intemperate. They came from a swift and cosmopolitan mind, and expressed his own frustration as much as anything else. He found the people's insularity crass and suffocating. They were manacled by their own arrogance, he said. Their structures of thought were so rigid and impervious to influence they were condemning the Andaluz to death. Every Spanish characteristic, Berenguer felt, was seen in Andalucía at its most extreme. If the Spanish were proud of their country, the Andaluz carried pride in the region to the point of parody. Whenever I thought Berenguer was exaggerating, I remembered an incident that happened to me on a Rocío pilgrimage.

I was introduced to a middle-aged lawyer from Sevilla who, discovering I was British and a writer, asked me what I was currently working on. I told him and added conversationally that one day I'd like to write about Andalucía. When he heard that his face turned crimson, he began to tremble and sweat, his voice became incoherent, and he started reeling round the room like a man convulsed by a massive coronary attack. As I watched shocked and astounded – for several moments I thought I might have brought on his death – his friends seized a chair, forced him to sit, and eventually calmed him down. Later we got to know each other better and in the end he came close to accepting it might be possible for a foreigner to write about Andalucía. But the outrage of his immediate response to the idea was so extravagant and theatrical that in any other race it could only have been staged as a joke. Not in the case of an Andaluz. Both the emotion and its expression were real.

I once rashly told Berenguer what had happened. Ever afterwards he delighted in throwing the incident back at me as providing absolute proof of everything he said. When he talked or wrote about the country people, the *campesiños*, Berenguer's acid was transformed by some alchemy into sympathy and compassion. He understood them. He spoke their tongue. He knew their ways and customs and values. He was a wonderful guide to their minds and the forces that shaped them.

'The Andaluz are trapped,' he said once, speaking of the peasants. 'They are victims of a fraud worse than that inflicted on the Irish. The fraud is perpetrated by the church. A naturally brave, sane, kind, and laughing people has been cowed and cheated. They are told their only purpose in life is to be God's soldiers on earth. They are made to obey laws they know instinctively and pragmatically are absurd. But the land is hard, subsistence is difficult and the fraud is sanctioned by force. On the church's side is the army, the state, the vested interests. What chance do the *campesiños* have?'

As so often, Berenguer spread his arms wide in a gesture of impotence.

'Every day of my life I am forced to watch a fundamentally decent people degraded and corrupted by fear and superstition. They are like children who having been told babies are delivered by storks, grow up to learn babies result from copulation, nine months in the womb, and a harsh delivery in pain and blood. And still as adults they are told babies come from storks. There is the patent lie and the witnessed truth, and the church demands they accept the lie.'

Right from the start of our life in the Guadalmesi I was made aware of the extent of the church's authority over the country people. The younger ones, like Ana, might deride and abuse it in private, insisting they didn't believe in religion, but publicly they accepted it without question. When we first moved into the Huerto it was spring, work was still being carried out in the house, and the tiled floors were soon coated with mud from the garden. To keep them clean Elisabeth engaged three women from Pelayo who came in daily with their mops. The following week the local priest paid us a visit to see how the women were getting on. When he arrived they were on their knees scrubbing. He ordered them to stand up, leave the house and come back only when they were wearing trousers beneath their skirts. The women were all married and their heavy, black ankle-length skirts could hardly have been described as immodest, but he was obeyed instantly. Afterwards even on the hottest summer days they always wore two layers of clothing.

Birth, marriage and death were of course dominated by the church. Baptism was not only a sacrament. It provided children with godparents, *copadres* and *comadres* whose role in an Andalucian child's life was nearly as important as that of its own parents. In becoming a godparent a person assumed what was effectively a blood relationship with the child with almost all the powers and responsibilities of a real parent. Even for the most defiant unbeliever it was unthinkable for a child to grow up in Andalucía without them, and they lay exclusively in the church's gift. Marriage in a country without divorce was another of its monopolies. Burial completed the cycle.

One afternoon Manolo the dustman came panting up the valley towards the house. Unusually for him he was not only on foot but running. He stopped at the kitchen door and his normally smiling face was grim.

'*Una tragedia, señora,*' he said to Elisabeth.

It was a tragedy indeed. Crossing the road in Algeciras Ana's father had been knocked down and killed by a truck. The funeral took place the next day in the blazing sun of an August morning: for reasons of health Spanish law strictly requires the

237

dead are buried within 48 hours. The ceremony was divided into two parts. During the night the coffin had been placed in the family house, a tiny two-room dwelling in one of Algeciras' poorest *barrios*. As Elisabeth and I walked up the dusty cratered track towards it past fly-blown dogs and scrawny chickens, a clamour filled the air above the low roofs ahead. Unlike the shrill mourning keening of the Moroccans across the straits, the sound was solemn but vigorous.

Turning the corner before the house we saw two lines of facing chairs had been placed in a long narrow funnel leading up to the door. The chairs were occupied by the family's female friends and relations, the most distant taking the furthest seats and the nearest those closest to the house. The men in their blue or grey working overalls stood smoking and talking together beyond. Threading both groups were dozens of running, playing, crying, quarrelling and laughing children. We moved slowly along the funnel offering our sympathy to the women until we reached the door. Inside, Ana's mother was sitting by the coffin surrounded by her daughters and the two grandmothers. Like the women outside they were all dressed in black. Their faces were drawn with grief and the tears flowed, but there was no ostentation in the sorrow, only strength and resolution.

After Elisabeth had embraced them and I had shaken hands we went outside. We had been delayed by a puncture on the way down and the men had been waiting for our arrival. As we stepped back into the sun the chairs were drawn aside and the men went into the house to bring out the coffin. The women had no further part to play. While they stayed behind the men carried the coffin down the track and long the road to the church. We walked with them. Elisabeth's presence was accepted without comment because, as Ana explained afterwards with typical Andaluz courtesy and the imaginative sympathy which is the other side to Andaluz insularity: 'Everyone knew that in your *pueblo* it must be customary and proper.' The service was short and simple. While the priest committed the soul of Ana's father to his maker, the men knelt or stood with bowed heads, caps clasped in their hands, shuffling occasionally, their faces sombre and pensive.

Afterwards, with the service over, the congregation filed out into the street. There they soon dispersed. There were no more formalities to be observed. The mortal remains of their dead companion would be taken to the municipal cemetery. His spirit had been entrusted to God. They had done their duty. Now it was back to work leaving the bereaved family, its chief breadwinner gone, to struggle as best it could although they, as friends, neighbours and members of the same *pueblo*, would do what they could to help.

༤ 16 ༤

ONE HOT JULY morning I was driving across the little plain beyond the Almoreima forest on some errand to Jimena de la Frontera. As the trees ended I saw parked ahead of me by the roadside a gleaming new British-registered Range Rover. I slowed and looked at it. A Range Rover was an unlikely car to find on the remote approaches to the sierras, and this one appeared to have been abandoned. There was no one in sight, the plain was silent and undisturbed in the midday sun, and after a few moments I drove on puzzled. An instant later I had to brake sharply. A man who'd been lurking in the shadows of a cistus bush had suddenly hurled himself out into the middle of the road, and was furiously waving me down.

I swerved into the side and stopped. The man was one of the most remarkable figures I'd ever seen. About 65, he was extremely short, colossally fat, weighed well over 20 stone, and had a bristling halo of long white hair that surrounded a scowling and pugnacious face. Dressed in a high-buttoned black suit he looked like an angry Mr Pickwick who'd somehow been plucked from his Thames-side slumbers and inexplicably dropped by a time-warp into the searing heat of an Andalucian summer's day.

'Carr, J. W.,' he bellowed, leaning in through the window. 'Botanist by inclination, deaf as a post, and bloody nuisance to all concerned. You've got an honest face, which I always distrust, but the car's buggered and I'd be grateful if you could spare a moment.'

Before I could answer he bustled back to the Range Rover, snapped up the lid of its trunk, and started heaving a collection of books, microscopes, plant specimens and gin bottles into the back of my own car.

'Where are you bound for?' he asked heaving himself in beside me. 'Ronda, no doubt. Excellent. Just where I'm headed. We can unload this junk at the hotel. Then on the way back you can take a couple of my miserable penny-pinching accolytes and toss them out at Antequera. Point them up the hill, kick their bums hard, and tell them to concentrate on the *Ranunculus* family. Have a quick snort and we'll be on our way.'

He offered me a bottle of gin which he'd been drinking from through the neck. I refused but I started the car and set off. I wasn't going anywhere near Ronda; Antequera was hours further away still, and the round trip would take the entire day. Somehow, confronted by a J. W. Carr, the abrupt rearrangement of one's plans seemed entirely normal.

Mr Carr-the-botanist, as I soon discovered, was a member of that dwindling species, the great British eccentric. An impoverished schoolmaster in a small Suffolk village, he'd woken one morning and decided that as the world seemed to nourish the rich and the poor equally, there was no good reason why he shouldn't join the ranks of the rich. He examined the commercial possibilities open to a Suffolk teacher, opted for a mail order business and, in due course, helped by his loyal and long-suffering wife, made himself a small fortune. At which stage he was faced with the problem of what he should do with it. For most of his life Mr Carr had been a student of ornithology.

'But the trouble with birds is the little buggers keep moving,' he explained to me. 'Flapping their wings, always on the bloody go, they're never satisfied. If you get as fat as I am, nothing glandular, all happily due to gin, it makes them rather less than lovable. Plants on the other hand tend to stay right where they're put. You can creep up on a plant, pull its petals off, stuff its roots in a bag, kick the little sod to death if you want, and it won't bat an eyelid. For someone like me that's very appealing.'

During the war Mr Carr was serving on a destroyer when his ship was torpedoed by a German U-boat off Gibraltar. As it sank he jumped overboard. Surfacing in the sea he saw two other destroyers standing by to pick up survivors. Both were the same distance away and it was a question of which one to head for. Carr made his decision and struck out. It wasn't a good choice. An hour later the destroyer he'd picked was also torpedoed and for the second time that day he was back in the water. He was eventually saved again and shipped back to Britain. Strangely, his most abiding memory of the day was not the two sinkings but the lush and mysterious Andalucian shoreline he'd glimpsed between the waves as he swam.

With his fortune made and serious bird study ruled out by his ballooning girth, Carr decided to concentrate on botany and to make his life's work the compilation of a distribution atlas of Andalucía's flora – the haunting landscape he'd seen so long ago from the sea. In fact, the scope and range of both Andalucía and the plant kingdom proving in the end too daunting even for Carr, the project was finally limited to the flora of the provinces of Sevilla and Málaga. Within these two great tracts of land that reached from the sea to the high sierras Carr was determined to identify and record every plant, grass and flower. For an elderly English schoolteacher, short-sighted, stone deaf and barely mobile because of his gargantuan weight, it was still an epic task. Carr tackled it by first dividing the region into 10-kilometre squares. Then each year he organized a series of botanical package holidays. Carr would arrive in advance and set up a mobile base-camp in a pair of large caravans complete with reference library, herbarium, scientific equipment, and artists' studio – every species logged which was not already illustrated in the standard European reference works was painted in colour by specially commissioned artists.

Behind Carr at two-weekly intervals came fifteen-strong groups consisting mainly of elderly British amateur botanists, spiced occasionally with an academic. Each morning they'd be transported to a different square and spend the day on foot cataloguing what it contained. Meanwhile Carr would sit in his caravan, a huge brooding presence with a gin bottle in his hand, directing operations. The wretched botanists had paid for their trip and were nominally there on holiday, but he treated them like a slave-driver.

'Higher, you silly old goat, higher!' he'd bellow at the distant silhouette of some grey-haired spinster frantically trying to scramble up a crag. 'There should be some *Oxalis pescaprae* above you. I can damn near see it from here.'

Rude, intemperate and irascible, Carr feuded with everyone from the members of his parties and the local British consul to the University of Sevilla and the Royal Horticultural Society in London. Year by year as his obsession about the atlas grew so did his enemies multiply, at least in Carr's mind, and he became ever more stubborn, provocative and contrary. Yet he was also a rare and, in his own way, a great man. He was a true scholar, a wit, a gourmet, a passionate romantic and a visionary. Apart from wild flowers death, alcohol and learning were his principal preoccupations. Death, of which he was entirely unafraid, hovered constantly about his head. The gin bottles accompanied him everywhere. Learning and scholarship, above all learning that concerned language, were constant delights. A fine academic linguist himself, he was continually frustrated by the deafness which made it difficult for him to communicate through speech. Nonetheless his pleasure in words remained. I'd often come into the caravan to find him chuckling happily over a new dictionary of New York Yiddish street-slang or the argot of a Serbo-Croat farming community.

One spring Mr Carr arrived in Algeciras, his base as on so many occasions in the past, and checked into the Reina Victoria. He told the desk clerk he was heading up the hill to visit us, climbed back into his Range Rover and set off. Midway along the road he pulled into the side. There, quickly and apparently without any pain, he died of the coronary failure he'd predicted for so long. His last sight must have been of the straits where forty years earlier he'd twice escaped drowning and seen Andalucía first. Beside him on the passenger seat were a wild iris, the inevitable bottle and a pile of academic books. Apart from the completion of the distribution atlas, which was taken on by the formerly much-abused University of Sevilla, they were the only memorial he would have wanted.

My own legacy from Carr was an introduction to the extraordinary wealth of Andalucian natural history and wild-life. When he first wedged himself into my car on the Jimena plain, Elisabeth had just tentatively returned to painting which she'd studied until our marriage and the arrival of six children in almost successive years had temporarily put paid to it. Carr, discovering what she was capable of, promptly bullied and cajoled her into joining the artists who were painting the flora for him. For both of us, in Elisabeth's case much more certainly than my own, Carr's appearance in our lives opened a window on to botany. It also pushed wider open still, because in spite of his grumbling protestations about his bulk Carr remained an

interested and informed ornithologist, another window already and inevitably ajar – a window on to Andalucía's birds. The inevitability came from the Huerto Perdido's site above the straits.

Twice every year, in spring and autumn, millions of birds migrate from Africa to breed in Europe, and then as the summer wanes return south again. They range in size from tiny warblers to storks and eagles. Most species, whatever their size, prefer to make as much of the flight as possible above land, using the narrowest channels wherever they're forced to cross the sea. In the case of larger birds, notably the birds of prey, a narrow sea-channel is essential. Heavily dependent for flight on the buoyant warm air thermals that only form over land, they can seldom survive for long above an ocean. Without the lift provided by thermals they lose height, tire and quickly plane down to be drowned in the waves. Accordingly the broad migrant front, sweeping up across Africa or returning over Europe, splits into two narrow and densely concentrated bands as it approaches the Mediterranean. One band heads for the Bosphorus; the other, for the Straits of Gibraltar. On the far side in either direction the concentrations dissolve and the flocks ripple out laterally again.

The Huerto Perdido, at the centre of the straits, stood immediately below the western flight-path in its shortest and most crowded sector. Day and night from March to October the sky above the house was a tumultuous flickering highway for unending caravans of aerial passengers. Some species crossed the sea regardless of weather, sun or darkness. Others, mainly the birds of prey again, were more demanding. They needed not only a short sea-crossing, but sun and an absence of wind, sun to raise the thermals and a lack of wind to allow them to glide the channel without being buffeted back. Often, to the frustration of visiting ornithologists, the straits were troubled in mid-migration for days on end by cloud, *levante* and rain. Whenever that happened the migrant flocks, unable to move, would build up like damned water on the far shore. Then one morning the sky would clear, the sun emerge, and the pent-up birds, suddenly released, would cascade out across the sea-lane.

The best place to watch the migration from the Guadalmesi was on the shore at the valley's foot. During a major raptor passage, a day of irruption after a spell of cloud and wind, Africa seemed to be shackled to Europe by innumerable ropes of beating eagles. Reaching the near shore the ropes appeared to sag as the exhausted birds glided down, swirling in only a few feet above my head. Then, as they searched for and found new thermals on the Spanish coast, they'd start to soar again, winding laboriously upwards until they gained enough height above the forest to spiral away and disperse in the sierras. The southern movement from the late summer onwards could be even more spectacular if, as frequently happened, a head-wind was blowing from out of Africa. One September I drove westwards beyond Tarifa and got out to walk in the pastures between the hills and the sea. One of the fiercest *levantes* I can remember was blowing across the straits. The wind was so strong that the returning migrant birds were forced down to within a few feet of the ground. Exhausted after their journey south and struggling to avoid being blown into the ground they ignored me. For an hour I walked through waves of eagles, hawks, falcons, kites and harriers, so close to them that again and again their wing-tips brushed my shoulders and their glittering topaz eyes gazed from inches away into mine.

Another year there was thick cloud over the straits for several weeks at the time of the storks' movement north. When the weather finally cleared and the passage took place, the birds made an uninterrupted arc across the sky 22 miles in length. As they dropped to rest briefly in Andalucía they covered the pastures like a snowfall. Field after field was turned white, with an occasional bull rising like a black island amid waves of surf. Among the larger birds the most notice-able during the migration through sheer weight of numbers is the scavenging V-tailed black kite – the more elegant and less common red kite is a resident – followed by the booted eagle in its two phases, dark and light. But with time and a little luck

the keen birdwatcher can see a whole spectrum of other, often rare species including the black vulture, Egyptian vulture, black-winged kite, golden eagle (some species often thought of as wholly resident are occasionally forced to migrate by competition for territory), osprey, and even, as I did once, an imperial eagle.

Although the autumn and spring crossings are the best known and most dramatic of Andalucía's bird sights, the whole region is a cornucopia for ornithologists. The reasons are its natural richness, the diversity of habitats that include coastal marsh, lagoon, open plain, scrubland, hill and high montane forest, and the relative lack of human interference with the landscape. Many adaptable species are widespread throughout most of the region. Others with more specific requirements are localised. After a time I began to learn that every part of Andalucía nurtured or harboured its own singular speciality. In the rolling parkland countryside near Andujar, a blend of meadow and pine, there were always azure-winged magpies. On the grass plains beyond Tarifa, great bustards with their astonishing spring courtship display, when the males seem to turn upside down and transform themselves into quivering umbrellas of black, white and chestnut-coloured feathers. On the shore below Tarifa itself, the occasional passing greater flamingo, or perhaps a group of them standing pink-legged and improbable on the sand. At the Cape of Trafalgar, Audouin's gull and the roseate tern, one with a scarlet yellow-tipped bill and the other with a pink blush on its breast and a long forked tail. Along the Sevilla motorway, black-winged kites perched on telephone poles; rainbow-coloured rollers round Jimena de la Frontera; dazzling bee-eaters nesting in colonies in the hills behind. The list is almost endless. Andalucía even has birds that officially don't exist in mainland Europe.

One August evening I was sitting on the patio of a house overlooking a river near Algeciras. In the early dusk I noticed a group of half a dozen birds hawking the air above the water for insects. They were clearly falcons but ones I'd never seen before. After a while I decided they could only be Eleonora's falcon, although when I checked the reference books they all

Bee-eaters

stated firmly the species was unknown there. Finally I consulted a neighbour, a veteran and expert ornithologist, and found he'd seen the birds and also identified them unmistakeably as Eleonora's falcon. The most likely explanation for their appearance, he suggested, was they were nesting on the African coast and something had interfered with their local food supply. In order to support their young they'd been forced to cross the straits and fly a hundred miles every day to hunt.

As well as its prodigal bird populations Andalucía supports a rich and diverse range of other forms of wildlife. The most noticeable are its mammals. The native brown bear of the sierras, although still surviving in some other mountainous areas of Spain, was an early casualty of human colonisation. The next significant loss was the wolf, which again precariously clings on in a few remote parts of the country. In *South From Granada*, his account of the years he spent in the Alpujarras during the twenties, Gerald Brenan tells how caged wolves, trapped nearby, were regularly brought down and exhibited in the villages. The last known Andalucian wolf was shot not long afterwards, before the Civil War, in the marshes south of Sevilla, where it had strayed from the sierra in search of prey during a hard winter. Most of the region's other indigenous animals were still thriving, at least when we first came to Guadalmesi. In the valley the commonest and most striking were the two European members of the carnivorous family, *Viverridae*, the Egyptian mongoose, and the genet, *Genetta genetta*.

Both used to be considered relic populations, descendants of native animals left behind when Africa parted from Europe. More recently zoologists have decided neither of the two are indigenous and both were introduced. The evidence, scanty at best, seems to me to be evenly balanced either way. I tend towards the earlier view for no good reason other than that both species seem perfectly fitted to the climax community of the valley's cork-oak forest. The genet, a sinuous and graceful cat-like creature with a smoke-grey coat dappled with black spots, is wary and nocturnal. A ferocious and efficient hunter, often trapped for its pelt, it reminded me of a tiny, shadowy leopard. The mongoose, in contrast, is a creature of daylight. I used to see it often as I walked the forest when, bold and inquisitive, it would rise on its hindlegs and inspect me fearlessly as I passed. When the females have young, the maternally-led family travel like centipedes, their eyes closed and their noses pressed into the rectum of the animal in front — a habit which gives them their Andaluz country name of 'politicians'. Intrepid, aggressive, hard-muscled and heavily built, a mature male can weight up to 28 pounds, and its strength, as I once discovered, is remarkable.

One evening Gaspar, the herder of the dubiously owned pigs whose boar had leapt through the bedroom window, arrived at the house with the news that a wounded and unidentified *bicho* had been delivered to the Mesón de Sancho. I hurried down with him to the roadhouse to find a cluster of the valley's inhabitants warily prodding a large cardboard carton. It was dark and the box had been placed in a dimly lit shed. Shining a lamp inside I made out two huge and defiant orange eyes above a pair of talons each of which could have spanned my face, locked into a hastily-cut section of oak branch.

Eagle Owl

'I was out hunting, Don Nicholas,' an anxious voice from the group explained. 'The *bicho* got up in front of me from a tree. I fired, thinking it was a partridge. Then I realized it was something else.'

The *bicho*, the beast, as everyone there must have known, was an eagle owl, the largest of the world's owls with a five-foot wingspan and capable of taking young deer as prey. For an Andalucian countryman to have confused it with a partridge was about as likely as an experienced plane-spotter mistaking a Boeing for a hang-glider. The young peasant must have fired with his eyes shut, the bird had tumbled, and then, because all owls were potent, mysterious and menacing creatures, rather than killing it he'd brought it in panic to the Mesón. I examined the bird. Its wing was broken but apart from that it seemed to be in reasonable condition. Gaspar and I put a splint on the fractured bone and carried the owl back to the house.

For a month as the wing mended it lived in one of the guest rooms, perched on the lowered clothes' rail of a high walk-in closet. Then we moved it a room-sized cage I had built by the Tarifa carpenter, Ramón, in an outhouse below the bedroom patio. Every night I fed the owl by hand with raw chunks of rabbit or pigeon including the fur and feathers needed to help its digestive system form pellets. Feeding time was an awesome and unnerving experience. As I walked into the cage the two orange globes of its eyes would blaze out at me through the darkness, the owl's beak would snap repeatedly with a sound like a slamming door, and its feathers would bristle out, making its size appear to be doubled. Then, still snapping and bristling, it would start to bob and sway, lashing its head from side to side. I was an intruder and it was using all the most intimidating gestures at its command to frighten me away. Moving very slowly I would come forward until I was close enough to avoid an attack from the talons which were quite capable of stripping most of the flesh from my face. Finally, stroking its breast with one hand and lifting up the meat with the other, I would give it its meal.

251

Four months later I found myself in what seemed to be an unresolvable quandary. The owl's wing had healed and it appeared to have regained the ability to fly. It could plane down from its perch to the cage's floor and then beat back up again. Flying twelve feet across a cage was very different from the distance it would have to cover hunting wild in the forest. There was no means of judging the owl's capabilities. Setting it free might mean restoring the owl fit and whole to its natural environment; on the other hand if the wing bone had been permanently damaged, it would simply be condemning the bird to a squalid and lingering death from starvation. The problem was made even more difficult by its species. There were so few eagle owls left that every individual was important. It wasn't possible to gamble on its survival as I'd done with other more common birds I'd released in similar circumstances. In the end, and very reluctantly, I decided to send it to the Madrid zoo where it might at least breed with one of the other eagle owls already there. Sadly – the owl was the most magnificent creature I'd ever known and it belonged to the valley – I made ready for its departure. Then, the very night before it was due to leave, two things happened.

The bird had been wounded in December. By then it was early April and the start of the breeding season. As dusk fell another eagle owl, which could only have been the captive's mate, began to call to it from the forest. The caged owl answered and for hour after hour the valley rang with their deep booming cries. I went to bed anguished, trying to shut the calls out of my head, but still convinced that what I'd decided was right. In the morning Gaspar arrived to help me crate the bird up and we walked down to the cage together. There we stopped bewildered. A great hole had been smashed in the cage's side and the owl had gone. No bird could have made the hole – at my request Ramón had built the cage so strongly it was even proof against Gaspar's mighty pigs. There was no sign of a fight. If a human had been involved he would simply have unbolted the door. Whatever had happened seemed inexplicable. Gaspar and I started to search.

Over the past few weeks it had as usual rained heavily, and the ground outside the outhouse into which the cage was built had been turned into a flat sheet of mud. Twenty minutes later, interpreting prints left on the mud and other signs in the cage itself, we had the answer. After the owl's wing had healed and while I'd still hoped to release it, I'd given up feeding the bird by hand. Instead, I'd leave a dead pigeon or rabbit on the cage floor so the owl could fly down and take the prey itself, re-accustoming it to the conditions it would have had to face again in the forest. As its farewell meal in the Huerto the evening before I'd left a particularly plump rabbit. Normally the bird fed quickly and hungrily. When I'd visited it for the final time before going to bed I noticed the rabbit was untouched. For once the owl, presumably tense and unsettled by the presence of its mate calling in the forest, had ignored its meal.

During the night a hunting mongoose must have scented the rabbit. It had entered the outhouse and done what I had thought was impossible – smashed the wooden frame, dragged down the wire, and battered its way into the cage. Then beneath the eyes of the no doubt still preoccupied owl, it had picked up the rabbit and carried it out, eating it later in the *monte* beyond. The mongoose's tracks were unmistakable as too were the distinctively-barred shreds of fur left behind on the wire. Afterwards the owl had swooped down from its perch and walked out through the hole the mongoose had made. For a few moments it had paced across the mud – the spoor of its talons was equally unmistakable. Then it had spread its wings and drifted away towards the stars.

Gaspar, my co-trustee of the owl from the start, had shared all of my anxieties over what to do about the bird as its wing healed.

'You should never have worried, Don Nicholas,' he said as, the puzzle resolved, we both gazed down over the valley in the April sunlight. 'Left to themselves, matters resolve themselves. The choice was never yours to make. The mongoose got his supper and the *bicho*'s free again. *Se acabó la cosa* – the matter's ended.'

253

It hadn't quite. Later in the summer an immensely excited birdwatcher came up to the house, where he'd been sent from the Mesón de Sancho. He'd made his lifetime's discovery – he'd found a successfully nesting pair of eagle owls. One of the pair, the larger female, had a wing that seemed to be slightly deformed. Was I, according to the Mesón the local authority on the valley's birds, aware they were there? For an instant I hesitated. I thought of the December evening, the figures clustered round the crate, the nervous voice explaining why the shot was fired, the long winter nights when the magnificent creature with its burning sunset eyes had perched inside the cage as the broken wing mended; and then of the mongoose's intervention only hours before the owl started a lifetime's incarceration in Madrid. Finally I shook my head, smiled and said only I was delighted to hear eagle owls were still breeding in the valley.

Perhaps the richest area in Andalucía not only for birds but for most other forms of its wildlife is the now internationally known Coto Doñana reserve. As the Guadalquivir river approaches the sea south-west of Sevilla it spreads out in a huge swampy delta known generally as *las marismas*, the marshes. Parts of the delta are permanently under water, parts flood seasonally after the winter rains, and parts consist of large 'islands' of wood, plain and pasture. The soil everywhere is exceptionally rich and as a result the delta's human history is extremely ancient. Some classical texts record it as the site of the legendary city of Tartessus, and the area successively formed part of the Etruscan, Phoenician, Greek and Roman civilisations, none of which left any significant print of their presence. In 1294 Sancho IV gave part of the delta to Guzman the Good in gratitude for his defence of Tarifa against the Moors. By then it was already noted as a royal hunting ground. Guzman was also rewarded with the title of Duke of Medina Sidona.

Three hundred years later his descendant, the seventh duke, re-acquired the land which by then had passed from the hands of the family into the ownership of the village council of

Almonte. The seventh duke was married to a daughter of the Princess of Eboli. The Princess was a bold, attractive and ambitious woman who carried on a number of liaisons at court and even intrigued against the king, Philip II. Outraged by her mother's behaviour her daughter, Ana, retired to the remote delta estate where her husband built her a retreat named El Palacio. In the course of her time there, Ana's name and title – she was known formally as Doña Ana – were abbreviated by the locals into Doñana, giving the land and the modest palace the name by which they are still known. The palace, rebuilt in 1624, was visited at the end of the eighteenth century by Goya whose portrait of the new owner's wife, the Duchess of Alba, hangs in the rooms of the Spanish Society of America in New York. At the same time he may, or may not, have used the Duchess as a model for his two great works, now in the Prado in Madrid, the naked and the clothed *maja*. Most outsiders would consider it a signal honour to count among their ancestors an extraordinarily beautiful woman who one of the world's finest painters chose to portray not merely once but twice, the second time in all the glory of her nakedness. The Andaluz, not least the Duchess's descendants, see the matter very differently. The question is constantly and passionately debated, and the suggestion she was Goya's model almost always bitterly repudiated. It is almost impossible to reach a final answer but on balance I tend to believe she was – if only because the mood of those two superb studies accords so well with the brilliance of the Coto's spring landscape, and Goya was there in the spring, beyond the Palacio's walls.

Just over a hundred years later the Coto Doñana experienced another era of splendour when the Duke of Tarifa, to whom it then belonged, renovated the Palacio and invited the king, the mournful Alfonso XIII, to hunt. Alfonso thought the Coto's deer, bear and birds provided the finest sport in Europe, and returned there again and again. Yellowing photographs of his hunting parties still line the Palacio's hall and corridors. With the outbreak of the Civil War the whole delta reverted to the wilderness it had been for most of its history. Then in 1961 a concerned Spanish scientist, Dr José Valverde, seeing the devastating effect on the *marismas* of development round Sevilla, set out to try to save the Coto as a largely self-contained ecological unit. His efforts coincided with the foundation of the World Wildlife Fund. With the fund's financial support a part of Doña Ana's original estate was bought on behalf of the Spanish people, and a reserve created. The reserve was enlarged and its status changed by governmental decree to that of a National Park in 1969. Since then it has been enlarged further still. In Doña Ana's time the Coto, which loosely means 'park', consisted of about 56,000 acres. Today the reserve with its buffer-zones covers 155,000 acres.

What in my experience is one of the wonders not just of Andalucía or even Spain but of all Europe is not at first sight very prepossessing; at least not to those who think of wilderness landscapes as rugged and dramatic. The most immediately noticeable feature of the Coto Doñana is its monotonous flatness, a level plain that seems to be resting precariously on dirty brown marsh-water. In winter the cold can be chilling, in summer the heat is torrid and merciless, in spring the air often dank and heavy. Drab grey scrub seems to cover most of the exposed terrain, the riverways look dark and sullen, and spirals of dust and sand swirl through the air. For the unprepared a first visit to the Coto can be bewildering – Doña Ana's park looks like a wasteland. Then as the eye adjusts to the landscape it quickly registers something quite different. The entire place, every bush, sand-pit, pool, lagoon and stretch of plain, even the sky above, is churning with wildlife. There are great herds of deer and wild boar, foxes, otters, genets, mongooses, wild cat, the last of Europe's pardel lynxes, even the occasional half-feral camel – introduced from north Africa, shunned by the locals as the devil's beast, and still stubbornly reproducing itself. The ground beneath and between the scrub is thick with reeds, grasses and flowers, and blanketed by insects. Most striking of all are the birds. Kites, hawks, falcons, vultures and eagles throng the air – the last few pairs of the Spanish imperial eagle survive on the marshes. Flamingoes and

herons crowd the pools and lagoons. Bee-eaters breed in great colonies in the sand-banks. Flights of duck are constantly beating down or planing up from the lakes. In places, clumps of trees are so heavy with nests of egrets and spoonbills their branches are collapsing beneath the weight. Hundreds of thousands, even millions, of smaller birds, warblers, larks, thrushes and finches, make the undergrowth clamour and vibrate.

The extravagant wealth of the Coto's life owes its existence to the deposit-enriched silt along the delta's waterways. Plants root and blossom prodigally. The plants nurture insects and support the grass-eaters. Insects and herbivores in their turn supply the ascending layers in the food-chain up to the lynxes and eagles, and beyond them to the vultures – among the noblest and most important of all birds. Like the world's other great deltas, the Camargue at the Rhone's mouth in France or Lake Ngami in the Kalahari, the Guadalquivir basin functions like a gigantic bellows, filling and contracting seasonally. After the winter rains the waters ripple out to irrigate and fertilize the raised banks and islands. Multitudes of birds then descend to nest and breed, drawn not only by the food supplies above the surface but those below – the spawning frogs, fish and larvae. When the water evaporates in summer and the marsh plains dry out to mud-caked flats, the birds head south. As winter comes other species replace them, duck and geese driven from their northern range by snow and arriving to crop the permanent pasture-land. With the spring's return the pattern is reversed. The breeding birds come back from Africa, the northern ducks and geese head towards the Arctic to rear their own broods, and the cycle starts again.

Until a few years ago a trip to the Coto Doñana was what the reserve's own information rightly described as: 'Something to be undertaken only after careful preparation and even then to be regarded in the light of an adventure.' Our expeditions there from the valley usually involved a two or three-night stay, and planning started several weeks in advance. First there was accommodation. The Palacio, which had become the reserve's HQ in the centre of the marshes, kept a few small bedrooms for visitors. There was no telephone, so bookings had to be made through the Doñana's tiny and unpredictably-open office in Sevilla. Then another set of arrangements had to be made to enter the reserve – the Palacio was an hour's hazardous drive on a track across the *marismas* from a locked boundary gate beside a keeper's cottage. The keeper was often away herding bulls. In his absence the gate's key could be found under a certain rock or flower-pot. His cottage was surrounded by innumerable rocks and flower-pots. If the position of the right one wasn't precisely understood, a Coto expedition could be stalled outside the gate for forty-eight hours or more.

Finally there was the provisioning for the trip. The Palacio's kitchen staff were a willing local couple from the marshes. They would do their best, heating up pre-cooked dishes or making simple omelettes from eggs that also had to be brought in, but they had no supplies of their own to prepare and sell. Most visitors, guided by the reserve's warning advice, arrived with the barest of iron rations. The parties from the Guadal-mesi, particularly after the staff became friends, adopted an entirely different approach. A Doñana expedition was not a survival course but a celebration. Its food should echo the splendours of the wild. For days beforehand Elisabeth, normally in company with our neighbours Milet and Cristi, both fine ornithologists and frequent companions on the trips, would prepare meals to be eaten in the Palacio. All three were outstanding cooks. The evening before an expedition set out, the cars and Land Rovers were loaded with fragrant-smelling pots, casseroles, baskets, hampers and crates. The convoy left the valley at dawn. On the way to Sevilla we paused at Chiclana for breakfast, thick black coffee, freshly made and mouth-watering sugared *churros*, and a belly-warming glass of sweet raw *anís*. Beyond Sevilla the road circled west. There was a stop at the keeper's cottage for the hidden key, a bone-shaking ride into the *marismas*, and finally the arrival at the rambling white and ochre palace, a spacious but unpretentious dwelling for the sixteenth-century noblewoman who'd chosen to live in the wilderness. That night, after a day's intoxicating experience of the Coto's water, flowers, deer, wild boar and spiralling columns of birds, we'd feast in Doña Ana's dining-hall, as she must have done herself, on a goose stuffed with a guinea-fowl stuffed with a partridge accompanied by the red wine of Rioja.

Since then the Doñana has undergone considerable changes. Some, notably the extension of the protected areas and buffer zones in 1979, have been welcome. Others are less happy. After the retirement of its founder, Dr Valverde, the reserve went through a long period of uncertain management. Today the Palacio is closed to visitors and the most people see is what they manage to glimpse through the windows of a Land Rover during a short guided drive over one small section of the reserve. It is a sorry substitute for days of walking, watching and listening, and long evenings beside the Palacio's log fires. The present régime is explained by shortage of funds, as with many reserves a longstanding difficulty, and an understandable wish to limit direct human impact on the marshes. Unfortunately there is a much greater threat to the Coto's survival than lack of money or the pressure of visitors, which in any event is negligible. The fragile ecology of the *marismas* depends upon water and the water is inexorably disappearing, being lost outside the reserve to industry, tourism, development, and in drainage programmes. If the flow along the Guadalquivir's arteries is allowed to dry up the Coto Doñana will collapse and die of its own accord, whatever its theoretical status as part of the nation's and the world's heritage. The issue, in the end a political one, will be decided by public opinion formed largely, on one side, by those who've seen and experienced the Doñana's magic. The reserve's management does not have an easy task. But until it can devise a better and more rewarding policy for visitors, the weight of public opinion it so desperately needs behind it will be difficult to acquire.

The problem of the vanishing water is not the Doñana's alone. It crops up again and again all over Andalucía. A map of the region drawn by the nineteenth-century sportsmen and naturalists Chapman and Buck, the American consul in Sevilla and his British companion who described their exploits in a number of books, would look very different today. They were chiefly interested in hunting waterfowl and many of their favourite haunts – lagoons, estuaries and rivers – have either disappeared altogether or shrunk beyond recognition. During our years in the valley we witnessed a significant change even in the Guadalmesi. When we first arrived the valley supported otters. Five years later the last was shot by Domingo and otters never returned. The reason was not the pressure of local hunters but the drop in the level of the river. As the valley was gradually developed and buildings grew up along the coastal road, more and more water was drawn for domestic use. The fall in the level of the Guadalmesi had already driven out the straggling little human community along its banks. Now it was dispossessing the wildlife too.

There are many other pressures on Andalucía's birds and animals. Poison, still randomly scattered on the hillsides, takes a terrible toll on foxes. During the spring and autumn migration, hundreds of thousands of small birds are trapped by decoys. A caged bird surrounded by nets of lime is left out in the open – the reaches round Tarifa were a noted hunting-ground. When the migrant flocks settle, drawn down by the caged bird's song, they either smear themselves on the limed twigs or get caught in the nets. Hundreds of thousands more are killed throughout the year for food. Approaching a little village in any month it is common to see an old woman or a child step forward from the roadside and hold up a garland of dead robins or larks for sale. *Pajarritos*, little birds fried and eaten whole, bones and all, are available as a *tapa* in most country *ventas*. Land clearance for prairie-farming through mechanized agriculture is an even greater threat. Mile after mile of ancient mixed habitat is uprooted and swept away, and the ground beneath given over to a leading monoculture.

Several species have already disappeared. As well as the wolf and the bear, the lynx can probably be considered extinct – at least biologically extinct in the sense that the surviving individuals are too few to form a successful breeding population. Europe's largest vulture, the lammergeier or bearded vulture with its distinctive habit of dropping bones from a height onto rock to crack them for their marrow, clung on in the sierras until the early 1960s. Then it retreated from Andalucía. The massive black vulture may well have gone too. The outlook even for the griffon, one of the sierras' most enduringly familiar sights, is bleak. Like the wolf it seems to need a large range and a network of associated family groups to survive. Improved veterinary medicine has meant a steep decline in stock mortality and consequently in the availability of carrion. Coupled with all the other accelerating changes in Andalucian land use, it has made the griffon's traditional hold precarious. The future for the Egyptian vulture looks equally gloomy, and the Doñana's imperial eagle may well be no more than a living museum piece.

Although the view ahead for much of Andalucía's wildlife is dark, it is far from being uniformly black. In contrast to many other more remote and apparently less vulnerable wildernesses like the Kalahari plateau, Andalucía has its built-in defences –

the valleys, crags, ravines and hidden table-lands of the sierras. Below the hills the countryside will continue to be cleared, the rivers drained, the concrete spread, and intensive agriculture increased. Whole ecological shelves will vanish and so will the communities of flowers, insects, birds and animals that used them as their larder. Higher up many other species, however diminished in numbers, will hold on. The most sophisticated modern technology hasn't yet begun to solve the problem of expanding human territory vertically, or even up the slopes the mountain ibex, *Capra hispanica*, would consider no more than a gentle gradient. Until it does a wide range of plants and creatures, possibly more diverse than anywhere else in Europe, will continue to have a sanctuary.

At the same time Andaluz attitudes to the wild, which means no more than the living landscape they share with every other organism it supports, are changing. The most important instrument of change has inevitably been the much-abused medium of television. For several years in the mid-1970s the state-controlled network broadcast an excellent series of wild-life films produced by a passionately-committed conservationist, a former dentist named José Luis Rodriquez de la Fuente. Rodriguez de la Fuente was impressively bearded, bold, articulate, and a superb communicator who died in a plane crash at the peak of his success. He was the first person to show a mass audience of the Spanish people that the country's wildlife was as much a cause for pride and preservation as the paintings of Velasquez or Goya; and to warn them of the dangers it faced. One Sunday evening after one of his series finished Juani came up to my study on her return from a weekend visit to her uncle's little farm beyond Tarifa.

'His donkey died on Friday,' she told me. 'Usually it would have been taken to the lime-pits or sold to the agent at the abbattoir. But my uncle dragged it out into the *campo* and left it there for the vultures. During the weekend there were about forty of them on the carcass. Many people from the *pueblo* came to watch.'

A few years earlier the reaction of the average Andaluz

262

towards a vulture, or any other bird, would have been to find a gun and shoot it. The idea of pulling into the fields a carcass that might at least have been worth a few *duros* from the slaughterhouse would have been inconceivable. After Rodrigues de la Fuente's programme Juani's uncle had taken the animal's body out unprompted.

Juani's normally pale and puckered little face was flushed with pleasure as she finished the story. She had good reason to be pleased. The television series and her uncle's response to them meant Andalucía's wildlife has abundant hope yet.

WHEN I FIRST saw the Andalucian landscape along the Straits
of Gibraltar on that bright summer morning in 1963 with
caravans of eagles migrating overhead and dolphins leaping in
the sea below, the Guadalmesi valley was an almost untouched
scoop of green cork forest in the hilly shoreline. The coastal
road that crossed it was narrow, cratered with potholes, and
largely deserted apart from the occasional mule-train or an
ancient grinding fish truck which left a snail's track of slime
and melting ice in its wake. At one end of the sea-lane Algeciras
was an uncompromisingly sturdy and cheerful working port,
with its neighbour across the bay, the sleeping British lion of
Gibraltar, selling reliable kippers and echoing to the sound of
military bugle calls. At the other the walled town of Tarifa,
'most loyal and most noble', was a little lost enclave, half
Moorish and half Andaluz, where the older women wore Arab
veils, the windy streets smelled of coriander and sea-salt, and
from the upper floor of every other house, it seemed, came the
demented wailing of some deformed and inbred child.

Twenty years later Tarifa's women have lost their veils but
otherwise the little town is unchanged. Almost everywhere else
the landscape has been transformed. In the upper half of the
valley, Rochford Scott's 'romantic dell', unaltered until the
1960s since his visit 130 years earlier, metalled roads overhung
by cold sodium street lamps spear through the trees. Tracts of
the forest, the supposedly sacrosanct Patrimonio National,
have been hacked down with the approval of the state in the
interests of development. The spiny rosin-scented maquis,

once brimming with birds and butterflies and brilliant in spring with flowers, has gone, and rows of trim villas with large gleaming cars in their driveways are rising from the cleared earth. The waters of the Guadalmesi have dwindled to a trickle. The old coastal road has become a major highway along which day and night roar convoys of giant container trucks. Gibraltar is still partially blockaded in spite of years of negotiations between Britain and Spain. Algeciras is almost unrecognisable.

Approaching Algeciras from the east by car at night is like driving through an inferno. For mile after mile the bay is lined with oil refineries, steel plants, paper mills and textile factories. Huge derricks and towering structures of metal and concrete rear up into the darkness, blazing with lights several hundred feet above the ground. Pillars of fire from burning waste gases rim the horizon and the air is thick with oily black smoke and the stench of sulphur. Some of the streams and rivers that run into the bay are polluted with such high concentrations of industrial acid waste that the remaining local villagers can no longer ford them on foot. After a few crossings the poisoned water eats away the stout leather of their *campo* boots. Even the migrating birds have been forced to change their million-year-old routes, circling to east or west to avoid the rising clouds of discharge.

Further to the east beyond the Campo de Gibraltar the resorts of the Costa del Sol have fused into one unbroken belt of concrete. Beyond Málaga further east still the coastal plain is being transformed by the application of 'controlled climate' agricultural techniques, through which higher-yielding crops can be raised by cultivation under plastic tenting. For miles on end along the coast the landscape appears year-round to be covered in drifts of dirty snow. To the west round Huelva, another smoke-bleared and flame-lit Algeciras, even more advanced scientific methods are being used. Borrowing from pioneering Israeli hydroponic technology, a variety of crops including citrus fruits are now being grown in heavy sand on land that has always been considered not merely marginal but dead. Throughout Andalucía the migration from the country-side to the cities, for long the cause of one of Spain's most serious social problems, has intensified as, amid increasing bitterness, the huge ranches are mechanized and turned over to cereal monoculture, throwing the casual farm labourers out of jobs they have considered their inheritance and right for several hundred years.

The changes have inevitably been reflected in the lives of those we knew in the Guadalmesi. Ana married her glum *novio*, Juan the iron-worker, and moved back into the *barrio* in Algeciras where she was born. Juan then discovered there was much more money to be earned in the construction industry. Overnight he abandoned the craft he had spent years learning and became a hard-hat labourer. Our gardener, the courteous bespectacled José, did the same. Marrying the beautiful sempstress Juana, his *novia* of twelve years, he left the beloved farm where he'd grown up on the spur in the middle of the valley, moved into town, and became a mixer of cement for the extension to the refinery. Juani, Ana's prim and worried 'fallen' cousin, made to my surprise the boldest break of all with the past. As a grown woman of 27 she'd meekly accepted her peasant parents' refusal to allow her to come to Britain with us for a month's summer holiday. Five years later she'd set up house with a married professional man, borne him a child, trained as a nurse in an old people's home, and become the staff's union organizer.

The changes, particularly the industrialisation of Algeciras Bay, had started before 1978 when the forty years of the Franco régime came to an end, but they accelerated dramatically almost from the moment of his death. His prolonged death itself had a bizarre and pagan quality like the passing of some ancient mighty warlord who, whatever their differences, somehow embodied the spirit of all the tribes he had ruled so ruthlessly and for so long. For day after day, unconscious, barely breathing, wasted almost to a skeleton, he clung to life with the same stubbornness he'd shown throughout his years of power. As the end approached the tension throughout the country, the awareness that something vast and charged with unknown portents was happening, became almost tangible. One morning I saw old Curra, the valley's witch, trudging up through the trees with two heavy baskets in her hand.

'Where are you going?' I asked her.

'Up there,' she pointed at the hills behind the Cabrito ridge. 'I'm hiding enough to last me for a month in the same place I used during the Movimiento. You'd be wise to do the same, Don Nicholas. They won't be able to find us in the sierras.'

All that day a stream of peasants from the valley passed the house carrying supplies to hide in caches in the hills. It was happening throughout the Andalucian countryside. Until then, time might have blurred the memories of the horrors of the Civil War, but the defiant death-bed struggle of the old man in Madrid had brought them back as vivid and chilling as they had ever been.

If his funeral after the end eventually came was an accurate omen, the future for the various Spains was to be as bitter and blood-soaked as the darkest of the country people's recollections of the war. The faces of the mourners gathered outside the immense tomb in the Valle de los Caidos, the nationalist war memorial in 'The Valley of the Fallen', were convulsed by a welter of passions that ranged from grief and despair through raging anger to a terrible unfocussed desire for vengeance as if Franco's death had been caused not by time but by his and their enemies. They did not so much sing the nationalist war hymns as at first chant and then bay them. When the gates finally closed on the coffin the crowds' response, relayed across the country by television in images of violence and hysteria, belonged not to modern Europe or even to modern history. It surged up in a tide of implacable frenzy for Spain's remote past. The mourners were neither acknowledging a death nor celebrating a life. Like Viking *berserkers* they were goading themselves into madness for battle.

Fortunately for Spain, the gathering in the Valley of the Fallen, huge as the crowds seemed at the time, was representative of only a tiny proportion of the country as a whole. For once in Spain's history madness failed to prove contagious. It abated, the peasants collected their caches from the hills, and the national life continued, although in a radically different form from before and in spite of periodic attempts to resurrect the past. Within a year of Franco's death the first political meeting to be held in Andalucía for forty years took place in Algeciras. It was addressed by Fraga Irribane, a cabinet minister under Franco who had since become the leader of a 'reformed conservative alliance'. Fraga's speech to the packed audience was bland and cautious. At the end he asked for questions. From one side of the hall a young long-haired architect asked for his undertaking that marijuana would be legalised under a Fraga government. From the other, a local landowner demanded his assurance that the death penalty would be extended to cover all crimes of theft and violence. Fraga was eloquent but noncommittal on both issues. It was an index of the maturity of the new post-Franco Spain that when the meeting ended the audience filed peaceably out into the night, and there was no need to summon the Guardia Civil to separate warring supporters of the two sets of values, which only months before would have been achieved by clubbing the young architect to the ground and escorting the landowner to his car with respectful salutes.

The real nature of Franco's legacy is likely to be debated almost as long and passionately as that of the Moors. His defenders claim that he understood the different Spains better than anyone since the Catholic Kings. He held the country together, gave it an almost unprecedented forty years of peace, virtually abolished crime, raised the people's standard of living to a level unknown in their history, and won time for the wild, impetuous nation to grow up enough to take its place among the western democracies after he died. In direct contrast, his critics charge that he was a man utterly without sympathy or imagination who even failed to grasp that different Spains existed. All he had was a suffocatingly narrow vision of a wilful childlike people who could only be ruled by fear and violence. His régime was oppressive, brutal and corrupt. While his police hounded and tortured the ordinary citizens, his cronies cynically enriched themselves at the country's expense. The famed peace and stability of the Franco years were an illusion. They masked the reality of a nation deprived, as if imprisoned for four decades, of its youth and manhood.

While acknowledging some truth in his defenders' assertions, my own assessment of the Franco era is closer to that of his accusers. I met him only once. He looked, as he always did, like a Soviet newspaper caricature of a capitalist factory manager, tricked up for a fancy-dress party in military uniform, sly, posturing and greedy. There was no aura of the soldier or statesmen about him. He belonged unashamedly to the world of small businessmen, to the fraternity of chemists, grocers, innkeepers and undertakers. He puffed out his chest, strutted forward, stroked his moustache, uttered a few banalities, and vanished amid a clatter of salutes and stamping heels. Chaplin in *The Great Dictator* could not have played his role better. What Franco had was not so much the vision and sense of destiny he has been credited with by friends and enemies alike, as a petty merchant's cunning and boundless self-confidence. In spite of all his sonorous rhetoric he had little real concept of Spain's magnificence, fragility and complexity. He simply saw a country that constantly threatened to fly apart and which in his view needed to be severely disciplined. With his remarkable energy and organisational skills, he set out first to subdue it under God and then to mould it according to his, God's servant's, views.

Andalucía, which as elsewhere in Spain gained its own regional government after Franco's death, emerged from the Franco years on the surface to some extent brutalised and coarsened, as were the other Spains. No proud and free-spirited people could survive four decades of rule by a distant, authoritarian and largely alien government, which appointed local administrators on whim and used the hated para-military Guardia Civil to enforce its laws, without developing a carapace of hardness. At the same time Andalucía had to absorb the impact of mass tourism and, later in the régime, the arrival of industry and advanced technology. Meanwhile, no attempt had been made to tackle the region's crucial problems: the desperate need for land reform and the deadly intransigence of its institutions, failings it shares with the rest of the country.

Yet to a quite extraordinary extent Andalucía survived Franco with its spirit unbroken and its heart unbruised. It had, of course, long experience of outliving remote dictators. Even so the challenge posed by Franco, armoured as so often in the past by the church but this time underpinned by modern communications, weapons and propaganda, was of a different kind from any it had confronted before. Andalucía stared it down. The changes Franco imposed, and the torrent of them that poured in after he died, have inevitably altered its life and landscape as the face of the Guadalmesi valley today shows. They have brought a higher standard of living, measured by hours of leisure and consumer goods, to many Andalucians, but they are far from universally popular in spite of that.

'No, *señor*,' Manolo the La Ahumada dustman said with emphasis when I asked him not long ago if he'd thought of moving into Algeciras. '*Claro*, of course, I could sell my little farm, go to the city and there I would be a rich man. But for what? To be deafened by the trucks, to be choked by the pollution, to have the Guardia Civil as my neighbours, to pay taxes to Madrid? Don Nicholas, it would be madness! I was born in La Ahumada, but I stay here not because it is my birthplace and my *pueblo*. I stay here because I am fortunate.'

Domingo the hunter from further down the valley echoed Manolo's views.

'To live in the *campo* is the only way for a man to live,' he told me. 'Unfortunately to be able to do that it is sometimes necessary to make money in the city first. If I ever went to Algeciras it would be for that one reason only. But as soon as I had the money,' Domingo made a swift chopping gesture with his hand, 'I would be back here in the Guadalmesi like that.'

The saddest reflections on city life came from our gardener, José, who had made the break with the valley on his marriage and moved to Algeciras. He went to live with his wife and two small daughters in a tiny house on the edge of one of the modern developments, balanced uneasily between the old and the new Andalucías.

'It was a terrible mistake,' he said to me unhappily. 'Yet even now I don't know what else I could have done. Here in the city the children have medicine, schools, the chance of another life. I thought it would be a better life. I don't believe so any longer. It's just a different life and *segun yo*, the way I see it, it's not as good as the one with all its problems I had.'

José paused. Then he looked up and smiled.

'Do you remember the owl, Don Nicholas?'

I nodded. José was referring both to the eagle owl we'd had at the Huerto Perdido, and to the birds whose nest he'd watched over as a child in the valley waiting to call his father if they brought back something the family could eat for supper.

'Well, I wish my daughters could have seen those *bichos*,' he went on. 'Maybe they will. Maybe one day I'll be able to take them back to the valley. I hope so. They're Andaluz like me, and like me they belong to the countryside. For us it is the only place to live.'

In conserving and perpetuating the best of their past the Andaluz have two enormous strengths. The first is one of spirit, of doggedness, resilience and tradition. They value their land highly, they know the way it works, and they hold hard to the ancient methods of tilling, seeding and cropping it. On the very summer night when the first sodium lamps were turned on above the newly-metalled roads of El Cuarton, eight hundred yards further down the valley the peasant farmers of the Guadalmesi were winnowing wheat on baked earth floors with the same wooden sleds that had been used by neolithic man thousands of years before. They endure and so do communities like theirs all over Andalucía.

The second strength belongs to the land. Andalucía in this sense is no different from any other part of the planet. Its earth is rich, robust and capable of almost unlimited regeneration. It can be despoiled and wasted, as huge tracts of the region are now, but it has an underlying buoyancy. Leave it alone for a year or two and it springs back to life. Plants colonise it, the *monte* seeps over it, trees invade it, birds and flowers and animals surge back into it. In spite of every attempt by man to pillage and degrade it, Andalucía blossoms again and again with each returning spring. For me its brightest petals show each May in the marshes south of Sevilla.

❧ 18 ❧

IN THE EARLY thirteenth century a hunter from the little village of Almonte was walking through the marshes south of Sevilla when his dog pointed at a thicket. Going forward to investigate he was surprised to find not a game-bird but a carved wooden statue of the Virgin hidden between the tree trunks. He pulled the statue out, lifted it onto his shoulders, and set off to carry it back to Almonte. Half an hour later overcome by the midday heat he stopped to rest and fell asleep with the statue beside him. When he woke he found the Virgin had vanished. The hunter started searching and eventually with the help of his dog found the statue again. It was back in the thicket where he'd first seen it.

By then it was too late to make another attempt to carry it back to Almonte that day. Instead the hunter returned to the village, described what had happened, and came back next morning with a group of companions. When they too tried to remove the Virgin the events of the day before were repeated. They rested midway to Almonte, fell asleep, and woke to find the statue had disappeared. Once again they found it back in the thicket. Thoroughly frightened by then, they hurried back to Almonte and told the story to the village priest. Equally out of his depth the priest issued an order that no one was to touch the Virgin, visited the thicket himself to see her, and then reported the incident to his ecclesiastical superior. The question of what to do about the recalcitrant statue dragged on for years. Finally the Bishop of Sevilla handed down judgement. The Virgin of the marshes, he announced, had chosen the thicket as the place where she wished to be worshipped. She was to be left there and a shrine was to be erected round her.

The shrine was duly built and a tiny settlement grew up beside it. Both the shrine and the settlement were named El Rocío, the dew, after the heavy morning dew that covers the marshes, while the Virgin became known as the Paloma Blanca, the white dove, after the doves that quickly colonized the village. Like a number of other miraculously discovered Spanish Virgins, it seems likely that the statue was hurriedly hidden in the marshes five centuries earlier as news of the Moorish invasion reached Andalucía's Christian communities. Where it came from originally no one knows. According to local legend it was carved in Rome soon after St Peter's arrival and sent from there to Africa to convert the heathen. From Africa it came to Spain to save the Spanish. When Africa's Arabs embraced Islam they were so fearful of the Virgin's power they crossed the straits to take her back. Frustrated by her disappearance, their eight hundred years in Spain were nothing more than a prolonged search to find her again.

Whatever her origins, from the moment of her rediscovery in the marshes the Virgin's magnetism was unquestionable. Not long after the erection of the shrine she became the focus for one of the most popular pilgrimages in Spain, rivalled only by that to the shrine of St James at Santiago de Compostella. In the spring of 1498 Columbus was forced to delay his departure on his third voyage of exploration to the New World because his sailors had gone on the Rocío, as the pilgrimage is colloquially known, and refused to return until it was over. Twenty-one years later Magellan, sailing from the same port at the Guadalquivir's mouth, Sanlúcar de Barrameda, drew strength from the knowledge that his own crew had paid their respects to the Virgin earlier that summer – Magellan left in mid-August and the Virgin's pilgrimage takes place at Whitsun, or Pentecost, in late May or early June.

For 51 weeks of the year Rocío is a ghost town, a little straggle of broad sand-covered streets and empty houses, silvery and garlanded with flocks of the Virgin's white doves, at the centre of the wastes of the *marismas*. In winter the chill Atlantic winds sweep through it. In summer it drowses hazy and deserted in the heat. Then in the fifty-second week it suddenly explodes into thronging and tumultuous life. If Sevilla's spring fair is the most brilliant expression of the urban or *pueblo* Andaluz' capacity for celebrating life, the Rocío is its countryside equivalent – an extraordinary act of faith which is also the largest, longest and most dazzling open-air party in the world. We first went on the pilgrimage in the early 1970s. Depending upon the starting-point – the pilgrims travel through the marshes to reach the shrine from every quarter – the journey there and back can last a week and preparations started long in advance. Over the centuries of the Rocío Virgin's veneration many of the near-by towns and villages have formed *hermandades* or brotherhoods. Originally loose associations of pilgrims who came together for companionship and mutual protection on the journey, the *hermandades* today are proud and well-organised clubs. Each has its own colours and standard and its own club-house in the village. We had been made honorary members of the brotherhood of Sanlúcar and given sleeping-space in Rocío for the two nights we would be there, but there were clothes, provisions, drink and transport for the journey to be organised.

About clothes there was little choice. The pilgrimage is also a major social occasion, as grand and formal as any full-dress ball with the difference that it goes on continuously for seven days and nights and the setting is the watery and open-skied Guadalquivir delta. All true Rocieros, as the pilgrims are called, are on display from dawn to dusk and then from dusk through to dawn again. To be superbly turned-out throughout the week is not merely a matter of convention, it is a duty to the Virgin in whose honour the pilgrimage is being made. The women wear the traditional long, flounced and vividly-coloured Sevillana or flamenco dresses, as most foreigners think of them, the men the severe *traje corto*, flat Sevillan hats, riding boots, short dark jackets and dark trousers protected by intricately-worked leather chaps. We had decided to take the three eldest children – Honey at five to her fury was considered too young – and everyone was dressed to the Rocío's lofty standards.

The provisions were relatively simple. The food was Andalucian country fare – huge and round Pelayo-baked loaves, asparagus and potato omelettes, chick peas, black pudding and *chorizo* for stews to be cooked over open fires, endless *tapas* of olives and smoked ham. The drink could only be sherry, the golden wine of the vineyards round the delta. Transport was more difficult.

Because of the terrain of the marshes, for centuries the Rocío remained of necessity a horseback pilgrimage with waggons drawn by mules or oxen to carry the pilgrims' supplies. Today Rocío is linked to Sevilla by road and thousands of those who now make the journey every year arrive in cars or coaches. But the serious Rociero, which includes all the members of the *hermandades*, still insists on travelling by horse or waggon. The few horses available for hire in southern Andalucía during Rocío week are prodigiously expensive, and in the end I decided to take a carriage instead.

The decision was easy. Finding a suitable vehicle for the marshes was much more complicated. Two weeks before the pilgrimage began I set off for Sanlúcar, found Juan Carlos Barbadillo, and together we scoured the town. Late in the evening we were directed to a gypsy who enthusiastically showed us what he called his *charet*. A carriage of the sort I had in mind it was not. On the other hand it had four serviceable wheels, two inward-facing bench seats at the back, a perch for the driver, and a gaily-striped canopy. Furthermore it was offered with its habitual means of power, a sullen but muscular mule. I rented it for Rocío week at an exorbitant price, the gypsy promised to deliver both cart and mule to the Sanlúcar ferry-point across the Guadalquivir from the marshes on the Friday morning of the pilgrimage's start, and Juan Carlos and I retired to the Bar Central.

Early Friday morning found all five of us standing in a

throng of other pilgrims on the river shore. The day even at
7.00 a.m. promised to be hot and clear. Black kites were
scavenging the waters and the opposite bank was hidden in
mist. Half an hour later, true to his word, the gypsy appeared
with the *charet* and the scowling mule.

'He's a good beast,' the gypsy said handing me the reins and
pocketing the money. 'Just don't count too much on his sense
of direction.'

He gave the animal an affectionate lash on the haunches
with a birch whip and loped off. I climbed up into the driver's
seat, guided the mule down to the water's edge, and we
splashed up the ramp of the waiting ferry. Ten minutes later we
disembarked on the other bank and set off for Rocío in a
procession behind the Sanlúcar brotherhood's supply wagons.

The landscape on the far side was a mixture of towering
dunes, sandy plains and corridors, lakes and inlets, and spiny
rosin-scented stands of umbrella pine. As the day wore on the
heat became intense. There were galloping horses everywhere.
The air was thick with dust and rang with the endless muffled
beat of hooves on sand. Sometimes a horseman would bring
his mount to a rearing halt beside the *charet*, scoop up
Elisabeth or one of the children, swing them on to the horse's
back, and plunge away into the trees, returning an hour or
more later to lower them into the cart again. Every twenty
minutes or so the procession, constantly spreading out into a
dozen different streams and then reforming, would come to a

halt. Someone would strike up on a guitar, a group of riders and the Sevillana-dressed ladies behind them would jump down, fandangoes would be danced in the pines' shadow or in the blazing sunlight, a bottle of ice-cold Jerez wine would be drunk, and the column would head on its way again.

Sometime during the afternoon we took a wrong turning on one of the winding lanes through the pines and became separated from the rest of the brotherhood. Half an hour later we were alone and hopelessly lost. Until then I had forgotten the gypsy's warning about the mule's sense of direction. Now peering over the dunes as the animal gazed perplexed and gloomy at the sand I remembered. The area of the *marismas* is not particularly large but more than once, even in the recent history of the Rocío, pilgrims who have strayed from their companions by no more than a few miles have failed to survive the rigours of the delta. In our case the challenge was never even put to the test. As I studied the barren horizon there appeared out of nowhere an extremely fat and scarlet-faced man, riding a small white pony and escorted by two mounted attendants who from their resemblance to him could only have been his sons.

'Are you lost, *señor*?' he asked. 'Never fear! We are Rocieros together and the white dove has sent me to guide you to safety. I am Pedro, a master-butcher from Sevilla. I know the *marismas* like the back of my hand. It is a small miracle that I chanced on you. Follow me and your problems are over.'

He pulled a bottle of sherry from his saddlebag, offered it to me, drank handsomely himself, and kicked his pony towards the setting sun. One of his sons cantered after him, took the pony's bridle and pointed the animal in the opposite direction. We followed. Two hours later, after winding through a maze of sandy gullies and ravines, we caught up with the tail-end of the Sanlúcar column. Pedro the bulky master-butcher, I learned from his son, had never been into the marshes before. It was the first Rocío for all the family.

'So maybe it is a miracle after all,' the son said, smiling shyly as we said goodbye in the dusk. 'I had no idea where we were going. I was simply operating by guesswork. I think the Virgin takes care of her own.'

By then we were in the middle of the Coto Doñana and the lighted silhouette of the Palacio, familiar from many visits in the past, was lifting above the scrub in the darkening air. We crunched towards it through bushes of rosemary whose scent rose up from beneath the wheels and whirled past our faces mingling with the smells of sweat and oiled leather from the ever-present cavalcade of horses. That night we slept fitfully against the Palacio's walls beneath the stars. All round us fires burned, guitars played, whirling figures danced in the light of the flames, rockets soared into the sky, and the night was full of the monotonous beat of drums and the haunting chant of flutes. As the sun rose the next morning the party continued uninterrupted as it would for the next five days. A bottle was opened, a young girl in a shining swirling dress paused briefly to wash her face and then with the beads of water still gleaming on her skin spun into a dance, a man joined her briefly, caught up the reins of his horse, vaulted into the saddle and cantered away singing.

The second day was like the first except the landscape had changed from sand dunes to delta marshland. A 15-year-old Jerez boy had attached himself to us and taken over the driving of the mule. Sometimes I sat beside him, sometimes I jumped down and walked. In the late spring the *marismas* were still green and damp. We travelled through great flower-spangled meadows fringed with mist out of which herds of deer and wild boar appeared and disappeared, fugitive rose and black silhouettes in the greyness. There were shadowy groves of eucalyptus; marshes bright with yellow flag iris and tiny jade-green narcissus; lagoons and riverways whose water turned the colour of peat shot through with flecks of bronze as the sun climbed higher. It was the height of the breeding season and the air was canopied by multitudes of birds. There were purple herons, white egrets, spoonbills, bee-eaters, rollers, hoopoes, larks, finches, skeins of duck and flamingo overhead, and high above them circling kites and eagles.

Rocío

As the sky began to darken again we reached Rocío. Its site had been marked for hours before by a huge cloud of dust on the horizon, formed by the horses and waggons of the thousands of pilgrims converging on it from every side. As the different brotherhoods enter the village – those from Sevilla are accompanied by immense two-tier ox-waggons covered in flowers – they ride past the chapel, salute the Virgin from outside, and circle the streets to announce their arrival before making their way to their individual club-houses. Later in the evening the brotherhoods assemble in a single parade, honour the Virgin once more, and then separate for the night's celebrations in rowdy hoof-drumming squadrons that turn Rocío into a wild west frontier town. During the pilgrimage sleep is almost impossible. The drums, rockets, flutes, guitar music, song, galloping horses and bellowing laughing voices overwhelm and deafen the nights. Occasionally someone, exhausted beyond endurance, staggers out from the village and collapses under the stars in one of the marshy pastures. Usually, within an hour or two, seeping damp and the chill night air send them scurrying back to Rocío's lights.

On the Sunday morning mass is celebrated in the open with the pilgrims attending on horseback and looking in their uniform of *traje corto* like massed regiments of cavalry gathered in prayer before battle. Next day comes the Rocío's climax. The Virgin is brought out from her chapel on a wooden float and carried in procession through the village. The task of carrying her belongs by tradition to the men of Almonte, one of whom first found her seven centuries before, but the honour is considered so great that every red-blooded man in Rocío battles to share it for at least a moment. Bobbing and swaying in a haze of dust above a throng of frenziedly struggling figures the Virgin slowly makes her way through the packed streets. In spite of the exhaustion, the drink and the intense passions aroused by the occasion, fights during the procession or at any time during the whole pilgrimage are almost unknown. The Paloma Blanca is the white dove of peace and permits no violence during her festival. Whenever an argument breaks out which looks like ending in blows, a shout instantly goes up, '*Viva la Paloma Blanca!*' The quarrellers are then honour-bound to stop and shake hands. Throughout the Rocío the Virgin's wishes are paramount.

The return of the float to the shrine technically signals the end of the pilgrimage. In practice, for most of the brother-

The Virgin of Rocío

hoods it has another two or three days to go, depending on the distance home. For the *hermandad* of Sanlúcar there was the two-day return journey across the marshes to the mouth of the Guadalquivir. During the stay in Rocío we had lost the boy from Jerez and acquired instead the wild-eyed Domingo from the valley, who took over the mule's reins. The atmosphere of the journey back was subtly different from the outward trip. The singing and dancing, the guitar-playing and drum-beating, went on as before, but it was less clamorous and insistent. A mood of contentment, almost of gentleness, had settled over the column. In part it was due to tiredness but more to a feeling of fulfillment. Once again the pilgrimage had been made in the true old-fashioned way. Things had been done properly and with due ceremony. The white dove had been honoured not as a formality, an excuse for a wonderful week-long *fiesta*, but with faith and love and belief. She stood at the very centre of life. She gave meaning to the year and the passing seasons, to birth and death and all that filled the road between the two. Now that she had been revered the pilgrims could return safely to their ordinary existence, sure in the knowledge that spring would come again and the grave-faced little wooden lady would be waiting for their adoration in the white shrine in the marshes.

The brotherhood made its final halt of the journey beside a charcoal-maker's hut in a glade in the pines near the ferry-point. There the new Rocieros, which included the five of us, were 'baptised' in one of the parodies of a sacrament that the Church of Rome from the Middle Ages on has felt secure enough to tolerate as a safety-valve on its severity. The baptism was performed by Juan Carlos Barbadillo. He mixed a fear-some improvised blend of lagoon mud, sherry and the previous evening's left-over stew in a brass pan, made the novice pilgrims kneel before him, and ladled the mixture generously over their heads while he intoned lascivious Andaluz benedic-tions. Before kneeling I handed my hat to Domingo. After-wards I scrubbed myself clean in the river and took the hat back. In his other hand Domingo had been holding the last of our provisions, six newly-laid eggs. Convulsed with delight by the ceremony and doubled up in laughter, Domingo had unwittingly broken all the eggs into the hat. When I put it on a wave of curdled yolk and white cascaded down my face. I cursed him, washed again, and climbed up beside him in the cart as he guided it down the shore towards the ferry.

'So how did it compare with last year, Domingo?' I asked.

'More people,' he said. 'Every year there are more people. But the Rocío never changes. How can it? Look at what it has. The most beautiful Virgin in Spain. The loveliest *campo*, the warmest sun, the sweetest air. The finest horses, the best wine and songs and music and dancing. And with just a loaf of bread and a few pesetas you can enjoy it all. Even a beggar can go on the Rocío and live like a king for a week. *Para mi el Rocío es Andalucía* – for me the Rocío is Andalucía. I mean no disrespect to your *pueblo*, Don Nicholas, which of course I don't know. But each time I go to Rocío I ask myself: how could a man wish to live anywhere else in the world than Andalucía?'

I glanced in the back of the cart. Under the shadow of the awning Elisabeth was dozing with the children, tangled round each other like young animals, fast asleep on the boards at her feet. The mule was standing patiently by the gunwhale. Someone had tied a Rocío medallion to the animal's headband. The silver-gilt image of the Virgin glittered in the dazzling sunlight reflected off the river. I opened the last bottle of sherry, drank and handed it to Domingo.

'*Viva la Paloma Blanca*,' I said. '*Salud* until next year.'

❧ INDEX ❧